THE DICTIONARY
of the
U.S. CONSTITUTION

Howard Chandler Christy painted this picture in 1937, portraying the Framers of the Constitution as he imagined them 150 years earlier. His view of the Constitutional Convention—that it was the cradle of liberty—is shared by many people, and it is not wrong to think of it that way. Yet it is also important to notice which groups of Americans were not "in the picture" in 1787. If new details were added to this painting today, it would look very different.

THE DICTIONARY
of the
U.S. CONSTITUTION

Barbara Silberdick Feinberg

Preface by Jack N. Rakove

Franklin Watts
A Division of Grolier Publishing
New York London Hong Kong Sydney
Danbury, Connecticut

For Gina Cane,
a cherished friend and an inspired, and inspiring,
teacher of schoolchildren.

I would like to thank the following people for assisting me in locating research materials: Gina Cane, Jeremy R. Feinberg, Esq., the Honorable John M. Ferren, Pat Milone, and Mark Piel, Director of the New York Society Library. I am especially grateful to Gina Cane, Jeremy R. Feinberg, Lorna Greenberg, and my editor, Douglas Hill, for their excellent suggestions and encouragement.

COVER AND INTERIOR DESIGN: Marleen Adlerblum Design
COPYEDITING: Richard Slovak
PHOTO RESEARCH: Laura Kreiss
FACT CHECKING: Noeme Garcia

CONSULTANTS:
Winton L. Wasson, Georgia State University and The Counterpane School, Georgia
James G. Marshall, The Hotchkiss School, Connecticut

Library of Congress Cataloging-in-Publication Data

Feinberg, Barbara Silberdick
    The Dictionary of the U.S. Constitution / by Barbara Silberdick Feinberg

        p. cm.
    Includes bibliographical references and index.
    Summary: A dictionary of terms and concepts related to the U.S. Constitution
and the Supreme Court decisions that have interpreted it.
    ISBN 0-531-11570-4
    1. Constitutional law—United States Dictionaries. Juvenile.
[1. Constitutional law Dictionaries.]   I. Title.

KF4548.5.F45   1999   99-14775
342.73 '02 '03—dc21   CIP

Printed in the United States of America

    2 3 4 5 6 7 8 9 10 R 08 07 06 05 04 03 02 01 00

Table of Contents

Along with the Declaration of Independence, the Constitution is one of the two great founding documents in the history of the United States. As drafted by the convention that met at Philadelphia in 1787, the Constitution consisted of seven articles divided into a number of sections and clauses. Six of these articles described the structure and powers of the new national government the Framers of the Constitution were proposing to create. The seventh article provided that the Constitution would take effect after conventions in nine of the thirteen states ratified it. By July 1788, eleven states had done so. Two others, North Carolina and Rhode Island, initially rejected the Constitution and did not join the Union until after its new government had begun operating.

To this original Constitution, Americans have added twenty-seven more articles in the form of amendments. The first group of ten amendments, known as the Bill of Rights, was proposed almost as soon as the new government was organized, and ratified in 1791. A second set of three amendments was adopted after the Civil War, largely to secure equality and justice for the freed slaves of the defeated Confederacy. Eight more amendments, two sets of four each, came out of the reforming spirit of the 1910s and, in part, the civil-rights movement of the 1960s. The other amendments have been adopted in piecemeal fashion.

When reading the many definitions offered in this dictionary, it is important to remember that the form of the U.S. Constitution—the fact that it is a single text—has had a powerful effect on Americans' very idea of a constitution. As Americans define the term, a constitution is a document, adopted at a particular moment in history, that establishes a government and the rules under which that government will act. A constitution is the highest form of law that a society possesses. It sets limits on the extent of governmental powers and the ways in which they may be exercised. When government acts lawfully, its decisions are consistent with the rules of the constitution. When government violates those rules, its acts are no longer valid; they become unconstitutional. The great advantage of having a written constitution is that it establishes basic rules and standards that everyone—citizen and official alike—can understand and respect.

These ideas are so familiar to us that we sometimes forget how new they were in the 1770s and 1780s. Then, the accepted definition of a constitution was very different. When political writers at the time discussed the British constitution, for instance, they were not referring to a single specific document. Instead, they described an entire system and tradition of government. Some documents—indeed, many documents—formed part of that constitution, including the famous Magna Carta of 1215 and the English Bill of Rights of 1689. But many other laws enacted by Parliament were also part of the constitution, and so were important legal doctrines that had evolved in the common-law courts of England. The structure of the government was also a major element of the constitution. But there was no single text to which citizens or officials could turn to determine exactly what the constitution required. In fact, the leading principle of the British constitution was that only Parliament itself could determine what the law finally was.

Americans increasingly rejected this idea during the constitutional quarrel that led to the American Revolution. Once they declared independence in 1776, they began to form the new definition of a constitution that the United States has followed ever since. The first experiments in developing this new definition came about from the simple need to replace the old colonial governments with new institutions. In the years after 1776, Americans also began to think of a constitution as a higher form of law—a document that would create and empower government, but also limit its authority in order to protect the rights of its citizens. The adoption of the U.S. Constitution in 1787–1788 was the dramatic culmination of this process.

The Constitution that the Framers produced can be read quickly. At first glance, it does not seem to make especially interesting reading. Its language is dry and formal; its clauses lack spice. Reading the Constitution closely is hard work, and understanding what it means takes even more effort. We have to examine each of its specific clauses, and ask how these clauses relate to each other. The Constitution does not tell us exactly how to do this; it simply assumes that we will read its clauses carefully to understand their meaning.

The whole Constitution is more than the sum of its parts, however, and the real constitution under which Americans live is more than its seven original articles and twenty-seven amendments. When we say that the Constitution is the foundation of our system of government, we mean just that. A foundation supports an entire structure, but the structure still has to be built over time, and often modified to meet new conditions. The original architects of the building—when they are called "framers" of the Constitution it is in the sense of "carpenters"—tried to describe their plans in the plainest language they could. But they could not even guess at every problem later occupants of their structure would face. Nor could they always imagine how the document they were writing would be interpreted. Sometimes their language proved less clear than they had thought. Sometimes later generations of Americans have simply disagreed about what that language originally meant, or about what it should mean now.

So in important ways the Constitution is not simply a document. It is also the interpretations that have been made of that document over time. Much of this interpretation takes place, as the Framers expected it would, in the courts. Article III of the Constitution gives federal courts the authority to try cases arising under the Constitution and the laws of the United States. Article VI also binds state courts to recognize the Constitution as "the supreme law of the land." In effect, the Framers asked both the national and the state courts to enforce the Constitution. This often requires judges to interpret both its language and the purposes that language was meant to serve. The other branches of government are also obliged to follow the Constitution. Together, their interpretations create the precedents and doctrines that enable the Constitution to remain something more than a quaint parchment from the eighteenth century.

Because the Constitution is both the foundation of our government and a source of ongoing interpretation, our obligation to read it carefully means that we have to carry out at least two tasks. First, we have to try to understand what its language meant to those who wrote and approved it. If we could impose any meaning we wished on its language, bending it to suit our own purposes or interests, the

> "Our Constitution is a covenant running from the first generation of Americans to us, and then to future generations. It is a coherent succession. Each generation must learn anew that the Constitution's written terms embody ideas and aspirations that must survive more ages than one."
> Justice Sandra Day O'Connor,
> *Planned Parenthood of Southeastern Pennsylvania v. Casey* (1992)

Constitution would quickly lose all meaning. Second, we have to understand that words and concepts do acquire new or different meanings over time. What we understand by the expression "freedom of speech, or of the press" cannot be exactly the same as what James Madison meant when he drafted the Bill of Rights. "Electors," to take another example, cannot mean the same thing at the dawn of the twenty-first century as it did in the late eighteenth century. In fact, we would not even say "electors" today, but "voters."

The true value of this dictionary of the Constitution is that it helps us use our political language correctly. It also reminds us how great a challenge it is to connect the words we use in the present with the words we have inherited from the past.

Jack N. Rakove
Stanford, California
February 1999

Each entry in *The Dictionary of the U.S. Constitution* begins with a definition of a word or phrase. This definition is followed by a discussion of the term and its place in the Constitution or constitutional law and history. The entries are in alphabetical order from A to Z. (The only exception to the rule of alphabetization is that the articles and amendments of the Constitution itself are placed in numerical order under the heading "U.S. Constitution.")

In a black band at the top of each two-page spread are heads that indicate the first and last entries on that spread. Words in *italics* at the end of each entry are cross-references to related entries. These cross-references are listed in alphabetical order. In the margins are picture captions and occasional quotes illustrating some aspect of an entry. The quotes are meant to serve as guideposts, but they express only the speakers' interpretations of the Constitution. There are also lists and explanations of other sorts that provide additional information useful to the reader.

At the back of the book, the index is a list of the many topics discussed in this dictionary, including people, events, groups, specific rights, and sections of the Constitution. Beside each word in the index are the pages on which that topic can be found. Page numbers in **boldface** indicate where in the book a major entry is discussed in most detail. The bibliography, also at the back of the book, lists other sources of information about the Constitution.

Accused, Rights of the

These safeguard people suspected of crimes and guarantee that they will be treated fairly.

The rights of the accused are listed in the Bill of Rights. The Fourth Amendment to the Constitution protects people from unreasonable searches of their property, possessions, or body. The Fifth Amendment includes assurances that no accused person has to testify against himself or herself. The Sixth Amendment details the right to a jury trial and the right to an attorney. Finally, the Eighth Amendment prohibits excessive bail.

Bail; Bill of Rights; Confession; Jury Trial, Right to; Searches and Seizures; Self-Incrimination;

U.S. Constitution, Fourth Amendment; U.S. Constitution, Fifth Amendment; U.S. Constitution,

Sixth Amendment; U.S. Constitution, Eighth Amendment

Adjournment

Action to end a meeting or postpone it until a later date.

According to Article I, section 5, of the Constitution, if either the House of Representatives or the Senate wants to adjourn for more than three days, the other house of Congress must agree. Article II, section 3, gives the president the power to adjourn Congress if the representatives and senators cannot agree on a common time.

Congress; House of Representatives; President; Senate; U.S. Constitution, Article I; U.S. Constitution,

Article II

Advice and Consent

> "[T]he president . . . appoints—but under a check; it is necessary to obtain the consent of the senate."
>
> Rep. Elias Boudinot, N.J.,
> Comments recorded in the
> *Congressional Register,*
> June 18, 1789

The constitutional requirement that the Senate accept or reject proposed treaties and presidential nominees.

The advice and consent clause is found in Article II, section 2, of the Constitution. The article gives the president authority to make treaties and appoint judges, ambassadors, and other high officials. The president does so, however, only with the "advice and consent" of the Senate.

The Framers borrowed the term from long-standing English law and made it part of the checks and balances of the Constitution.

Ambassadors; Cabinet; Checks and Balances; Framers; President; Senate; Treaties;

U.S. Constitution, Article II

Ambassadors

A government's official representatives to foreign governments and to international organizations such as the United Nations.

United States ambassadors are in charge of other U.S. diplomats, specialists from government agencies and executive departments, and a staff of assistants. They often hold negotiations with foreign governments and send the U.S. government information about conditions abroad. According to Article II, section 2, of the Constitution, the president nominates ambassadors, who are confirmed in their posts through the advice and consent of the Senate. Article III, section 2, states that all lawsuits involving ambassadors must be tried before the Supreme Court.

Henry Cabot Lodge, the U.S. ambassador to the United Nations from 1953 to 1960, is shown here holding up the Great Seal of the United States in a meeting of the U.N. Security Council on May 26, 1960. This session of the Security Council came during an international crisis involving a U-2—a U.S. spy plane—that was shot down over the Soviet Union. The event was a great embarrassment to the United States, and Lodge and other U.S. ambassadors around the world were called upon to offer official explanations about the spying incident. By his gesture, Lodge seems to be commenting on the central element of the Great Seal, an American bald eagle, and on what the eagle is holding in its claws—arrows, symbolizing preparedness for war, and an olive branch, symbolizing a desire for peace.

Advice and Consent; Jurisdiction; President; Senate; Supreme Court; U.S. Constitution, Article II; U.S. Constitution, Article III

Amendment Process

The method of changing the Constitution, laws, or other documents by adding to or subtracting from their contents.

Amending the Articles of Confederation was almost impossible because all of the states had to approve any change. The Framers of the Constitution rejected this requirement. They agreed instead that if three-fourths of the states approved an amendment, it would take effect. By doing so, they made it possible for a Constitution handwritten with quill pens to survive into the age of computers.

Article V of the Constitution describes the process of amending it. Amendments may be proposed to the states following a two-thirds vote in both houses of Congress (which now means 290 members of the House of Representatives and 67 senators). Alternatively, the legislatures of two-thirds of the states may call for a special convention to propose amendments. In either case, ratification (final approval) occurs when three-fourths of the states' legislatures, or special conventions held in three-fourths of the states (currently, thirty-eight states), vote their approval. In 1921, the Supreme Court upheld a seven-year deadline on votes for ratification. Congress is informed when an amendment has been ratified. The Archivist of the United States, an official in charge of national documents, certifies the amendment by checking to make sure everything is in order. Then the amendment is published in the *Federal Register*, an official publication that prints all U.S. government laws and rules. To date, twenty-seven amendments have been added to the Constitution.

Articles of Confederation; Congress; Framers; House of Representatives; Ratification; Senate; States; Supreme Court; U.S. Constitution, Article V; U.S. Constitution, individual amendments

Amendments

See: U.S. Constitution, individual amendments

Amendments, Unratified

Changes to the Constitution that have been offered by Congress but never approved by three-fourths of the states.

Up to the present, six amendments have been passed by Congress and submitted to the states but not ratified. (More than 2,000 other proposed amendments have been voted down in Congress—or not considered at all—and never been presented to the states for ratification.)

The first ten amendments, the Bill of Rights, were among twelve proposed amendments that the First Congress sent to the states in 1789. The first two of those twelve proposed amendments were not approved at the time, although the second one was finally resubmitted and ratified in 1992, becoming the Twenty-seventh Amendment. The remaining, never-ratified amendment proposed in 1789 related to the size of the House of Representatives. It would have restricted the authority of Congress to regulate the size of the House of Representatives by requiring that the House grow by specific proportions as the population grew.

Since then, five other amendments have been sent to the states but not ratified. In May 1810, the Eleventh Congress proposed an amendment to the Constitution that would have revoked the citizenship of any U.S. citizen who accepted a title of nobility from a foreign government.

In March 1861, the Thirty-sixth Congress proposed an amendment to the Constitution that would have prohibited any later amendments giving Congress the power to abolish slavery. It is interesting to note that this amendment protecting slavery would have been the Thirteenth Amendment to the Constitution. Since it was not ratified, the next ratified

These boys were photographed working on a mechanical loom in the early 1900s. The fast-moving parts of machines posed great dangers for working children in that era. The drive belt of this loom, for instance, could easily catch a boy's arm. Or the moving parts could catch his foot, particularly dangerous for the boy shown in the foreground here, since he is barefoot. In 1916, Congress passed the Federal Child Labor Act. The law barred interstate commerce of goods made in factories employing children under the age of fourteen or employing sixteen-year-olds for more than eight hours a day or six days a week. Two years later, in *Hammer v. Dagenhart* (1918), the Supreme Court ruled that Congress had no authority to pass a law against child labor, since child labor was not "harmful." Congress then went ahead and passed an amendment to the Constitution banning child labor, but that amendment was never ratified by the states. In 1938, Congress passed another child-labor law, and this time, in *United States v. Darby Lumber* (1941), the Supreme Court ruled it was constitutional.

amendment became the Thirteenth Amendment—the one ending slavery, not perpetuating it.

In 1924, the Sixty-eighth Congress proposed an amendment giving Congress authority to outlaw child labor and specifying that state laws allowing child labor were to be suspended.

Almost a half century later, in 1972, the Equal Rights Amendment was proposed. It would have guaranteed equality of rights to women. At first, this amendment seemed headed for ratification, but growing opposition halted its early momentum. Congress extended its deadline for ratification, but in 1982 it formally failed to become the Twenty-seventh Amendment.

In 1978, the Ninety-fifth Congress submitted an amendment to give the District of Columbia representation in Congress "as though it were a State." It failed to win ratification within seven years.

Apportionment; Bill of Rights; Congress; District of Columbia; Equal Rights Amendment; House of Representatives; Nobility; Ratification; Senate; Slavery; States; U.S. Constitution, Thirteenth Amendment; U.S. Constitution, Twenty-third Amendment; U.S. Constitution, Twenty-seventh Amendment; Voting Rights

Annapolis Convention

An unsuccessful meeting about trade problems that led to the call for a Constitutional Convention.

In September 1786, delegates from Delaware, New Jersey, New York, Pennsylvania, and Virginia assembled in Annapolis, Maryland, to discuss common problems of trade and commerce. The Virginia legislature had requested the meeting. In 1785, Virginia had successfully negotiated its differences with Maryland over navigating the Potomac River. Such disagreements occurred because the Confederation Congress lacked the power to regulate trade among the states.

Originally, nine states agreed to send representatives to Annapolis. Delegates from only five showed up, however, too few to settle existing trade disputes. Instead, New York's Alexander Hamilton proposed that a Constitutional Convention be held to strengthen the national government. The other delegates agreed to submit the proposal to their state governments. They also sent a copy to the Confederation Congress in New York City. It called for the convention to meet in May 1787 in Philadelphia.

Commerce Clause; Confederation Congress; Constitutional Convention

We "suggest . . . the appointment of Commissioners, to meet at Philadelphia on the second Monday in May next, to take into consideration the situation of the United States."
Annapolis Convention Report, September 1786

Antifederalists

The name given to those who opposed ratification of the Constitution in 1787–1788.

They claimed that the delegates at the Constitutional Convention in Philadelphia had no authority to write a new Constitution; they had been instructed to improve the Articles of Confederation, not to scrap them. Some Antifederalists also insisted that if the Constitution were to take the place of the Articles, it had to be approved not by just nine states but by all thirteen. This was the way the Articles provided for change.

The Antifederalists had other objections to the Constitution. They feared that the state governments would lose their independence and become agents of the national government. They were especially concerned about the so-called elastic clause (which gave Congress seemingly broad power to pass all laws "necessary and proper" to carrying out the Constitution) and the supremacy clause (which says that the Constitution is "the supreme law of the land"). To avoid what they saw as a dangerous concentration of power in the federal government, the Antifederalists wanted to strengthen state governments and keep them responsible to the people. They preferred to keep the United States a confederation of small independent republics rather than a large country ruled by a strong national government.

The Antifederalists also warned that the American people would lose their liberties under the new Constitution, which lacked a Bill of Rights to guarantee their freedoms. In addition, they said, the national government was isolated from the interests of the public. Six-year terms for senators would turn them into an upper class who lost touch with the people; federal judges appointed for life would have little in common with those they were supposed to serve. Some Antifederalists complained that the president had too much power, but others disagreed. They all wanted the people to make changes in the Constitution before it was ratified. However, they also agreed to press for amendments to the Constitution once it was approved.

The Antifederalists included such patriots of the American Revolution as Samuel Adams, George Clinton, Elbridge Gerry, Patrick Henry, Richard Henry Lee, Luther Martin, George Mason, Melancton Smith, and Robert Yates. They and their followers published pamphlets and articles under such pen names as "Agrippa," "Brutus," "Cato," "Centinel," and "Federal Farmer." They drew support from farmers, frontiersmen, city

An impassioned Patrick Henry is shown here during a meeting of the First Continental Congress in 1774. Shortly after the scene depicted here, he would deliver his famous call for independence from Great Britain: "Give me liberty or give me death."

After independence was won, Henry was a strong defender of states' rights. An Antifederalist even before the Constitutional Convention, he refused to attend the meeting in Philadelphia because, as he said, he "smelt a rat."

During debates in the Virginia Ratification Convention in June 1788, Henry opposed the Constitution on a number of grounds, including the planned creation of a national judiciary.

"In what a situation will your judges be," he asked, "when they are sworn to preserve the constitution of the state and of the general government! If there be a concurrent dispute between them, which will prevail? They cannot serve two masters struggling for the same object. The laws of Congress being paramount to those of the states, . . . the judges must decide in favor of the former. . . . The judiciary are the sole protection against a tyrannical execution of the laws. But if by this system we lose our judiciary, and they cannot help us, we must sit down quietly, and be oppressed."

This creature, a "gerrymander," is the invention of a political cartoonist in the 1810s. It pokes fun at Governor Elbridge Gerry of Massachusetts and the oddly shaped electoral districts he helped to create. After the 1810 census, the state's congressional districts were redrawn to favor Gerry's political party, the Democratic-Republicans. Critics said one district looked like a salamander. Today, the word *gerrymander* (from "Gerry" + "salamander") means creating an electoral district to help one political party over another.

More than twenty years earlier, Gerry was one of the wealthiest men to attend the Constitutional Convention. He refused to sign the Constitution, but later supported its ratification in the Massachusetts ratifying convention.

workers, and debtors. They later formed the core of the Democratic-Republican Party, led by Thomas Jefferson.

Amendment Process; Articles of Confederation; Bill of Rights; Constitutional Convention; Elastic Clause; Federal Government; Federalism; Federalists; Judicial Tenure; Ratification; States; Supremacy Clause

Appointment to Office

The selection of people for positions in the government. The president chooses ambassadors, heads of executive departments, consuls, justices of the Supreme Court, and other federal officials.

As the Constitution provided, Congress has extended the list to include judges of lower federal courts, heads of government agencies, and other officials. Article II, section 2, of the Constitution requires that the president's appointments get Senate approval. When officials resign or die, the president may fill these vacancies on his own authority if the Senate is not in session. Such appointments expire at the end of the next Senate session.

Advice and Consent; Ambassadors; Congress; Consuls; Executive Departments; Federal Courts; President; Senate; Supreme Court; U.S. Constitution, Article II

Apportionment

The distribution of seats in the House of Representatives (or any other popularly elected legislature), and the distribution of direct taxes (such as a poll tax).

Article I, section 2, of the Constitution states that the number of a state's seats in the House and the amount of taxes a state collects for the national government shall be based on the size of its population, excluding Indians not taxed. Until ratification of the Fourteenth Amendment, every five slaves were counted as three free persons for the purpose of calculating population.

Originally, there was one representative for every 30,000 people, but by the year 2000 each member of Congress represented about 630,000 people. In 1910, the total number of seats in the House was set at 435, to keep it from becoming unmanageable. A census, taken every ten years, counts the population. This is used to determine how many of the 435 seats are given to each state. No matter how small its population is, each state gets at least one representative. In *Wesberry v. Sanders* (1964), the Supreme Court held that the districts that elect representatives to Congress within each state must have as close to the same population as possible. In this way, everyone's vote has the same weight. If one district were to have many more people than another, its votes would count less.

Because each state must have at least one representative, however, exactly equal districts are impossible. For example, Montana has one election district of 803,655 people (according to the most recent census) while Wyoming's one district has only 455,975 people.

Census; House of Representatives; Poll Taxes; Ratification; Supreme Court; Three-Fifths Compromise; U.S. Constitution, Article I; U.S. Constitution, Fourteenth Amendment

Appropriations

Money voted on by Congress to pay for government activities.

Article I, section 8, of the Constitution gives Congress the power to spend funds on national defense and the well-being of the citizens. According to section 7, all proposals to raise money must originate in the House of Representatives. In the original Constitution, the House was the only branch of government directly elected by the people (until the Seventeenth Amendment, ratified in 1913, changed the way the Senate is elected). By having money bills start in the House, the Framers sought to make sure that government funds were used for projects that were acceptable to the public.

Congress; Defense; Framers; House of Representatives; Revenue; U.S. Constitution, Article I; U.S. Constitution, Seventeenth Amendment

Arms, Right to Bear

The guarantee that ordinary citizens can keep private firearms.

This right is found in the Second Amendment to the Constitution. During the War for Independence, many states included the right to bear arms in their bills of rights. Later, during debates over ratification of the Constitution, Federalists and Antifederalists agreed that armed citizens were the best defense against a tyrannical government. Where they differed was over the existence of a federal army or state militias. Antifederalists feared that a standing national army could be used to take away citizens' freedoms. Federalists argued that when armed citizens belonged to state militias, a federal army could not turn on them. Only if people were disarmed could this danger arise. Five state ratifying conventions demanded that the right to bear arms be added to the Constitution. A debate continues about whether this right can be limited by the federal government.

Antifederalists; Bill of Rights; Federal Government; Federalists; Militia; Ratification; U.S. Constitution, Second Amendment

Article

See: U.S. Constitution, individual articles

Articles of Confederation

The first written constitution of the United States (1781–1789).

It was drafted in 1776–1777 by a committee of the Second Continental Congress headed by John Dickinson of Pennsylvania. By 1779, twelve states had approved it. The Articles took effect in 1781 when Maryland finally signed them, after settling land claims with Virginia.

The Confederation was governed by a Confederation Congress of delegates from each state. However, meetings of Congress were uncertain at best. Delegates from seven states had to be present for business to take place, but attendance was irregular. The states were slow to pick delegates, and distances were great in those days of horses and primitive roads. Nine states had to agree before Congress could pass most laws. Nine states rarely agreed on anything. Even if they did, the "laws" of Congress were little more than recommendations for state action. There was no executive; instead, committees of delegates carried out Congress's decisions.

Under the Articles, the United States arranged a peace treaty with Great Britain in 1783, ending the War for Independence. The Confederation Congress also passed the Land Ordinance of 1785 and the Northwest Ordinance of 1787. These laid down rules for settling and governing American territories between the Allegheny Mountains and the Mississippi River. They also arranged for the orderly admission of new states to the Union. Nevertheless, the Confederation was too weak to solve problems of trade among the states. Nor could it deal effectively with the European nations that controlled other parts of the North American continent.

The Articles of Confederation are described below:

Article I designated the official name of the country. The Confederation called itself "the United States of America."

John Dickinson served in the Delaware and Pennsylvania colonial legislatures in the 1760s. His *Letters from a Farmer in Pennsylvania,* which was widely read, argued that the British Parliament had the right to tax the colonies' foreign trade, but not their local businesses. Dickinson always hoped to avoid war with Britain, and this is why he refused to sign the Declaration of Independence in 1776.

When the colonies declared their independence anyway, Dickinson chaired the committee that drafted the Articles of Confederation. He served in Congress and as president (governor) of Delaware, elected to the post by the state legislature. In 1786, members of the Annapolis Convention chose him as their chairman.

Later, as a delegate to the Constitutional Convention, Dickinson argued for a strong national government. Early in the debates, he suggested a Congress with one chamber based on population and another granting equal membership to the states. His other ideas included restricting voting rights to property owners, letting the national government limit the slave trade, and giving the national government the power to veto state laws.

Article II concerned states' rights. The Articles preserved the sovereignty, freedom, and independence of the states. The Confederation government could do only what the states had specifically permitted it to do. The states kept all other powers, rights, and jurisdictions.

Article III described the formation of a confederation, or league, among the states. The states agreed to join together for purposes of their common defense, protection of their freedom, and their general well-being. They had to come to each other's defense if any of them was attacked.

Article IV detailed the mutual obligations of states toward their citizens. Free people (not slaves, the poor, vagabonds, or fugitives from the law) could travel anywhere within the states. Such visitors to any state were to be treated like citizens of the state in matters of trade, business, court judgments, and personal liberties. At the request of a state, its fugitives had to be returned from another state. States had to recognize as legal the records, judgments, and acts of other states.

"The fundamental defect is a want of power in Congress. It is hardly worth while to show in what this consists, as it seems to be universally acknowledged, or to point out how it has happened, as the only question is how to remedy it."
Alexander Hamilton,
Letter to James Duane,
September 3, 1780

Article V had to do with creation of a confederation government. A congress would meet yearly. State legislatures would name no less than two and no more than seven delegates for one-year terms to the Congress, but each state could cast only one vote. The states had the power to recall their delegates and replace them. No delegate could serve for more than three years out of every six. States would pay the delegates' expenses, and no delegate could hold another paid office in the United States government while serving in Congress. Delegates' freedom of speech was protected while they attended Congress.

Article VI dealt with restrictions on states. The states could not conduct diplomatic relations with other nations except with the permission of the United States. Nor could they make treaties or alliances among themselves without the consent of Congress. They could not charge tariffs on foreign goods. No state officials could accept noble titles, positions, honors, money, or gifts from foreign countries. The states and the Confederation government could not grant titles of nobility either.

States could keep their own navies only with the consent of Congress, for purposes of self-defense or trade. States could have militias, but they could not raise armies in peacetime except to man forts. This required the consent of Congress as well. States could go to war without the permission of Congress only if they were invaded or were about to be invaded.

Article VII concerned military officers. All officers at or under the rank of colonel were to be appointed by state legislatures in time of war.

Article VIII dealt with the Confederation government's finances. A common treasury would pay for matters of mutual defense and well-being voted on by the Congress. States would contribute to the treasury in proportion to the value of their land holdings.

Article IX described powers of the Confederation government. The government had the sole power to declare war or peace. The government could enter into treaties with foreign nations. Congress could decide how to divide up ships and cargoes captured on land or water, set up courts to try piracy, and appeal cases arising under the law of the seas. Congress would serve as the last court of appeals in disputes between states.

Congress had the power to regulate the content of coins issued by the states or the Confederation. It could fix standards of weights and measures, regulate trade, and manage affairs with Indians—provided the rights of states over Indians within their lands were preserved. Congress could set up and regulate post offices. It had the power to appoint army and navy officers in service to the United States, make rules for their conduct, and direct their operations.

A Committee of the States, appointed by the delegates, would handle matters when Congress was not in session. One delegate from each state would serve on it. Congress could appoint additional committees to manage the nation's business. The delegates would name a chairman, called a president, to preside over their meetings. He could serve for only one year out of every three.

Congress had the power to determine how much money was needed to meet public expenses and to vote to appropriate the money or borrow it. The government could build up and equip a navy. It could agree on the number of armed forces needed and require each state to contribute and equip its quota. These troops would be paid by the United States.

Nine states had to consent before Congress could sign treaties, declare war, coin money, appropriate money for defense and citizens' well-being, borrow money, raise an army or navy, or appoint a commander in chief of the army. Congress could adjourn at any time and to any place, but no period of adjournment could be longer than six months. Congress would publish a journal of its discussions, activities, and votes. The delegates could request copies and send them to their state legislatures.

Article X described powers of the Committee of the States. The committee or any nine members could exercise any powers given to it by a majority of Congress except powers requiring the approval of nine states.

Article XI had to do with Canada, which could be admitted to the Confederation if it chose. The votes of nine states would be necessary for the admission of any other colony.

Article XII concerned debts. The government would pay all debts owed by the Congress of the United States before the Articles of Confederation went into effect.

Article XIII dealt with amendments. Every state was expected to obey the decisions of the Congress and the Articles of Confederation. Changes in the Articles required the consent of every member state.

Adjournment; Appropriations; Breach of the Peace; Commander in Chief; Confederation; Confederation Congress; Continental Congress; Debts; Defense; Executive Branch; Felonies; Journals; Jurisdiction; Letters of Marque and Reprisal; Militia; Nobility; President; Speech, Freedom of; Tariffs; Treason; Treasury, U.S. Department of the; Treaties

Assembly, Freedom of

The guarantee that people can gather peacefully in private homes, meeting halls, public streets, and parks without government interference.

It is found in the First Amendment to the Constitution, a part of the Bill of Rights, which limits the national government. Later, the Supreme Court interpreted the Fourteenth Amendment to place similar restrictions on the states as well as the national government. Most early state constitutions did not protect freedom of assembly in their bills of rights. John Adams, however, insisted that the New Hampshire and Massachusetts constitutions include this right. He remembered that the British Intolerable Acts had forbidden colonial meetings.

No one has an absolute right to assembly. In *Cox v. New Hampshire* (1941), the Supreme Court ruled that permits may be needed to hold public parades and demonstrations. Courts have to balance people's right to assemble with the need for public order, peace, and quiet. For the most part, however, courts have protected the right of groups to march and demonstrate. In the 1960s, judges often had to intervene to let Dr. Martin Luther King Jr. hold peaceful protests for blacks' civil rights.

The Supreme Court has divided the places where people may freely gather into three categories, with three different sets of rules. First, marches and picketing are permitted in

The Rev. Martin Luther King Jr. is shown here during a civil-rights march in Mississippi on June 7, 1966. One day earlier, James Meredith, the first black student to attend the University of Mississippi after court-ordered desegregation there, was shot during the march. Meredith survived the attack, the latest in a series of violent acts directed against civil-rights demonstrators. King's own experiences with violent opponents went back at least to the period of his leadership of the Montgomery, Alabama, bus boycott in 1955–1956. King's house was bombed before he and his fellow demonstrators saw the Supreme Court declare Alabama's segregation laws unconstitutional. King and the thousands who worked with him toward the objectives of equality of rights under the Constitution would be subjected to many brutal encounters along the way. King himself was assassinated in April 1968, less than two years after this photograph was taken.

public places, such as streets and parks, where people have traditionally gathered to state their views. Second, picketing and demonstrations are allowed in public places intended for other uses, such as airports, courthouses, schools, and libraries. Third, picketing and other demonstrations on private property are not so acceptable. In *Frisby v. Schultz* (1988), the Court held that peaceful picketing may be broken up when a homeowner's privacy is invaded. In the case of privately owned shopping malls, the Court has ruled that states and cities may require the owners of these centers to let people use their grounds for peaceful purposes. The Court reasoned that, for many communities, shopping malls serve the same role as town squares. So far, the right to deliberately but nonviolently disobey the law is not protected by freedom of assembly.

Bill of Rights; Civil Rights; Privacy; Supreme Court; U.S. Constitution, First Amendment; U.S. Constitution, Fourteenth Amendment

> "[T]he immunity from state scrutiny of membership lists which the [NAACP] claims on behalf of its members is here so related to the right of the members to pursue their lawful private interests privately and to associate freely with others in so doing as to come within the protection of the Fourteenth Amendment."
>
> **Justice John Marshall Harlan, NAACP v. Alabama, 1958**

Association, Freedom of

The right to form and join groups of one's choice.

This right is not found in the Constitution or the Bill of Rights. The Supreme Court has ruled that it is part of the First Amendment right to assemble, further guaranteed by the equal protection clause of the Fourteenth Amendment. In the 1950s, rivalry and tensions existed between the United States and the Soviet Union. As a result, some Americans were penalized for belonging to organizations sympathetic to the Soviet Union. In *Yates v. United States* (1957) and other similar cases, the Supreme Court decided that simple membership in such groups was not a sufficient reason to punish people. At the same time, some state legislatures had been harassing the National Association for the Advancement of Colored People (NAACP), a black civil-rights organization. In *NAACP v. Alabama* (1958), the Court ruled that the members of the group had a right to associate. In the 1980s, the Court took on the challenge of private clubs that excluded people because of their gender or race. In cases such as *Roberts v. U.S. Jaycees* (1984), it upheld laws forbidding clubs from doing this.

Assembly, Freedom of; Bill of Rights; Civil Rights; Equal Protection of the Laws; Supreme Court; U.S. Constitution, First Amendment; U.S. Constitution, Fourteenth Amendment

B

Bail

Money or property pledged to guarantee that a person arrested for a crime will show up for trial if he or she is released from jail.

In 1689, the English prohibited excessively high bail. Americans followed their example in the Eighth Amendment to the Constitution. The right to bail is based on the idea that a person is innocent until proven guilty. Innocent people do not belong in jail. Sometimes, however, a court will deny bail if the accused is considered likely to flee or to pose a serious danger to the community.

Accused, Rights of the; Searches and Seizures; U.S. Constitution, Eighth Amendment

Bankruptcy

Financial ruin that occurs when debts, or money owed, cannot be repaid.

Article I, section 8, of the Constitution gives Congress the power to pass uniform bankruptcy laws for the United States. In the 1700s, people could be imprisoned when they were bankrupt. One of the Framers of the Constitution, Robert Morris, was held in debtors' prison from 1798 to 1801. He was freed under the first federal bankruptcy law, passed in 1800. Modern law sometimes allows a bankrupt person's debts to be forgiven and failed businesses to close down. More often it gives people and businesses time to reorganize their finances to enable them to pay back at least some of what they owe.

Congress; Debts; U.S. Constitution, Article I

Bear Arms, Right to

See: Arms, Right to Bear

Bicameral Legislature

A term describing a lawmaking body with two houses or chambers.

Article I, section 1, of the Constitution created a bicameral Congress for the United States. The two chambers are called the House of Representatives and the Senate. Under the Articles of Confederation, the United States was governed by a single-chamber legislature. The Framers, however, returned to the British tradition of a two-chamber legislature. In Great Britain, the lower house of Parliament represented the people, and the upper house contained members of the nobility and the clergy. In the United States, the upper house (the Senate) was originally designed to protect the interests of the monied and propertied classes; the lower house (the House of Representatives) was intended to represent the people.

The Framers did not want either or both houses to become more powerful than the other branches of government. Applying the principle of

checks and balances, they gave the two houses joint and separate responsibilities. For example, the cooperation of both houses is needed for a bill
to become a law. On the other hand, only the Senate can approve presidential appointments, and only the House can introduce money bills.

Appointment to Office; Appropriations; Articles of Confederation; Bill; Checks and Balances;
Congress; House of Representatives; Senate; U.S. Constitution, Article I

Bill

A proposed law.

Article I, section 7, of the Constitution states that every bill must pass
the House of Representatives and the Senate and be sent to the president
for signing before it can become a law. If the president refuses to sign it,
the bill can still become law. This time, two-thirds of the members of each
house must vote to pass the bill. The names of the members of Congress
and how they voted must be written into the records kept by the two
chambers. In addition, all bills for raising revenue must be introduced in
the House.

House of Representatives; Journals; Law; President; Revenue; Senate; U.S. Constitution, Article I

Bill of Attainder

A law passed by a legislature punishing a specific person or group without
giving the benefit of a trial.

In sixteenth- and seventeenth-century England, bills of attainder usually called for capital punishment, or the death penalty. They were used
against people thought to be guilty of trying to overthrow the government. They were also used to punish the king's ministers who abused their
powers. This was an early, if harsh, step toward making ministers responsible to Parliament rather than to the monarch. In Article I of the
Constitution, sections 9 and 10 forbid Congress and the states from passing bills of attainder. For the most part, such legislative punishments have
been rare in American history. In 1943, however, Congress ordered that
three government employees suspected of disloyalty receive no pay until
the president reappointed them, subject to Senate approval. With the president's support, the men kept on working and sued to be paid. In *United
States v. Lovett* (1946), the Supreme Court ruled in their favor. The Court
found that Congress had violated their rights by passing a bill of attainder
against them.

Congress; President; Senate; Supreme Court; U.S. Constitution, Article I

Bill of Rights

James Madison served in 1776 at the Virginia Constitutional Convention. A decade later, urging changes in the Articles of Confederation and a stronger national government, he called for a series of conferences among the states, which led to the Constitutional Convention.

Madison is often called the "Father of the Constitution." He had asked for the Convention to be held. He kept the most complete notes of discussions and debates. Most important, he had prepared an outline for a new government, the Virginia Plan, which was presented by Edmund Randolph. Under Madison's guidance, the delegates changed the relationships among the states, the national government, and the people, replacing the Confederation with federalism.

During the debates over ratification, Madison worked hard to defeat the Antifederalists in Virginia and other states. He contributed to a series of important essays, collectively called the Federalist Papers. Published in newspapers throughout the states, the essays answered Antifederalist criticisms. They successfully defended and explained the new Constitution.

Although at first he thought a Bill of Rights was unnecessary, Madison soon changed his mind. As a representative in Congress from 1789 to 1797, he was mainly responsible for getting Congress to pass the Bill of Rights. He later served as secretary of state and president of the United States.

Written guarantees of basic freedoms. In the United States, these are found in the first ten amendments to the Constitution.

In 1689, the English had passed a bill of rights, legally protecting the basic liberties they had enjoyed for centuries. It prohibited the king from suspending laws, imposing taxes, or keeping a standing army in peacetime without the consent of Parliament. It also guaranteed members of Parliament freedom of speech and free elections. All citizens were guaranteed the right to petition the monarch to undo wrongs. In addition, excessive bail and fines were banned. The English Bill of Rights was part of a religious and political settlement that replaced one monarch with another.

During and after the War for Independence, the thirteen states wrote bills of rights into their individual state constitutions. However, the Articles of Confederation did not include them, because the national government had little or no power over the people. It could act only through the states.

A majority of the Framers of the Constitution, including Alexander Hamilton, Roger Sherman, and James Wilson, similarly reasoned that the people already had all the protection they needed. They believed bills of rights were necessary to protect people from kings, not from governments the people created to serve them. These Framers also thought that since the powers of the national government were limited and enumerated, the government would be unable to oppress its citizens. Elbridge Gerry, James McHenry, George Mason, and Charles Pinckney were leading spokesmen for those who disagreed. Through their efforts, the Constitution prohibited bills of attainder and ex post facto laws, which would have violated personal freedoms. Still, these Framers were not satisfied and demanded a bill of rights. In fact, it was precisely because some rights were spelled out in the Constitution that many people feared the national government would restrict other rights—the ones that were not mentioned. During debates over ratification of the Constitution, those who opposed the document because it lacked a bill of rights were joined by other Antifederalists, such as Patrick Henry and Richard Henry Lee. To win their support, Federalists promised to add one.

State ratifying conventions sent Congress more than two hundred proposals for safeguarding American freedoms. From these, Representative James Madison prepared a series of changes to the Constitution. By now, he was convinced that the people wanted a bill of rights. He had to wait five months before the lawmakers discussed his recommendations, because they were too busy setting up the new government. During the debates, Madison argued that guarantees of citizens' rights should be made part of the text of the original Constitution. Roger Sherman, however, persuaded the lawmakers to treat them as amendments. The states had already ratified the Constitution, so any additions to the document would require their approval. After reviewing and rewriting Madison's proposals, the House and the Senate came up with twelve amendments that were sent to the states in 1789. (He carefully avoided amendments that would alter the shape of the newly formed federal government.) Ten of the twelve proposed amendments were ratified in 1791; one of the two failed amendments was finally added to the Constitution in 1992.

In *Barron v. Baltimore* (1833), the Supreme Court decided that the Bill of Rights did not apply to state governments, but only to the national government. Between 1925 and 1972, however, the Court gradually reversed its earlier decision. To do this, it relied on the Fourteenth Amendment, which requires that each state give its citizens due process and equal protection of the laws. The Court interpreted those phrases to include parts of the Bill of Rights. This process is known as *incorporation*. Currently, only the Second, Third, Seventh, and Tenth amendments have not been incorporated, as well as the grand jury requirements of the Fifth Amendment.

Antifederalists; Articles of Confederation; Bill of Attainder; Due Process of Law; Equal Protection of the Laws; Ex Post Facto Laws; Federalists; Incorporation of the Bill of Rights; Press, Freedom of the; Ratification; Speech, Freedom of; Supreme Court; U.S. Constitution, individual amendments

Breach of the Peace

Disorderly behavior or any other actions that disturb the public order.

According to Article I, section 6, of the Constitution, committing a breach of the peace is one of the few crimes for which members of Congress can be arrested while the legislature is meeting. Delegates who served in the Confederation Congress were subject to the same rule, found in Article V of the Articles of Confederation.

Articles of Confederation; Confederation Congress; Congress; U.S. Constitution, Article I

Bribery

Illegal gifts, payments, or other benefits used to gain favors from officials.

Article II, section 4, of the Constitution makes bribery one of the offenses punishable by impeachment. All federal-government officials may be removed from office for giving or receiving bribes. For example, in 1876, a congressional committee wanted to remove President Ulysses S. Grant's secretary of war, William W. Belknap, from office. He had taken bribes from men eager to be placed in charge of Indian trading posts at western forts. Belknap resigned before Congress could take further action.

Impeachment; U.S. Constitution, Article II

Cabinet

A group of presidential advisers, including the heads of executive departments, the vice president, and others the president may choose.

The term *cabinet* can be traced to England. At first, it referred to a small room where the king met with his closest advisers; later it came to mean the advisers themselves.

The development of the American cabinet is an example of an informal amendment to the Constitution. During the Constitutional Convention, the delegates discussed formally creating a group that would advise the president, but this idea was not included in the final draft of the Constitution. Instead, Article II, section 2, of the Constitution gives the president the power to appoint the heads of executive departments, subject to Senate approval. It also allows the president to ask for their opinions in writing. In the 1790s, President George Washington simply asked the secretaries of state, the treasury, and war and the attorney general to meet with him and advise him. These four officials made up his cabinet. Other presidents followed Washington's example. As the nation's responsibilities increased, Congress added more executive departments. In the 1990s, President Bill Clinton's cabinet included fourteen heads of departments and four other officials.

Appointment to Office; Constitutional Convention; Executive Departments; President; Senate; Supreme Court; U.S. Constitution, Article II; U.S. Constitution, individual amendments; Vice President

President Ronald Reagan is shown here with some advisers in 1981. The people in this photograph were concerned with defense and foreign affairs—from left to right: the director of the CIA, secretary of defense, president, vice president, secretary of state, counsel to the president, and national security adviser. This particular group of advisers, the National Security Council, was created by act of Congress in 1947 and modeled on the cabinet, the larger (but not legally established) body of presidential advisers. Membership in both groups is in part up to the president.

Capitation Tax

A head tax, meaning a direct tax on each person, as opposed to taxes on property or merchandise.

It is one of the oldest forms of taxation, used even in biblical times. Article I, section 2, of the Constitution requires that such taxes be divided among the states according to their population, with every five slaves to be counted as three free people in a state's population. This was a compromise between southern slave-owning states and northern commercial states, which lasted until the Thirteenth Amendment banned slavery in 1865. The Twenty-fourth Amendment eliminated the poll tax, a capitation tax that was used by some states to keep people—especially blacks— from voting.

Poll Taxes; Slavery; U.S. Constitution, Article I; U.S. Constitution, Thirteenth Amendment; U.S. Constitution, Twenty-fourth Amendment

Population of the United States in Selected Census Years

Year	Population
1790	3,929,214
1840	17,069,453
1890	62,947,714
1940	131,669,275
1990	248,709,873

Census workers are shown here questioning U.S. residents during the 1970 census. The count of the population, conducted every ten years since 1790, has changed considerably over time— both in its methods and the kinds of information it collects. At first, heads of households were asked to count their own families (and the families of any slaves they owned). Later, Congress required that every U.S. resident be counted and asked about occupation, place of birth, education, and the like. The count determines states' representation in Congress, but the information is also very useful to historians and government policymakers.

Census

An official count of the population, often including information on people's age, sex, race, and occupation.

Article I, section 2, of the Constitution requires that a census be taken every ten years for purposes of distributing seats in the House of Representatives. This was intended to adjust for changes in population growth and the movement of people from one state to another. The census was also used to calculate the amount of direct taxes to be contributed by the states. This has been modified by the Sixteenth Amendment regarding income taxes.

Capitation Tax; House of Representatives; U.S. Constitution, Article I; U.S. Constitution, Sixteenth Amendment

Checks and Balances

A constitutional arrangement that gives each branch of government—the executive, legislative, and judicial branches—some degree of power over the others.

The government cannot function unless the three independent branches cooperate. The French philosopher Montesquieu had recommended checks and balances as a way of limiting government power. The Framers of the Constitution adopted a version of his ideas.

They made sure that each independent branch could check, or stop, the actions of another branch. For example, Article I, section 7, of the Constitution permits the president to refuse to sign a law passed by Congress. Under certain conditions, Congress can pass the law again despite the president's objections. Under judicial review, the Supreme Court has taken on the power to reject laws passed by Congress and approved by the president. Of course, an amendment to the Constitution can overturn a Court decision. The Framers also thought to provide balances within the government. For example, they expected the Senate, originally chosen by the states, to balance the democratically elected House of Representatives and the more monarchlike executive. As a result of checks and balances, the three branches of government often must negotiate and compromise their differences. This delays government actions and makes them less likely to oppress the people.

Advice and Consent; Appointment to Office; Congress; Executive Branch; House of Representatives; Judicial Branch; Judicial Review; Legislative Branch; Senate; Separation of Powers; Spirit of the Laws; *Supreme Court; U.S. Constitution, Article I; Veto*

Chief Justices of the Supreme Court
John Jay, 1789–1795
John Rutledge, 1795
Oliver Ellsworth, 1796–1800
John Marshall, 1801–1835
Roger B. Taney, 1836–1864
Salmon P. Chase, 1864–1873
Morrison R. Waite, 1874–1888
Melville W. Fuller, 1888–1910
Edward D. White, 1910–1921
William H. Taft, 1921–1930
Charles Evans Hughes, 1930–1941
Harlan Fiske Stone, 1941–1946
Frederick M. Vinson, 1946–1953
Earl Warren, 1953–1969
Warren E. Burger, 1969–1986
William H. Rehnquist, 1986–

Chief Justice

The presiding judge of the Supreme Court.

The chief justice is mentioned in Article I, section 3, of the Constitution as the official in charge of presidential impeachment trials in the Senate. The chief justice and the other members of the Supreme Court interpret the Constitution and the nation's laws. In doing so, they help shape the American legal system and American history.

Impeachment; Senate; Supreme Court; U.S. Constitution, Article I

Citizenship

The right to be treated as a member of a country or state, to enjoy the protection of its laws, and to participate in its politics.

According to Article I, sections 2 and 3, of the Constitution, citizenship is a qualification for election to Congress. Article II, section 1, also makes citizenship a qualification for election as president or vice president. The Fourteenth Amendment extended citizenship to all people born in the United States, including former slaves.

Those who are not born citizens of a country may choose to become *naturalized citizens.* They may have to fulfill certain requirements. In the United States, these include living in their adopted country for a specified

period of years, reaching a certain minimum age, taking a test about American history and customs, and swearing allegiance to the nation.

Congress; President; U.S. Constitution, Article I; U.S. Constitution, Article II; U.S. Constitution, Fourteenth Amendment; Vice President

Adult naturalization classes such as this one, photographed in the 1920s, offer both daytime and evening instruction to future U.S. citizens. Many communities also sponsor classes to help immigrants learn English.

The Constitution refers to citizenship in many places, but it was not until ratification of the Fourteenth Amendment in 1868 that U.S. citizenship was truly defined. The amendment equates state and national citizenship, saying that "All persons born or naturalized in the United States" are citizens both "of the United States and of the State wherein they reside."

It is still up to Congress, however, to pass laws applying this definition of citizenship, at least for the rules of naturalization. As a result, some groups have been denied not only the benefits of citizenship but even the opportunity of citizenship. The Chinese Exclusion Act of 1882, to cite just one example, stipulated that "no State court or court of the United States shall admit Chinese to citizenship."

Today, no racial or ethnic group is barred from citizenship. However, there are still rules of naturalization that must be followed. Congress has also had to define the status of children born to U.S. citizens abroad. In most cases, those children are considered natural-born U.S. citizens.

Civil Law

In the American legal system, noncriminal law, such as property law and commercial law.

Civil law is referred to indirectly in Article III, section 2, of the Constitution, which gives the Supreme Court the right to hear cases between states and citizens of different states or between citizens of the same state claiming land from different states. The Eleventh Amendment changed the Court's jurisdiction in civil-law cases to exclude lawsuits against a state by citizens of another state or by foreigners. Such suits cannot be brought in federal court, but a state court may still accept them.

Federal Courts; Jurisdiction; Jury Trial, Right to; Supreme Court; U.S. Constitution, Article III; U.S. Constitution, Eleventh Amendment

Civil Liberties

The basic freedoms secured by the Constitution and the Bill of Rights.

These include such First Amendment guarantees as freedom of religion and freedom of speech. Other freedoms not listed in the Constitution are reserved to the people by the Ninth Amendment.

Bill of Rights; Religion, Freedom of; U.S. Constitution, First Amendment; U.S. Constitution, Ninth Amendment

Civil Rights

Guarantees of equal treatment under the law.

For almost one hundred years, the promises of equality for blacks and other minorities offered in the Fourteenth and Fifteenth amendments to the Constitution were not kept. For example, in *Plessy v. Ferguson* (1896),

These people participated in a civil-rights demonstration in the 1950s. Backed up by the National Association for the Advancement of Colored People (NAACP), an organization promoting equality of rights for African Americans, they protested school segregation.

Separation of the races was imposed by law in the South in the decades from the 1870s well into the 1960s. In the North, state legislatures eliminated discriminatory laws early in that period. Still, racial segregation continued to be practiced there in fact.

In some ways, it proved easier to end segregation in the South than in the North. As the Supreme Court noted in *Swann v. Charlotte-Mecklenburg Board of Education* (1971), the objective of the federal government was, from the mid-1950s on, "to eliminate from the public schools all vestiges of state-imposed segregation."

What proved harder to change was racial and ethnic separation resulting from differences in wealth and neighborhood housing patterns. Even today, student enrollment in many schools is 80 or 90 percent just one race or ethnic group.

the Supreme Court decided that blacks could be given what was called separate but equal treatment. As a result, over the next half century blacks in many parts of the country, especially in most of the former slave-owning South, were separated from whites at school, in public transportation, at various places of entertainment, in housing and hotels, and even at public rest rooms and water fountains. However, schools, bus and movie seats, hotels, and most other facilities available to blacks were very inferior to those set aside for whites. At the same time, various laws such as poll taxes were applied in a discriminatory way to deny a large number of blacks the right to vote. Finally, in *Brown v. Board of Education of Topeka* (1954), the Court overturned *Plessy* and ruled that because separate schools were unequal by their very nature, black and white children should go to school together. Between the 1950s and the 1970s, civil-rights protests, including marches, demonstrations, and boycotts, led Congress to pass a series of laws in an effort to right old wrongs involving segregation and in order to make it possible for blacks to vote. The Twenty-fourth Amendment swept away another obstacle to voting, the poll tax.

Poll Taxes; Segregation and Desegregation; Slavery; Supreme Court; U.S. Constitution, Fourteenth Amendment; U.S. Constitution, Fifteenth Amendment; U.S. Constitution, Twenty-fourth Amendment

Commander in Chief

The head of a nation's armed forces.

Article II, section 2, of the Constitution names the president as the commander in chief of the U.S. Army and Navy as well as any state militia when it is called up for national service. The Constitution does not mention the Air Force, of course, because airplanes did not exist until the twentieth century. Now the president commands this service too. The president shares responsibility for the nation's defense with Congress. According to Article I, section 8, only the lawmakers may declare war, set regulations for the armed services, and vote funds to support them.

Congress; Militia; President; U.S. Constitution, Article I; U.S. Constitution, Article II

Commerce Clause

In this cartoon, the United States is being swallowed by Monopoly, a ferocious giant, as the eye of the public looks down in judgment. The drawing was done in 1890, the year Congress passed the Sherman Anti-Trust Act, which declared illegal every "combination in the form of trust . . . in restraint of trade or commerce among the several States."

A trust, or monopoly, is a company or combination of companies that controls a product or market so completely that it has no real competition. Monopolies can demand whatever price they want for their products. Monopolies in essential goods (like gasoline or food) can harm the public.

The judicial and executive branches have at different times been active or reluctant in wielding power to break up monopolies. In the 1990s, a celebrated antitrust case was brought against the computer giant Microsoft.

Commerce Clause

The power of Congress to regulate business and trade.

Article I, section 8, of the Constitution gives Congress the right to control commerce between states, with foreign nations, and with Indians. The commerce clause is the result of a compromise arranged by members of the Constitutional Convention's Committee on Commerce. Under Article I, section 9, Congress is forbidden to tax items exported by any state. This pleased southern states whose citizens sold agricultural products, such as tobacco and cotton, overseas. Article I, section 10, prevents states from passing laws affecting business activities in other states or nations without the consent of Congress. This pleased the northern states whose citizens were involved in manufacturing and shipping.

The Articles of Confederation had not allowed the national government to regulate *interstate commerce,* business dealings affecting two or more states. The states, eager to protect local businesses, then set up barriers against goods made in other states. For example, Connecticut charged higher duties on Massachusetts-made items than on goods manufactured in Great Britain. Trade quickly became so difficult that first the Annapolis Convention and then the Constitutional Convention were called to remedy the situation.

Between 1789 and 1950, the commerce clause produced more lawsuits than any other part of the Constitution. In *Gibbons v. Ogden* (1824), the Supreme Court defined interstate commerce very broadly to cover transportation, navigation of waterways, and traffic among states. The Court excluded only trade that took place entirely in one state (*intrastate commerce*) and did not extend at all to any other states. At the turn of the century, Court interpretations of the commerce clause also made it possible for the federal government to regulate intrastate activities that affected interstate commerce. These included activities related to the public's health, morals, and safety. In *Champion v. Ames* (1903), for example, the Court upheld a federal law banning lottery tickets sent across state lines because the tickets could be harmful to public morals.

In *Hammer v. Dagenhart* (1918), however, the Court reduced the number of activities included as interstate commerce and struck down a law prohibiting interstate shipment of goods produced by child labor. The Court reasoned that the child-labor law was not an appropriate regulation because the kind of workers a company hired—adults or children— touched on the way a product was made, not how it was marketed. If a product was made entirely inside a state, the Court decided, then the method of making the product could not be regulated by Congress. In the early 1930s, such reasoning led the Court to prevent the federal government from setting wages and limiting the hours that people worked.

In the late 1930s, the Court finally reversed itself and allowed the government to set standards for wages and hours. It also used the commerce clause to uphold laws encouraging businesses to bargain with unions over employees' rights, as well as laws adjusting the amount of food that farmers sent to market. Overall, interpretations of the commerce clause have contributed to the growth of the national government by letting it regulate the way goods are made and sold.

Annapolis Convention; Articles of Confederation; Congress; Constitutional Convention; Duties and Imposts; Supreme Court; U.S. Constitution, Article I

> "The [anti-child-labor] act does not meddle with anything belonging to the States. They may regulate their internal affairs and their domestic commerce as they like. But when they seek to send their products across the state line, they are no longer within their rights. If there were no Constitution and no Congress, their power to cross the line would depend upon their neighbors. Under the Constitution, such commerce belongs not to the States, but to Congress to regulate."
>
> Justice Oliver Wendell Holmes, Dissent, *Hammer v. Dagenhart,* 1918

Common Law

Law based on people's customs, usual ways of doing things, and widespread beliefs.

Common law is taken into account when judges decide lawsuits. Such judge-made law was first applied in England and then brought to the American colonies. Common law is mentioned in the Seventh Amendment to the Constitution.

U.S. Constitution, Seventh Amendment

Annual Salaries of Selected Public Officials, 1998

President: $200,000
Vice President: $171,500
Senator: $136,600
Representative: $136,600
Chief Justice: $171,500
Associate Justice: $164,100

Compensation

Payment for services or workday activities.

Article I, section 6, of the Constitution states that the members of Congress will be paid by the U.S. Treasury. During the debates in the Constitutional Convention, some of the Framers wanted the states to pay the lawmakers, in order to make them more responsive to the states' needs. Others argued that this would allow the states to control Congress. The Constitution also sets the rules for compensating the president and federal judges, but it fails to mention the vice president. Article II, section 1, provides that the president shall be paid by the government, with pay neither increased nor decreased during a term of office. The president may not accept any additional fees from the government or the individual states. These arrangements are designed to prevent presidential pay from being used to influence presidential decisions. Article III, section 1, protects the impartiality and independence of federal judges. It makes sure that their salaries will not be cut while they are serving on the courts.

Confederation Congress; Congress; Constitutional Convention; Framers; Judicial Branch; President;

Treasury, U.S. Department of the; U.S. Constitution, Article I; U.S. Constitution, Article II;

U.S. Constitution, Article III; Vice President

Concurrent Powers

Powers shared by the national and state governments.

One example of a concurrent power is the power to tax. Another example is found in the Eighteenth Amendment to the Constitution. It permitted both the states and the national government to enforce a ban on drinks containing alcohol.

Taxation, Power of; U.S. Constitution, Eighteenth Amendment

Confederation

A league of independent states.

Member states share a common government, which they direct and control. The government does not have any power over the people living

A confederation "is a convention by which several smaller states agree to become members of a larger one."

Montesquieu, *The Spirit of the Laws*, 1748

in the states. The thirteen independent American states formed such a league under the Articles of Confederation from 1781 to 1789. The eleven southern states that left the Union from 1861 to 1865 also created a confederation, called the Confederate States of America.

Articles of Confederation; Confederation Congress; States

Confederation Congress

The single-chamber legislature created in Article V of the Articles of Confederation.

Lacking a permanent home, the Congress met in Philadelphia; Princeton, New Jersey; Annapolis, Maryland; Trenton, New Jersey; and New York City. It was made up of delegates from the member states. To keep them accountable to their states, the delegates were forbidden to hold another paid office in the government of the United States. The states paid their expenses.

Nine states had to consent before the Congress could use its most important powers. Since it was difficult to get nine states to agree to anything, the Congress did not do very much. In any case, business could be conducted only when a quorum of delegates from seven of the thirteen states were present. This was not always possible. The membership changed frequently because the states could recall their delegates and replace them at almost any time. In addition, the delegates could serve for only three one-year terms in a row, so a lot of people were coming and going in Congress. Each state could send no less than two and no more than seven delegates, but each delegation could cast only one vote.

Each year, one delegate from a different state was chosen to serve as the presiding officer of the Congress. He was called the president. There was no executive branch of government, but the delegates formed committees to carry out the decisions of Congress. The Congress appointed three secretaries to handle important matters. Benjamin Lincoln served as secretary of war until he was replaced by Henry Knox. Robert Morris was superintendent of finance. Robert Livingston was the first secretary for foreign affairs; John Jay succeeded him.

Articles of Confederation; Constitutional Convention; Executive Branch; Quorum; Territories; Treaties; Unicameral Legislature

Confession

An admission of wrongdoing.

> "Our . . . system of criminal justice demands that the government seeking to punish an individual produce the evidence against him by its own independent labors, rather than by the cruel, simple expedient of compelling it from his own mouth."
>
> **Chief Justice Earl Warren, *Miranda v. Arizona*, 1966**

The Fifth Amendment to the Constitution protects people accused of crimes from self-incrimination, meaning it protects them from having to testify against themselves. The Supreme Court established a series of guidelines in *Miranda v. Arizona* (1966) to keep the police from applying excessive pressure to get suspects to confess. People arrested for crimes must be given the following warnings: (1) You have the right to remain silent. (2) Anything you say can and will be used against you. (3) You have the right to talk to a lawyer before being questioned and to have a lawyer present during questioning. (4) If you cannot afford a lawyer, one will be provided for you if you so wish.

Self-Incrimination; Supreme Court; U.S. Constitution, Fifth Amendment

Congress

The name the Constitution gives to the two-chamber legislative branch of the United States in Article I, section 1.

Membership in the two chambers of Congress was fixed by the Connecticut Compromise, which settled differences between the large and small states at the Constitutional Convention. Seats in the House of Representatives are distributed according to the population in each state. In the Senate, each state is treated equally and given two seats.

In Article I, sections 2 and 3 set the lawmakers' terms of office and their qualifications for office. The entire membership of the House is elected to office every two years; senators serve six-year terms, with one-third of the body elected every two years. Representatives must be at least twenty-five years old, a citizen of the United States for at least seven years, and a resident of the state that elects them to office. Senators must be at least thirty years old, a citizen for at least nine years, and an inhabitant of the state that elects them.

Article I also describes how the members of each chamber are elected. Section 4 lets states regulate the "times, places, and manner" of these elections. Congress then set a uniform election date: the first Tuesday after the first Monday in November of even-numbered years. The Twentieth Amendment to the Constitution set January 3 as the date when newly elected members of the House take office. Article I, section 2, requires representatives to be elected by people divided into districts within their states. A compromise between northern and southern states at the Constitutional Convention originally counted every five slaves as three free persons for purposes of representation. Slavery was eliminated by the

Thirteenth Amendment. The Fourteenth Amendment states that when people are counted to see how many representatives a state gets, everyone must be counted, except untaxed Native Americans. Senators were originally elected by their state legislatures, according to Article I, section 3. After about 125 years, the Seventeenth Amendment provided that they be elected by the voters of their state.

Congressional privileges are included in Article I. Members of Congress are entitled to organize and manage their own affairs. They choose their presiding officers as well as such officials as a chaplain and clerk. Section 5 directs them to judge their own election results, handle questions about members' qualifications, keep a record of their proceedings, and punish members for inappropriate behavior.

Under Article I, section 6, the lawmakers are forbidden to hold another office in the government while serving in Congress. This promotes separation of powers. As an example of checks and balances, both chambers share the power to make law, found in section 7. Both also take part in the impeachment process. According to section 2, the House formally charges a public official with misconduct, but under section 3, the Senate then holds a trial to decide whether the official is guilty or innocent and should be removed from office. In addition, section 5 states that neither chamber can adjourn for more than three days without the consent of the other.

Unlike pre-Constitution congresses, the members can pass laws, by a simple majority vote, that affect the people as well as the states. The procedure for doing this is outlined in Article I, section 7.

Congressional powers are listed in Article I, section 8, including the right to raise and collect taxes, borrow money, regulate commerce, establish uniform laws on citizenship for foreigners, set up courts, and declare war. The Framers realized that if the Constitution were to last, they had to give Congress flexibility to provide for the future. This is why they added a so-called elastic clause to section 8, permitting Congress to make all laws that "shall be necessary and proper for carrying into execution the foregoing powers." Under its terms, as just one example, the lawmakers have used their power "to promote the progress of science and useful arts" to set up and fund the National Aeronautics and Space Administration (NASA). The Framers never imagined that the government would send astronauts to the moon.

Among the powers denied to Congress in Article I, section 9, are passage of bills of attainder and ex post facto laws, as well as any laws banning

The American astronaut Edwin E. ("Buzz") Aldrin posed on the surface of the moon in July 1969. Aldrin and Neil A. Armstrong were the first men to go to the moon. They were sent there as part of a program funded by U.S. tax dollars, as budgeted by Congress.

The earliest example of the government's funding a similar endeavor was the Lewis and Clark Expedition of 1804–1806. There followed the Coast Survey, the Smithsonian Institution, the National Academy of Sciences, and an increasing number of scientific studies carried out by the Army and by executive departments.

The government's authority to carry out these and many other activities is established by a phrase in the Constitution giving Congress power to "promote the progress of science and the useful arts."

By this authority, Congress has funded theater productions and other arts projects, both during the Great Depression of the 1930s and since then, through such means as the National Endowment for the Arts. This spending has been criticized in some circles.

Roger Sherman served for many years in the Connecticut colonial legislature. A highly respected and experienced delegate to the Continental Congresses, Sherman sat on a number of important committees, including those that prepared the Declaration of Independence and the Articles of Confederation. He later drew up a series of amendments to strengthen the Confederation. These would have given the Confederation Congress the power to regulate commerce, impose tariffs, set up a Supreme Court, and make laws affecting the people as well as the states. The states rejected them.

As a delegate to the Constitutional Convention, Sherman was an important spokesman for the small states and one of the authors of the New Jersey Plan. When it was not accepted, Sherman introduced the Connecticut Compromise and gave it his full support.

the slave trade until 1808. In addition, the members may not grant titles of nobility or accept such titles or offices. They also may not receive payments from foreign governments. Under Article IV, section 3, Congress has the power to admit new states and to protect federal property. In Article V, Congress is given the right to propose amendments to the Constitution.

Adjournment; Bicameral Legislature; Bill; Bill of Attainder; Breach of the Peace; Checks and Balances; Citizenship; Commerce Clause; Confederation Congress; Connecticut Compromise; Constitutional Convention; Continental Congresses; Elastic Clause; Ex Post Facto Laws; Express Powers; Felonies; House of Representatives; Immunity; Impeachment; Law; Legislative Branch; President; Senate; Separation of Powers; Treason; U.S. Constitution, Article I; U.S. Constitution, Article IV; U.S. Constitution, Article V; U.S. Constitution, individual amendments

Connecticut Compromise

An agreement between the large and small states at the Constitutional Convention concerning representation in Congress.

The large states' delegations supported the Virginia Plan, drawn up by James Madison and presented by Edmund Randolph. It recommended a lower house based on population and an upper house also based on population, but elected by the lower house. The smaller states' delegations, led by William Paterson, preferred a proposal called the New Jersey Plan. That plan called for a one-chamber legislature with each state given one vote, like the Confederation Congress. Roger Sherman sponsored a compromise that benefited small states with an equal vote in the Senate and the larger states with representation by population in the House of Representatives. Sherman's proposal was eventually accepted by the delegates.

Bicameral Legislature; Confederation Congress; Congress; Constitutional Convention; House of Representatives; New Jersey Plan; Senate; Unicameral Legislature; Virginia Plan

Constitution

A basic law that creates, organizes, and defines a government's powers.

Unwritten constitutions are the oldest kind. They developed gradually over time, based on customs, traditions, judges' decisions, or laws passed by legislatures. Usually the people did not formally vote their approval of unwritten constitutions. They showed their approval by living under a constitution's rules without protest.

Great Britain has an unwritten constitution. The government evolved over centuries into the form it has today. Certain important documents,

Junius Brutus Stearns did this painting, *Washington Addressing the Constitutional Convention,* in 1856, almost seventy years after George Washington chaired the Convention of delegates who drafted the Constitution. Eighty years later, in 1937—the 150th anniversary of the Convention—the U.S. Postal Service reproduced this painting on a commemorative stamp. In May of that year, at the opening of a summer-long celebration in Philadelphia, Washington's own copy of the Constitution, with corrections in his own hand, was put on public display. By then the Constitutional Convention had become for many a revered symbol of a glorious past.

Nevertheless, as the historian Michael Kammen points out in his book *A Machine That Would Go of Itself,* the Constitution "emerged as a symbol"—that is, as something else besides as an instrument of government—"both slowly and inconclusively." Very few artists, he says, illustrated scenes from the Constitutional Convention. And there are very few ships, newspapers, counties, or streets named "Constitution."

such as the Magna Carta and the English Bill of Rights, stated rights Englishmen thought they had already. Originally, when Americans protested their treatment by Great Britain, they were trying to restore their own rights under the British constitution.

Written constitutions are documents that actually create governments and, usually, limit their powers. The offices and procedures in written constitutions are not necessarily the result of slowly developing customs and traditions. They are usually the product of deliberate decisions made at one time by a group of individuals. Because these constitutions are written down, they may be more detailed and more rigid than unwritten constitutions. That is why they usually contain sections outlining how they may be amended, or changed. Written constitutions typically go into effect after they are approved by the nation's citizens.

Amendment Process; Bill of Rights; Magna Carta; Republican Form of Government; U.S. Constitution

Constitutional Convention

A meeting from May to September 1787 in the State House (now called Independence Hall), Philadelphia, to write a new plan of government for the United States.

The weaknesses of the Articles of Confederation—the document under which the United States was governed in 1787—were well known. The government could not get Spain to open its American rivers and ports to

Demonstrators came to the Lincoln Memorial in Washington, D.C., in June 1970 to voice anger at the government. Their gathering recalled the one held almost 200 years earlier. Both events were attended by people with common goals who represented different communities of interests.

The men with the banners proclaiming this a "Revolutionary People's Constitutional Convention" were members of the Black Panther Party. The Black Panthers called for armed resistance in defense of blacks, whose rights they said were systematically trampled in American society.

Others shown here—members of the Students for a Democratic Society, for instance—were motivated by President Richard M. Nixon's expansion of the Vietnam War and call for more draftees. Soon after his announcement, four students were killed by National Guardsmen at an antiwar demonstration at Kent State University in Ohio.

The assembly in Washington in 1970 did not produce a new constitution, but the participants' right to call for one was protected.

American traders, or Great Britain to abandon its forts south of the Canadian border. The Annapolis Convention had failed to settle trade problems among the states, and the Confederation Congress was unable to muster troops to help put down Shays's Rebellion, a farmers' insurrection in Massachusetts in 1786. Property owners, businessmen, and conservative politicians were demanding that something be done. In response, the Congress called for a meeting in Philadelphia.

Fifty-five delegates from twelve states attended. They became known as the Framers of the Constitution. After choosing George Washington as their chairman, they began discussions. They were originally instructed to make changes to improve the Articles of Confederation, but they soon concluded that the task was impossible. Besides, amendments to the Articles required the approval of all thirteen states, and Rhode Island refused to attend the convention. So the Framers began to prepare a new document. They worked in secrecy, to avoid pressure from the public and the state governments. Some delegates, however, kept journals of the proceedings. James Madison's record of the events was the most complete.

By keeping their discussions private, they were able to negotiate their differences in a series of compromises. The large states supported the Virginia Plan. The small states offered the New Jersey Plan as an alternative. The delegates finally accepted the Connecticut Compromise to settle their differences. Other problems soon developed over such issues as

Gouverneur Morris helped to write New York State's Constitution in 1776. At his insistence, it included a measure on freedom of religion.

In 1787, Morris attended the Constitutional Convention as a delegate from Pennsylvania. His humorous comments amused the delegates and influenced their opinions on crucial issues. He made more speeches than any other delegate.

Morris added the requirement to the Three-Fifths Compromise that slaves be counted for taxing states as well as determining their representation in Congress. He wanted a strong president, holding office for life, with a final veto over acts of Congress.

Morris served as the "penman of the Constitution." His eloquent wording and flowing handwriting gave the document its distinctive style.

By the time of his death, Morris had become deeply disillusioned with the government he had helped to create. Like many people with economic ties to New England, Morris opposed the War of 1812 because it disrupted trade with England. Opponents of the war convened the Hartford Convention in Connecticut from December 1814 to January 1815. Morris supported both the convention and the minority view expressed there—that New England should separate from the Union and draft its own constitution.

slavery and the slave trade, taxation, commerce, the rights of the states, and the election of a president. The delegates divided into a number of committees to find solutions. These included committees on commerce, rules, the slave trade, bankruptcy, representation, and state debts. Some of the most famous of the committees are described below.

The Committee of Detail wrote the first draft of the Constitution, changing general grants of power given to the new government into express powers. Committee members copied sections from the Articles of Confederation when they described the powers of Congress, denied powers to states, and outlined relations among the states. Oliver Ellsworth, Nathaniel Gorham, Edmund Randolph, John Rutledge, and James Wilson served on the committee. Rutledge was chairman.

The Committee of the Whole followed a procedure inherited from Britain that turns the entire membership of a legislature or meeting into a large committee. It is used to suspend formal rules, encourage unlimited debate, permit nonbinding votes, and sometimes speed up decisions. The delegates used it to give tentative approval to the Virginia Plan and to review the New Jersey Plan. The chairman was Nathaniel Gorham.

The Committee on Postponed Matters was assigned to make recommendations on matters about which delegates had disagreed. Its most important accomplishment was finding an acceptable method of electing the president. Some of the delegates had wanted the president to be elected by state legislatures, some by Congress, and others by the people. While settling this problem, the committee members also arranged for the election of a vice president. The eleven committee members were Abraham Baldwin, David Brearly, Pierce Butler, Daniel Carroll, John Dickinson, Nicholas Gilman, Rufus King, James Madison, Gouverneur Morris, Roger Sherman, and Hugh Williamson. Brearly was chairman.

The Committee on Style was asked to rearrange and organize the articles of the Constitution agreed on by the delegates and to write them in a clear manner. Alexander Hamilton, William Samuel Johnson, Rufus King, James Madison, Gouverneur Morris, and James Wilson served on the committee. Johnson was chairman. However, it was Morris who reduced the twenty-three original articles to seven and created the constitutional phrases so familiar today.

Annapolis Convention; Articles of Confederation; Confederation Congress; Connecticut Compromise; Debts; Denied Powers; Express Powers; Framers; New Jersey Plan; President; U.S. Constitution, individual articles; *Vice President; Virginia Plan*

Constitutional Law

A set of rulings used to settle legal disputes about the way a government is organized, how officeholders are chosen or exercise power, and relationships between citizens and government, among other topics.

In the United States, these rulings also apply to relations between the national government and the states. American constitutional law is made up of judges' interpretations of the words and phrases of the Constitution and the amendments that have been added to it. Supreme Court decisions are an important source of constitutional law.

Construction; Judicial Review; Supreme Court; U.S. Constitution, individual amendments

Constitution of the United States

See: U.S. Constitution

Construction

An explanation or interpretation of the words in a law or the Constitution.

Through judicial review, the justices of the Supreme Court have interpreted laws and the Constitution. They have given meaning to words and phrases that may be vague or out-of-date. *Strict constructionists* are those who interpret the Constitution narrowly, often by trying to examine the original intent, or original meaning, of the Framers. *Loose constructionists,* on the other hand, are more ready to interpret the Constitution as a changing document, one that evolves as it is applied to new situations in modern times.

Framers; Judicial Review; Original Intent; Supreme Court

> **"We must never forget that it is a *constitution* we are expounding . . . a constitution intended to endure for ages to come, and consequently, to be adapted to the various *crises* of human affairs."**
> **Chief Justice John Marshall,**
> **McCulloch v. Maryland, 1819**

Consuls

Overseas agents of the U.S. government who promote American business and commercial interests.

They also protect individual citizens who are traveling abroad. Consuls are not treated as official representatives of the United States to foreign governments. That responsibility belongs to ambassadors. Consuls are mentioned in Article II, section 2, and Article III, section 2, of the Constitution.

Ambassadors; U.S. Constitution, Article II; U.S. Constitution, Article III

Continental Congresses

Assemblies of delegates that met on and off from 1774 to 1781.

They made recommendations for handling common problems faced first by the colonies and then by the independent states of North America. They provided an important first step toward creating a national government.

The First Continental Congress was an advisory council of fifty-five delegates from twelve colonies that met in Philadelphia from September 5 to October 26, 1774. Georgia chose not to send delegates. The delegates worked out a common response to the British Intolerable Acts. These had closed down the port of Boston and suspended self-government in Massachusetts, among other things. Declaring that the Intolerable Acts violated the British Constitution, the delegates refused to obey them. Before adjourning, the Congress advised Massachusetts to form an independent government.

By the time the Second Continental Congress met in May 1775, the battles of Lexington and Concord had been fought in Massachusetts. The Second Continental Congress became the acting government of the United States. Before it went out of existence in 1781, it organized the army, directed the War for Independence, and encouraged the states to cooperate. At first, many delegates from the Middle Atlantic colonies were not ready to separate from Great Britain. Led by John Dickinson, they sent King George III a Declaration of the Causes and Necessity of Taking Up Arms in July 1775. It explained that the colonists were prepared to stop fighting as soon as Britain recognized their rights. Britain's answer was to send more troops to the colonies.

Soon, even the most reluctant colonies changed their minds about separating from Britain. By the spring of 1776, their delegates in Congress were instructed to vote for independence. The Congress approved the Declaration of Independence on July 4, 1776. During the course of the war, meetings of Congress moved from Philadelphia to other cities that were safer from British attack. The accomplishments of the Second Continental Congress were limited because it could not raise funds or act without the consent of most of the states. In 1781, it was replaced by the Confederation Congress, which faced similar difficulties.

Adjournment; Articles of Confederation; Confederation Congress; Commander in Chief; Constitution; Militia; Quartering of Troops

Contract Clause

The section of the U.S. Constitution that speaks of contracts, which are legally binding agreements between people or groups.

Contracts are promises to do or not to do something under certain conditions, for a fixed period of time. Under Article I, section 10, of the Constitution, states are forbidden to make laws that break the promises made in contracts. As men of considerable wealth, the Framers probably included this restriction because they wanted to secure their property rights. They also wanted to be assured they would be repaid the debts they were owed according to the terms of their contracts.

In its early interpretations of the words and phrases of the Constitution, the Supreme Court prevented states from interfering with contracts. In *Fletcher v. Peck* (1810), the Court refused to let Georgia cancel a contract made by a corrupt previous state legislature, under which the lawmakers had sold public lands at an incredibly cheap price to people who then sold them for profit. In *Dartmouth College v. Woodward* (1819), the Court ruled that the New Hampshire legislature could not change the way Dartmouth College chose its board of trustees. This would violate the 1769 royal charter, a contract, that set up the college. For the first time, the Court had protected a private corporation (Dartmouth College) from a state law altering the terms of its contract. As a result of this decision, states could not regulate private contracts arranging business property rights, the ownership and management of companies. From the 1860s to the 1930s, the Court relied on other sections of the Constitution to protect business property rights from state regulators.

When the national economy collapsed under the pressure of the Great Depression in the 1930s, the Court held that a state's right to make rules protecting its citizens should be "read into all contracts." That is, states have an assumed right to change contracts to protect their citizens. In *Home Building & Loan Association v. Blaisdell* (1934), a bank wanted to seize the home of a couple who fell behind in their mortgage payments. This penalty was called for in their contract. However, a state law allowed people to keep their property and pay off their loans more slowly during the national economic crisis. The Court reasoned that during emergencies, public needs were great. As a result, states should be able to pass laws altering contracts. Even in the absence of emergencies, states' police powers had increased so much by then that the court later reinterpreted Article I, section 10, to give the states more flexibility. Today, the Court lets states make decisions about economic conditions and, when they consider it necessary, break or change the agreements made in contracts.

Construction; Debts; Police Powers; Property Rights; Supreme Court; U.S. Constitution, Article I

States "possess authority to safeguard the vital interests of [their] people."
Chief Justice Charles Evans Hughes, *Home Building & Loan Association v. Blaisdell,* 1934

Convention

A meeting of an organization, called for a special purpose.

For example, modern political parties hold a convention every four years to nominate candidates for president and vice president and decide the party's official position on the issues of the day. Other organizations also hold conventions of their membership to elect new leaders and approve important decisions. In the past, conventions did not meet regularly. The Annapolis Convention met to discuss trade problems among the states. The Constitutional Convention was originally called to revise the Articles of Confederation.

The Framers decided that the Constitution should be approved by special conventions in each state rather than by state legislatures. State legislatures would be less likely to accept the it, because they were going to give up some of their powers to the new national government.

The Framers also mentioned conventions in Article V of the Constitution. To propose an amendment to the Constitution, two-thirds of the states may call for a convention. To ratify an amendment, conventions may be held in the states, and three-fourths of them must approve the change. State conventions have been used only once to date, to ratify the Twenty-first Amendment.

Amendment Process; Annapolis Convention; Constitutional Convention; Framers; Parties, Political; Ratification; U.S. Constitution, Article V; U.S. Constitution, Twenty-first Amendment

Copyright

The sole right of authors and artists to control the publication or performance of their works.

According to Article I, section 8, of the Constitution, Congress can grant this protection in order to promote progress in science and the arts. Under the October 1998 copyright law, for works completed before January 1, 1978, a copyright lasts for the lifetime of the author plus seventy years (with the provision that it can in no case expire before December 31, 2002, or, if published by that date, before December 31, 2047). For works finished after January 1, 1978, a copyright lasts for the lifetime of the author plus seventy years. However, if the work was created by or for a corporation, then the copyright lasts for 120 years from the date of creation or ninety-five years from the date of publication, whichever is earlier.

Congress; Patents; U.S. Constitution, Article I

Corruption of the Blood and Forfeiture

Punishment of a person's heirs by preventing them from inheriting that person's property.

Article III, section 3, of the Constitution forbids Congress from making this a penalty for treason. In Great Britain, when a bill of attainder was passed, the attainted person and his descendants were denied their property rights. People felt that the descendants had "bad blood," in that their blood was "corrupted" by their criminal ancestor. The penalty was abolished in the early 1800s.

Bill of Attainder; Treason; U.S. Constitution, Article III

Counterfeiting

Making an imitation and passing it off as real.

According to Article I, section 8, of the Constitution, Congress can determine the punishment for counterfeiting government bonds and monies. This is important because the widespread circulation of counterfeit currency or bonds could seriously disrupt the economy.

Congress; Money and Coinage; U.S. Constitution, Article I

Crimes and Misdemeanors

Acts that break the law.

The term can be traced back to medieval England. Then the words *crimes* and *misdemeanors* were practically interchangeable. In modern times, crimes usually refer to more serious offenses than misdemeanors. According to Article II, section 4, of the Constitution, "high crimes and misdemeanors" are grounds for impeaching a president, vice president, or other government officials.

The Framers had wanted the president to be a strong and independent leader, but they did not want the chief executive to be above the law. The threat of impeachment was one way to hold presidents accountable for their actions. When the House of Representatives debated removing President Richard M. Nixon from office in 1974, defining "high crimes and misdemeanors" presented a problem. At first, it was unclear whether Nixon had broken any laws, although he had apparently abused his powers as president. Then a previously unreleased tape recording confirmed that he had illegally concealed evidence of a crime from law-enforcement officials. It was immediately clear that Nixon would be impeached, but he resigned before the House could act.

> "[T]he Constitution is designed to be a law for rulers and people alike at all times and under all circumstances."
> Senator Sam J. Ervin, Comments before the Senate Select Committee on Presidential Campaign Activities, 1974

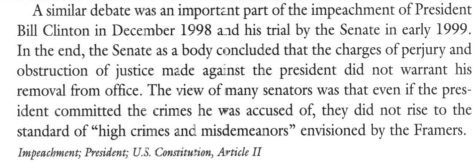

A similar debate was an important part of the impeachment of President Bill Clinton in December 1998 and his trial by the Senate in early 1999. In the end, the Senate as a body concluded that the charges of perjury and obstruction of justice made against the president did not warrant his removal from office. The view of many senators was that even if the president committed the crimes he was accused of, they did not rise to the standard of "high crimes and misdemeanors" envisioned by the Framers.

Impeachment; President; U.S. Constitution, Article II

This electric chair was photographed in the 1930s. Electrocution is the sole method of execution in six states. It is an accepted method in five other states. Lethal injection is a more common method of execution—the only method prescribed by law in fourteen states and an accepted method in eighteen others. In all, thirty-eight states have the death penalty.

D

Cruel and Unusual Punishment

This term is used to describe severe, barbaric, and excessive penalties for breaking the law.

For many centuries, people were branded with a mark burned into their skin, forced to have a hand amputated, or even executed for crimes as minor as petty theft. Until passage of the English Bill of Rights in 1689, criminals in England could be hanged but then taken down while they were alive so that their bodies could be divided into quarters or disemboweled. The Eighth Amendment to the Constitution prohibits such inhumane punishment. Nevertheless, in the early days of the American Republic, whipping and other penalties later regarded as excessively cruel were common. They were eventually abolished.

Bill of Rights; Death Penalty; Supreme Court; U.S. Constitution, Eighth Amendment

Death Penalty

Loss of life as a punishment for certain crimes.

Centuries ago, people were often hanged for petty crimes, such as stealing a loaf of bread, as well as for felonies, such as murder. Today, in the United States, people are executed only for very serious crimes, such as certain cases of murder. The Fifth, Sixth, Eighth, and Fourteenth amendments to the Constitution provide safeguards for people accused of felonies. Modern Americans disagree about sentencing people to death. In *Furman v. Georgia* (1972), the Supreme Court temporarily suspended the death penalty. The Court thought it was a cruel and unusual punishment because different juries often did not reach the same conclusion when deciding punishments for similar crimes. According to the Court, such arbitrary and often racially discriminatory action made it a violation of the Eighth Amendment. As a result of the *Furman* ruling, executions were halted in the thirty-nine states that had the death penalty. More than six hundred convicts on death row awaited further developments. In *Gregg v. Georgia* (1976), the Court allowed criminals to be sentenced to death once again. However, the juries must receive guidelines or instructions from judges, and sentencing is now separated from decisions about a suspect's guilt or innocence.

Cruel and Unusual Punishment; Felonies; Supreme Court; U.S. Constitution, Fifth Amendment; U.S. Constitution, Sixth Amendment; U.S. Constitution, Eighth Amendment; U.S. Constitution, Fourteenth Amendment

Debts

Money or services that are required to be repaid by a certain date.

Payment of debts was an issue that troubled the Framers of the Constitution. Fresh in their minds was Shays's Rebellion, an uprising of Massachusetts farmers in 1786 against state and local officials. The farmers were protesting court judgments against them for unpaid debts and overdue taxes, the result of a series of bad harvests. Led by a former captain in the Continental Army, Daniel Shays, they were trying to save their farms from being seized as payment for the money they owed. The state government of Massachusetts appealed to the Confederation Congress for help in putting down the rebellion. However, the Congress lacked the authority to order other states to send troops to Massachusetts; it could only make recommendations. The uprising was eventually put down by 4,000 members of the state militia.

For the most part, the Framers were wealthy men with little sympathy for those who did not pay back what they owed. They opposed state laws that eased requirements for paying debts or allowed debtors to make payments in paper money instead of gold and silver. (With the use of paper money, lenders received the full amount they were owed, but they could buy less with paper money than with silver or gold. This happened because the states kept printing more and more paper money, thereby reducing its value.) To protect lenders from these practices, Article I, section 8, of the Constitution gives Congress the right to coin money and fix its value. Article I, section 10, forbids the states from allowing anything but gold or silver coin as payment for debts and from changing or modifying contracts. Contracts often included arrangements for the payment of debts.

The Framers were also faced with the debts run up by the Second Continental Congress during the War for Independence. They knew that the government would have to borrow money from its European allies.

> "The government under the Articles of Confederation was not paying the interest on its debt and its paper [money] had depreciated. . . . The advantage of a strong national government that could discharge this debt at its face value is obvious; and it was fully understood at the time."
>
> Charles A. Beard,
> *An Economic Interpretation of the Constitution,* 1913

The allies had to be assured that their old loans would be repaid before they issued new ones. Article VI guarantees that the national government will honor the earlier agreements and debts.

The Constitution failed to provide for Revolutionary War debts owed by individual states. To solve this problem, the first secretary of the treasury, Alexander Hamilton, proposed that the national government accept the states' debts. Georgia, Maryland, New Hampshire, North Carolina, and Virginia opposed his plan. They had already paid off their debts by selling land and raising taxes. Connecticut, Massachusetts, New Jersey, New York, and South Carolina supported the plan, because they held a large number of debt certificates. In 1790, Congress voted $21.5 million to pay off all remaining war debts. To win votes for this measure, Hamilton and his followers agreed to let the nation's capital be located on the banks of the Potomac River, as the southern states wished. It seemed a fair exchange, because the debts held by northern states would be paid off by taxes collected mostly in the South.

Confederation Congress; Constitutional Convention; Continental Congresses; Contract Clause;
District of Columbia; Framers; Money and Coinage; Treasury, U.S. Department of the;
U.S. Constitution, Article I; U.S. Constitution, Article VI

Defense

Protection from invasion by foreign nations.

Both the Articles of Confederation and the Preamble to the Constitution made defense a duty of the national government. Following the principle of separation of powers, the Constitution divides responsibility for the nation's security between the president and Congress. According to Article II, section 2, of the Constitution, the president is the commander in chief of the armed services. The president may call up the state militias and can appoint the heads of military departments, subject to Senate approval. Article I, section 8, gives Congress the power to set up and fund an army and a navy and to declare war.

The Framers' outline for the nation's defense has changed over time. For example, in 1947, a secretary of defense was appointed to oversee the secretaries of the Army and the Navy. At the same time, the Air Force was organized as a separate military service.

Articles of Confederation; Commander in Chief; Congress; Foreign Affairs; Framers; Militia;
Preamble; President; Senate; Separation of Powers; U.S. Constitution, Article I; U.S. Constitution,
Article II; War Powers

Delegated Powers

See: Express Powers

Delegates

People who attend meetings with instructions from those who sent them.

Delegates act as agents for others. At the Continental Congresses and the Confederation Congress, the delegates spoke on behalf of their state governments. Delegates to the Constitutional Convention quickly found they could not carry out instructions from their states to improve the Articles of Confederation. They used their own judgment and replaced the Articles with the Constitution. Today, delegates attend many meetings. The most familiar of these are the Republican and Democratic national conventions, where the party delegates from each state choose a presidential and a vice presidential candidate every four years.

Articles of Confederation; Confederation Congress; Constitutional Convention; Continental Congresses; Convention; Parties, Political

Democracy

See: Representative Democracy; Republican Form of Government

Denied Powers

Limitations on Congress and the states, which prevent them from taking certain actions.

According to Article I, sections 9 and 10, of the Constitution, Congress and the states may not pass bills of attainder or ex post facto laws or grant titles of nobility. Section 9 prohibits Congress from suspending the writ of habeas corpus unless there is a national emergency. Other denied powers were the result of compromises made during the Constitutional Convention. Congress could not regulate the slave trade until 1808. Any direct taxes Congress raises must be based on the population of the individual states. In addition, it may not tax exports, show favoritism to one state over another in regulating commerce, or take money from the Treasury without passing an appropriation bill.

In Article I, section 10, the states are barred from taking part in foreign relations and foreign trade. They may not go to war independently either. Two or more states may not enter an interstate compact without the consent of Congress. They are also prevented from passing laws that would affect the payment of debts. So they may not substitute paper money for requirements that debts be paid in gold or silver. Further, they may not change the content of contracts.

Appropriations; Bill; Bill of Attainder; Commerce Clause; Congress; Constitutional Convention; Contract Clause; Debts; Export Taxes; Ex Post Facto Laws; Express Powers; Habeas Corpus, Writ of; Nobility; States; Taxation, Power of; Treasury, U.S. Department of the; U.S. Constitution, Article I

Direct Taxes

See: Capitation Tax; Poll Taxes

Discrimination

> "Distinctions between citizens solely because of their ancestry are, by their very nature, odious to a free people whose institutions are founded upon the doctrine of equality."
> **Chief Justice Harlan Fiske Stone, *Hirabayashi v. United States*, 1943**

Laws and actions that benefit certain groups and exclude others based on their race, gender, sexual orientation, religion, or national origins.

At one time or another, many different groups have been denied the equal protection of the laws and due process of law guaranteed by the Constitution. They have been victims of segregation and discrimination in education, jobs, housing, and transportation. Since the 1950s, the Supreme Court has interpreted passages in the Constitution in ways prohibiting discrimination. Since the 1960s, Congress has passed laws designed to end discrimination. While some discrimination continues, these laws have put the goal of full equality before the law within reach.

Civil Rights; Congress; Due Process of Law; Equal Protection of the Laws; Segregation and Desegregation; Supreme Court; U.S. Constitution, Fourteenth Amendment; Women's Rights

District of Columbia

The federal district in which Washington, the capital and seat of the government of the United States, is situated.

Article I, section 8, of the Constitution gives Congress the sole right to pass laws for the district. It states that an area not exceeding ten miles square will be set aside to serve as the capital, but it does not say where that will be. In 1790, Alexander Hamilton and Thomas Jefferson, two rival party leaders serving in George Washington's cabinet, agreed to locate the district on the banks of the Potomac River as the southern states wanted. In exchange, the southern states agreed to support Hamilton's plan to allow the federal government to pay off state Revolutionary War debts. This was what northern states wanted. President Washington chose the exact location of the capital and convinced landowners in Virginia and Maryland to sell their acreage to the government. The capital was named for him. The federal government ran the city of Washington. Most of

The U.S. Capitol, the building that is home to the Senate and the House of Representatives of the United States, is a familiar sight to many people around the world. The present building, with its impressive dome (topped by a nineteen-foot-tall Statue of Freedom, just visible) evolved slowly over many years.

In 1792, when the federal city that would become Washington, D.C., was just beginning to take shape, a competition was held to select a design for the Capitol. The building that won—and was built, serving as the first Capitol—was later burned to the ground during the War of 1812. It was rebuilt after the war under the supervision of Benjamin Henry Latrobe, who also designed the south wing, the one on the left in this photograph.

That wing, where the Senate now meets, and the north wing (the one on the right), where the House meets, were added to the Capitol between 1851 and 1865. The dome was added during the same period.

The Supreme Court met in the Capitol until 1935, when at last it moved to its own quarters across the street (toward the right side of this photograph). The street leading away from the Capitol to the northwest (toward the upper left of the picture) is Pennsylvania Avenue, along which the White House can be found.

the city's population lived there only when Congress was in session.

By the 1930s, the functions of the national government had expanded, and more people made their permanent homes in the District of Columbia. Yet they did not have their own local government. Only gradually did they even get national voting rights. The Twenty-third Amendment to the Constitution gives residents of the district the right to vote in presidential elections. In 1970, Congress passed a law giving them one nonvoting delegate to the House of Representatives. Finally, in 1974, they were permitted to elect their own mayor and city council. Congress kept the right to approve the city budget and to veto council decisions.

Amendments, Unratified; Cabinet; Congress; Debts; Federal Government; House of Representatives; U.S. Constitution, Article I; U.S. Constitution, Twenty-third Amendment

Domestic Violence

A rebellion or widespread disorder in one or more states.

Under the Articles of Confederation, the national government was too weak to act to put down Shays's Rebellion, an insurrection among Massachusetts farmers in 1786. With this problem in mind, the Framers of the Constitution wrote Article IV, section 4. It guarantees each state protection from domestic violence at the request of the state governor or state legislature. Congress has since given the president the power to send troops to a state. To enforce a federal law, the president no longer has to wait for states to ask for help. In modern times, most circumstances of domestic violence have involved federal issues. For example, President Dwight D. Eisenhower sent federal troops into Little Rock, Arkansas, in 1957 to carry out a federal decision to integrate schools. Angry crowds had threatened the lives of black students trying to enter Central High School.

There have been other domestic insurrections in American history. For example, in 1842, President John Tyler promised the government of Rhode Island to send in military aid if violence occurred during the Dorr Rebellion. The Dorr Rebellion was a protest against state election districts that gave more power to rural voters than to the more numerous city dwellers. Urban reformers held their own convention, drafted a new constitution, submitted it to the voters, and held elections under it. Thomas Dorr was chosen governor. However, the existing government refused to give up its power. State judges eventually convicted Dorr of treason.

In the *Prize Cases* (1863), the Supreme Court was asked to decide whether the Civil War was an insurrection (that is, a case of domestic violence) or a war. The Court ruled it was a war, even though it may have started as an insurrection. The Court reasoned that the Constitution did not discuss whether the federal government could declare war against a state. So a declaration of war by Congress was not needed. As commander in chief, the president could decide whether to treat the conflict as an insurrection or a war. Since President Abraham Lincoln treated it as a war, the Court accepted his judgment.

Articles of Confederation; Commander in Chief; Congress; Debts; Framers; Militia; President; Segregation and Desegregation; States; Supreme Court; Treason; U.S. Constitution, Article IV

Double Jeopardy

The guarantee that people may not be tried twice for the same crime.

Found in the Fifth Amendment to the Constitution, it can be traced to ancient Greek and Roman law. In *Benton v. Maryland* (1969), the Supreme Court ruled that this safeguard limited the states as well as the national government, through the Fourteenth Amendment. For the most part, double jeopardy applies only to criminal cases. It protects people from a second criminal trial for the same offense after they have been acquitted. It also forbids a second trial for the same offense after a person has been convicted of a crime. Finally, it prevents more than one punishment for the same crime.

Double jeopardy is one of the most confusing phrases in the Constitution because the Court has made so many exceptions to the general rule. At first it applied only to cases in which people were at risk of losing their lives. Later it was applied to cases that did not involve the death penalty. However, in *Heath v. Alabama* (1985), the Supreme Court ruled that the federal government could try a suspect after a state trial had been held for the same offense. This was acceptable to the Court because two different governments were involved.

Death Penalty; Federal Government; Incorporation of the Bill of Rights; States; Supreme Court; U.S. Constitution, Fifth Amendment; U.S. Constitution, Fourteenth Amendment

Due Process of Law

The guarantee that the government will treat people justly and fairly in matters affecting their lives, liberty, or property.

It can be traced to the Magna Carta. The Fifth and Fourteenth amendments to the Constitution offer the protection of due process to Americans accused of serious crimes. The Supreme Court has developed two approaches to due process.

Procedural due process focuses on the way government judgments and decisions are made. It includes the rights of the accused to be told the charges against him or her, to be heard in court, to present evidence in his or her defense, and to be tried before an impartial jury. Other safeguards are also provided in the Fifth, Sixth, and Eighth amendments, including the right to an attorney and to protection against excessive fines or punishments. Procedural due process has been extended to cover noncriminal disputes. For example, the Supreme Court has ruled in *Goldberg v. Kelley* (1970) that people cannot be deprived of government benefits, such as welfare, without due process, nor can they lose their driver's license without due process (*Bell v. Burson* [1971]). Under the requirements of due process, they are at least entitled to an official, impartial hearing.

Substantive due process is concerned with the content of laws. It seeks to ensure that laws themselves are reasonable and fair. Starting with the *Slaughter-House Cases* (1873), the Supreme Court overturned many government regulations of the economy because it ruled that they unreasonably interfered with businesses' freedom of contract, as well as with property rights, how business owners choose to manage their property. This is the reasoning the slimmest of Court majorities used to throw out both a state law limiting the hours people could work, in *Lochner v. New York* (1905), and a federal law setting the minimum wages people could be paid at their jobs, in *Adkins v. Children's Hospital* (1923). Finally, however, after the nation's economy had collapsed during the Great Depression of the 1930s, the Court reversed its earlier rulings and upheld a minimum-wage law in *West Coast Hotel v. Parrish* (1937).

In recent years, the Supreme Court has applied substantive due process to social rather than economic issues. The Court's attention has turned to privacy, people's rights to choose how they lead their personal lives. In *Griswold v. Connecticut* (1965), the Court supported a married couple's right to obtain information about birth-control devices, despite a state law against it. In *Roe v. Wade* (1973), it ruled that women have a right to end their unwanted pregnancies through abortion. The Court has adapted substantive due process to changing times and circumstances.

Accused, Rights of the; Commerce Clause; Contract Clause; Discrimination; Judicial Activism; Magna Carta; Privacy; Property Rights; Supreme Court; U.S. Constitution, Fifth Amendment; U.S. Constitution, Sixth Amendment; U.S. Constitution, Eighth Amendment; U.S. Constitution, Fourteenth Amendment

Duties and Imposts

Taxes collected on goods imported from abroad.

Article I, section 8, of the Constitution gives Congress the power to collect these taxes. According to section 10, the states may not tax imports, nor can they charge the *duty of tonnage*, a tax on merchant ships in their ports. The Framers had seen that during the Confederation, commerce among the states and foreign trade suffered when states collected these taxes. Further, the states had been reluctant to contribute money to pay the expenses of the Confederation government. These problems were corrected by giving the national government the sole power to collect duties and imposts.

Confederation; Congress; Framers; Imports; U.S. Constitution, Article I

Elastic Clause

The power given to Congress to pass whatever laws are "necessary and proper" for carrying out all of the national government's responsibilities.

This grant of implied powers is found in Article I, section 8, of the Constitution. In *McCulloch v. Maryland* (1819), the Supreme Court ruled that Congress could create a national bank. The Constitution did not specifically give Congress the power to do this. The Court, however, reasoned that the bank was a necessary and proper way for Congress to carry out its express powers to coin money and regulate its value. The elastic clause can be stretched to give Congress the flexibility it needs as times change. For example, Congress has voted funds for AIDS research. Medical research is not mentioned in the Constitution, but Congress does have the power "to promote the progress of science."

Congress; Express Powers; Supreme Court; U.S. Constitution, Article I

Elections

The process by which people vote their leaders into power for a fixed period of time.

E

"What is a legislative power but a power of making laws? . . . What are the proper means of executing such a power but necessary and proper laws?"
**Alexander Hamilton,
The Federalist No. 33**

These campaign signs dot the lawn of a home in Omaha, Nebraska. The United States and every state except Nebraska have bicameral, or two-chamber, legislatures. Peter P. Gutoski, the candidate endorsed by the sign at left, was running for a seat in Nebraska's unicameral, or single-house, state legislature.

Voter turnout—the percentage of people who vote from among all those eligible to vote—is traditionally higher in years when a president is elected. Off-year elections (those occurring between presidential elections) normally see much lower voter turnout.

Voter turnout has also been dropping over the past several decades. In 1960, 1964, and 1968—all presidential election years—voter turnout never dropped below 60 percent. Even in the off-year elections of 1962, 1964, and 1970, voter turnout was never less than 45 percent. Since then, voter turnout has never risen above 55 percent in presidential election years (it even dropped to 49 percent in 1996), and has never topped 40 percent in an off-year election.

In 1994, when the Republican Party won control of the House of Representatives for the first time in forty years, only 75 million people voted out of almost 200 million eligible. Two years later, when Bill Clinton, a Democrat, was reelected president, fewer than 100 million people voted.

Elections are vital to representative democracy because they allow the people to choose members of the government. Article I, section 4, of the Constitution lets the states regulate the "times, places, and manner of holding elections" for members of Congress. However, Congress has the right to alter state arrangements. The Framers of the Constitution did not set national requirements for voting. They thought that the states might resent this and refuse to sign the document. Most states had already restricted voting rights to white men who owned property. In the Framers' opinion, property ownership demonstrated that voters were solid, reliable citizens. (Since land was fairly easy to obtain, the number of voters would not be too limited.) By the 1820s, the states had abandoned property qualifications, but had kept or imposed other restrictions. The Fifteenth, Nineteenth, and Twenty-sixth amendments to the Constitution gave voting rights to black men, women, and eighteen, nineteen, and twenty-year-olds, respectively. In addition, the Twenty-fourth Amendment eliminated poll taxes, which had often been applied in a racially discriminatory way.

Originally, the House of Representatives was the only branch of the national government directly elected by the people within each state. Then and now, seats in the House are distributed among the states according to their population, calculated every ten years by the census. State legislatures divide states with large populations into districts. In each of those districts, qualified voters are entitled to elect one member of the House. In states with small populations and only one seat in the House, elections are held at large, or statewide. To keep the representatives accountable to the voters, elections are held every two years.

Since the Framers did not entirely trust public opinion, they did not provide for popular election of senators. Instead, state legislatures elected senators. However, the Seventeenth Amendment shifted the election of senators to the people of each state. Although senators hold office for six years, one-third of the members are elected every two years.

At the time the Framers wrote the Constitution, Americans were still reluctant to give too much power to any one person. They had seen how King George III, his ministers, and royal governors mistreated the colonies. Yet government under the Articles of Confederation had convinced them that an executive branch was needed. The Framers disagreed over how the president should be chosen. Some wanted him to be elected by Congress; others, by the people. In addition, the small states did not want the large states to dominate the presidential election. In a compromise worked out at the Constitutional Convention, an electoral college was created to elect the president.

Originally, under the new Constitution, officials in each state, sometimes selected by the people, elected the president for a four-year term. If they failed to give one candidate a majority of their votes, the House of Representatives would choose the president. This complicated method of electing a president was somewhat modified by the Twelfth Amendment and by the development of political parties, which changed the way the electoral college works. The Fifteenth, Nineteenth, Twenty-third, Twenty-fourth, and Twenty-sixth amendments extended the right to vote for president to all qualified Americans. The Twenty-second Amendment limited the number of terms a president could serve.

Apportionment; Articles of Confederation; Census; Congress; Constitutional Convention; Electoral College; Executive Branch; Framers; House of Representatives; President; Representative Democracy; Senate; U.S. Constitution, Article I; U.S. Constitution, Twelfth Amendment; U.S. Constitution, Fifteenth Amendment; U.S. Constitution, Seventeenth Amendment; U.S. Constitution, Nineteenth Amendment; U.S. Constitution, Twenty-second Amendment; U.S. Constitution, Twenty-third Amendment; U.S. Constitution, Twenty-fourth Amendment; U.S. Constitution, Twenty-sixth Amendment

Electoral College

A group of individuals, called electors, who meet every four years to officially elect the president.

The Committee on Postponed Matters of the Constitutional Convention created the electoral college as a compromise method of choosing the president. According to Article II, section 1, of the Constitution, each state is entitled to choose the same number of electors as the number of lawmakers—senators and representatives—that it sends to Congress. (States with large populations have more lawmakers and thus more electors than states with small populations.) State legislatures decide how the electors are chosen. Originally, some were appointed, while others were elected by qualified voters. Once the right of the people to choose electors became widespread, presidents were, in effect, elected by the people.

The Framers of the Constitution had expected the members of the electoral college, not the people, to choose the president and vice president. Originally, electors were given two votes for president. One vote had to be cast for someone outside that elector's home state. The Framers thought this requirement would encourage the election of the most capable people, people who were well known to electors in every state. According to Article II, section 1, the candidate with a majority of the electors' votes would become president; the first runner-up would become vice president. The Framers expected that few candidates would receive a majority of the votes. Instead, the House of Representatives would decide most elections, with each state casting one vote.

The rise of political parties complicated the way the electoral college worked. The election of 1796 produced a president and vice president of opposing parties. In 1800, there was a tie between the presidential and vice presidential candidate of the same party, so the House had to decide which one would become president. The Twelfth Amendment was passed to separate the voting for president and vice president.

Within a state, each political party now selects its own presidential electors, according to state law. The electors' names might not even appear on the ballot. On Election Day, people enter the voting booth and select the presidential candidate they prefer. The candidate with the most votes automatically is awarded the votes of all of his or her party's electors in the state. Losing candidates are not granted any electors from that state.

According to federal law, the electors in each state meet on the Monday following the second Wednesday in December. They cast separate ballots for president and vice president, make a list of the results, sign them, seal them, make sure they are correct, and send them to Washington, D.C. On January 6, the

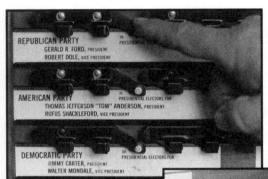

This voting machine shows the names of candidates for president and vice president in the election of 1976, together with their political party affiliations. Although he may not know it, the citizen whose finger is poised to vote (possibly the same person whose feet can be seen inside the voting booth at right) is really casting a ballot for "presidential electors." The electors—some state ballots list their names separately—have pledged to vote for particular candidates. Normally, they are members of the same political party as the candidates they support. However, the electors are not bound to vote for a candidate. It is not unknown for an elector to vote for a candidate who is not even on the ballot. In 1976, for instance, Gerald R. Ford won a majority in the state of Washington, but one elector there cast a ballot for Ronald Reagan instead. Such a switch has never changed an election.

Electoral College, 1992–2000

Alabama	9 votes
Alaska	3
Arizona	8
Arkansas	6
California	54
Colorado	8
Connecticut	8
Delaware	3
District of Columbia	3
Florida	25
Georgia	13
Hawaii	4
Idaho	4
Illinois	22
Indiana	12
Iowa	7
Kansas	6
Kentucky	8
Louisiana	9
Maine	4
Maryland	10
Massachusetts	12
Michigan	18
Minnesota	10
Mississippi	7
Missouri	11
Montana	3
Nebraska	5
Nevada	4
New Hampshire	4
New Jersey	15
New Mexico	5
New York	33
North Carolina	14
North Dakota	3
Ohio	21
Oklahoma	8
Oregon	7
Pennsylvania	23
Rhode Island	4
South Carolina	8
South Dakota	3
Tennessee	11
Texas	32
Utah	5
Vermont	3
Virginia	13
Washington	11
West Virginia	5
Wisconsin	11
Wyoming	3

outgoing vice president opens the ballots and counts the results in front of Congress. The vice president then formally announces the winner. At least 270 votes are needed for victory under the current makeup of Congress. If anyone fails to receive a majority of the electoral votes, the election is turned over to the House of Representatives, which is not required to select the person who finished first in either the popular or the electoral vote but must choose from among the top three vote-getters. This happened in the 1824 election, when the House gave the presidency to John Quincy Adams even though he came in second out of four candidates, behind Andrew Jackson, in *both* the popular and the electoral vote.

The electoral college does not precisely reflect the way people voted, since the winning candidate in each state receives all of that state's electors. If the electoral votes were tallied nationally, rather than by state, and on a proportional basis, the outcomes of some presidential elections might be quite different. For example, in the election of 1912, Democratic candidate Woodrow Wilson won 81.9 percent of the votes cast by electors in the electoral college but only 42 percent of the votes that people cast for president. (This was because a third-party candidate received almost 30 percent of the vote, more even than the Republican candidate.) Wilson won the most votes in forty states, but in some cases only by small margins.

Indeed, from 1828 through 1996, as a result of votes cast for minor-party candidates, the president has been elected sixteen times by the electoral college without receiving a majority of all the popular votes. Twice, in fact, the candidate who won a majority in the electoral college, and thus became president, did not even finish first in the popular vote. In 1876, a special electoral commission created by Congress granted Rutherford B. Hayes all of the electoral votes in several states where the outcome was in dispute, giving him a one-vote majority in the electoral college over Samuel J. Tilden—even though Tilden received nearly 300,000 more votes nationwide than Hayes. In 1888, President Grover Cleveland won about 100,000 more popular votes than Benjamin Harrison, but Harrison won the elections in twenty of the thirty-eight states and therefore ended up with 233 electoral votes to Cleveland's 168. (Cleveland got his revenge four years later, easily winning the vote in the electoral college while getting a larger margin of victory in the popular vote.)

Because of its winner-take-all nature, the electoral college favors large states that have the most electoral votes. This is why modern presidential candidates campaign so long and so hard in such states as California, New

York, and Texas, which have the largest populations and thus the greatest number of electors.

Congress; Constitutional Convention; Elections; Framers; House of Representatives; President; U.S. Constitution, Article II; U.S. Constitution, Twelfth Amendment; Vice President

Eminent Domain

Government seizure of private property for public use.

This was a British practice familiar to the colonists. The colonists themselves took away private land to build roads and bridges. The Fifth Amendment to the Constitution requires the national government to pay property owners a fair price for the land it seizes. At the end of the nineteenth century, this requirement was also placed on state governments, under the due process clause of the Fourteenth Amendment.

Due Process of Law; Incorporation of the Bill of Rights; Property Rights; U.S. Constitution, Fifth Amendment; U.S. Constitution, Fourteenth Amendment

Enumerated Powers

See: Express Powers

Equal Protection of the Laws

The obligation of states to make sure that one group of people within a state is not treated any differently from any other group under the law without a good reason.

This guarantee extends to the rights to own property, to enjoy personal freedoms, to be heard in court, and to have contracts enforced. It is found in the Fourteenth Amendment to the Constitution.

In 1868, Republicans in Congress passed the Fourteenth Amendment to protect newly freed slaves. Southern states had passed Black Codes, which kept blacks from serving on juries, testifying in court, and voting. Contracts between black servants and their white employers unfairly favored the whites.

At first, the Supreme Court interpreted the equal protection clause to allow social inequality between whites and blacks. The *Civil Rights Cases* (1883) permitted segregation in public accommodations, such as hotels, and *Plessy v. Ferguson* (1896) permitted separation of the races in public transportation, such as trains. The Court reasoned that as long as facilities for blacks and whites were equal, separation was acceptable. Only one justice dissented from the decision, which effectively legalized racism. In the late 1930s, the Court started to admit that separation had increased inequality between the races. In the 1950s, it began to use the equal pro-tection clause to overturn laws that kept blacks and whites apart. In *Sweatt v. Painter* (1950), for example, the Court ruled that a blacks-only law school in Texas violated the equal protection clause of the Fourteenth Amendment. Four years later, the Court handed down its historic decision in *Brown v. the Board of Education of Topeka* (1954), which ruled that blacks could no longer be kept from attending white schools.

More recent questions involving the equal protection clause have had to do with distinctions between state and private actions and with issues such as "reverse discrimination." States have the right to make some distinc-tions among citizens. For example, age is used to decide who may or may not qualify for a driver's license. The Supreme Court must decide which distinctions are reasonable and which are not. To do this, it established such tests as whether a law is reasonable. If facts support the classification, it will be upheld, such as an age requirement for driving. The *suspect clas-sifications* test identifies groups of people, such as blacks, foreign-born cit-izens, and women, who have suffered unequal treatment in the past. The Court is less likely to accept a law that singles them out for different treat-ment from that of other citizens.

Civil Rights; Congress; Discrimination; Incorporation of the Bill of Rights; Property Rights; Segregation and Desegregation; Supreme Court; U.S. Constitution, Fourteenth Amendment; Women's Rights

Equal Rights Amendment

A proposed, but never ratified, amendment to the Constitution banning discrimination based on sex.

The national government and the states are forbidden to treat men and women differently under the law, but existing protections are not always enforced or applied to all discriminatory situations. An early version of the Equal Rights Amendment was offered in 1923. Almost fifty years later, in 1972, Congress proposed the constitutional amendment to the states. Despite the efforts of women's rights groups, it failed to win approval in all of the thirty-eight states needed for ratification. Fears that it would lead to unisex bathrooms, the drafting of women into the military, and a decrease in family values helped defeat the amendment. Congress had already banned unequal treatment of females at their jobs in 1964, and in the 1970s the Supreme Court began to overturn laws that discriminated

Betty Friedan (third from right) and others (including noted television personalities) marched in Chicago in May 1980 to encourage the Illinois State Legislature to ratify the Equal Rights Amendment. Friedan, whose book *The Feminine Mystique* was published in 1963, is credited as one of the primary movers of modern feminism.

One year after her book was published—although completely unrelated to it—Congress passed the Civil Rights Act of 1964. Title VII of that legislation prohibited discrimination in employment based on sex, among other things. In 1966, Friedan and twenty-seven other women formed the National Organization for Women (NOW) in an effort to force compliance with Title VII through the courts. NOW also decided to push for an Equal Rights Amendment to the Constitution that would guarantee "equality of rights under the law" to women.

By the time this photograph was taken, NOW was more than 200,000 people strong. Although the amendment failed to win ratification in the thirty-eight states necessary to make it part of the Constitution, public support for the measure, as weighed by opinion polls, was never below 54 percent.

against women. Even today, however, women are often denied promotions and equal pay for equal work.

Amendment Process; Amendments, Unratified; Congress; Discrimination; Due Process of Law; Privacy; Supreme Court; U.S. Constitution, Nineteenth Amendment; Women's Rights

Equity

A set of judicial principles allowing judges to review cases and change awards of money or punishments that they decide are not fair.

Equity is based on rules developed many centuries ago in England. Injunctions are an example of a remedy under equity law. They are court orders to stop certain actions, and they have been used to halt strikes by workers either temporarily or permanently. Federal courts are given the power to hear equity cases in Article III, section 2, of the Constitution.

Federal Courts; Judicial Activism; U.S. Constitution, Article III

Excise Taxes

Federal taxes on items sold in the United States, such as automobiles, jewelry, and furs.

Setting, and collecting, these sales taxes is one of the express powers given to Congress in Article I, section 8, of the Constitution. The same tax rate must be applied nationwide. During the early years of the Republic, these taxes were a major source of revenue for the national government. The collection of excise taxes is a concurrent power, shared by the states and the national government. Under the Articles of Confederation, only the states could tax the sale of goods.

Articles of Confederation; Concurrent Powers; Congress; Express Powers; Revenue; Taxation, Power of; U.S. Constitution, Article I

Executive Branch

One of three major divisions of government. It is responsible for seeing that the laws are carried out.

The modern executive branch is made up of the president, vice president, their advisers and staffs, the members of executive departments, and members of various government councils and agencies. Congress has passed many laws gradually enlarging the executive branch. For example, in 1939 it created the Executive Office of the President. This now includes the White House staff, the Council of Economic Advisers, the Office of Management and Budget, the Council on Environmental Quality, and the National Security Council, as well as other advisory groups. More than three million civilians work in the executive branch of the government. The president is the nation's chief executive.

In 1787, the Framers of the Constitution realized that the lack of an executive branch weakened the Articles of Confederation. When they remedied this problem, they used the principle of separation of powers. According to Article II, section 2, of the Constitution, the executive branch has sole responsibility for putting laws into effect, commanding the armed services, and dealing with foreign governments. The legislative and judicial branches do not share these executive powers.

The executive and legislative branches do share other powers, following the principle of checks and balances. The Framers had seen how the British ministers of King George III and the royal governors of the colonies had abused their powers. They wanted to prevent this from happening in the new government formed by the Constitution. Article II, section 2, requires the Senate to give advice and consent to executive appointments to the government and to treaties. Under Article I, section 8, the House of Representatives must vote funds for executive programs. According to Article I, sections 2 and 3, Congress has the power to impeach and try members of the executive branch. The chief executive also has legislative powers found in Article I, section 7, and Article II, section 3. These include refusing to sign, or approve, laws passed by Congress, informing Congress about the state of the Union, recommending laws, and calling

---

Executive Office of the President
Central Intelligence Agency
Council of Economic Advisers
Council on Environmental Quality
National Security Council
Office of Administration
Office of Management and Budget
Office of National Drug Control Policy
Office of Science and Technology Policy
Office of the United States Trade Representative

Major Independent Agencies
Consumer Product Safety Commission
Corporation for National Service
Environmental Protection Agency
Equal Employment Opportunity Commission
Farm Credit Administration
Federal Deposit Insurance Corporation
Federal Election Commission
Federal Maritime Commission
Federal Mediation and Conciliation Service
Federal Reserve System
Federal Trade Commission
General Services Administration
National Aeronautics and Space Administration
National Foundation on the Arts and Humanities
National Labor Relations Board
National Mediation Board
National Science Foundation
National Transportation Safety Board
Nuclear Regulatory Commission
Office of Personnel Management
Securities and Exchange Commission
Selective Service System
Small Business Administration
Tennessee Valley Authority
U.S. Arms Control and Disarmament Agency
U.S. Commission on Civil Rights
U.S. Information Agency
U.S. International Trade Commission
U.S. Postal Service

Congress into special session. If the houses of Congress cannot agree on a date of adjournment, the chief executive may set the date.

Adjournment; Advice and Consent; Appointment to Office; Articles of Confederation; Checks and Balances; Congress; Executive Departments; Executive Powers; Framers; House of Representatives; Impeachment; Judicial Branch; Law; Legislative Branch; President; Separation of Powers; Senate; Treaties; U.S. Constitution, Article I; U.S. Constitution, Article II; Vice President

Department of Agriculture
1400 Independence Ave., S.W.
Washington, D.C. 20250

Department of Commerce
14th St. and Constitution Ave., N.W.
Washington, D.C. 20230

Department of Defense
The Pentagon
Washington, D.C. 20301

Department of Education
600 Independence Ave., S.W.
Washington, D.C. 20202

Department of Energy
1000 Independence Ave., S.W.
Washington, D.C. 20585

Dept. of Health & Human Services
200 Independence Ave., S.W.
Washington, D.C. 20201

Dept. of Housing & Urban Development
451 7th St., S.W.
Washington, D.C. 20410

Department of the Interior
1849 C St., N.W.
Washington, D.C. 20240

Department of Justice
950 Pennsylvania Ave., N.W.
Washington, D.C. 20530

Department of Labor
3rd St. and Constitution Ave., N.W.
Washington, D.C. 20210

Department of State
2201 C St., N.W.
Washington, D.C. 20520

Department of Transportation
400 7th St., S.W.
Washington, D.C. 20590

Department of the Treasury
15th St. and Pennsylvania Ave., N.W.
Washington, D.C. 20220

Department of Veterans' Affairs
810 Vermont Ave., N.W.
Washington, D.C. 20420

Executive Departments

Government divisions that put laws into effect and manage programs.

Each is led by a member of the cabinet, called a secretary. (The only exception is the attorney general, who is in charge of the Department of Justice.) Within each department there are undersecretaries, assistant secretaries, and government workers. They handle the department's programs, personnel, budget, and publicity.

In the Continental Congresses and the Confederation Congress, committees carried out the government's business. The Framers gave their new president more assistance, in the form of executive departments. According to Article II, section 2, of the Constitution, the president appoints heads of departments with the advice and consent of the Senate. He may ask them for written opinions on official matters. Heads of executive departments are also mentioned in the Twenty-fifth Amendment. A majority must agree if a vice president is to replace a disabled president who is unwilling to step aside. They must also agree on whether a disabled president is well enough to take up presidential duties again.

Originally, Congress created three executive departments—State, War, and the Treasury—as well as the post of attorney general. Today the list of departments includes State, the Treasury, Defense (which replaced War), Justice, Interior, Agriculture, Commerce, Labor, Health and Human Services, Housing and Urban Development, Transportation, Energy, Education, and Veterans' Affairs. The Post Office was a government department from 1872 to 1970, when it became an independent agency.

Advice and Consent; Appointment to Office; Cabinet; Confederation Congress; Congress; Continental Congresses; Delegates; Executive Branch; Framers; President; Presidential Disability; Senate; U.S. Constitution, Article II; U.S. Constitution, Twenty-fifth Amendment; Vice President

Executive Powers

Responsibility for managing the nation's foreign affairs, commanding the nation's armed services, and seeing that the laws are put into effect.

The Framers of the Constitution had experience with strong executives in the form of royal governors, ministers, and the British monarch. They also had experience with weak executives under the constitutions of some states during and after the War for Independence. To both stake out and limit the president's powers in the new federal system, the Framers borrowed heavily from the New York State Constitution of 1777. Article II, section 2, of the Constitution makes the president commander in chief of the armed forces, as well as of the state militias when they are called up to serve the nation. The president also has the power to grant pardons and reprieves; make treaties; nominate public ministers, ambassadors and consuls, judges of the Supreme Court, other federal judges, and heads of departments; and fill vacancies when Congress is not in session.

Because the Framers believed in the principle of checks and balances, the president shares powers with other branches of government. According to Article II, section 2, the Senate has to approve the president's appointees and treaties. Article I, section 8, gives Congress power to fund the armed services and declare war. Presidents have bypassed some of these restrictions. For example, President Franklin D. Roosevelt negotiated an executive agreement with Great Britain during World War II to exchange some aged American battleships for overseas bases. This executive agreement, made on his own authority, had the effect of a treaty but did not require Senate approval.

Appointment to Office; Checks and Balances; Commander in Chief; Congress; Framers; House of Representatives; Militia; Pardons and Reprieves; President; Senate; Supreme Court; Treaties; U.S. Constitution, Article I; U.S. Constitution, Article II; War Powers

Export Taxes

Taxes placed on goods to be shipped abroad.

In Article I of the Constitution, sections 9 and 10 forbid Congress and the states from collecting them. In *United States v. United States Shoe Corp.* (1998), the Supreme Court struck down a federal tax to maintain harbors. The Court reasoned that the fees charged to commercial shippers, based on the value of their ships' cargoes, was actually an export tax.

Under the Articles of Confederation, seaboard states had used export taxes to cripple the overseas trade of inland states. As part of a compromise with the South, the Framers of the Constitution agreed to eliminate these taxes. Southern states depended on exports to earn money. They shipped cotton, tobacco, and other agricultural products overseas, and the taxes would have reduced their profits. In return, the South agreed to give the national government the power to regulate commerce.

Articles of Confederation; Commerce Clause; Congress; Framers; Supreme Court; Taxation, Power of; U.S. Constitution, Article I

Ex Post Facto Laws

Laws punishing a person for an act that was legal when the act took place or that increase the penalties or punishment for a crime after that crime was committed.

For example, if children were arrested for a crime and charged as juvenile offenders, any law passed afterward requiring those same children to be treated as adults instead would be an ex post facto law. In Article I of the Constitution, sections 9 and 10 prevent Congress and the states from passing ex post facto laws.

Congress; Denied Powers; U.S. Constitution, Article I

Express Powers

A list of seventeen specific actions Congress may take, as outlined in Article I, section 8, of the Constitution.

These include the power to borrow money, coin money, declare war, and establish post offices. Under the Articles of Confederation, only state governments had these powers. States could also regulate commerce and collect taxes, duties, and imposts from individual citizens. The Constitution gave these powers exclusively to Congress.

Articles of Confederation; Congress; Debts; Denied Powers; Duties and Imposts; Inherent Powers; Money and Coinage; Postal Service; Taxation, Power of; U.S. Constitution, Article I; War Powers

Extradition

The obligation to return fugitives from justice to the state where they were accused or convicted.

If the fugitive will be punished unfairly, he or she might not be sent back. Extradition is found in Article IV, section 2, of the Constitution. Until passage of the Thirteenth Amendment to the Constitution, escaped slaves had to be returned if their owners claimed them. This was a concession to the southern states to help win their support for the Constitution. Northern states, however, for the most part ignored the obligation even after Congress passed laws to enforce it.

Congress; Slavery; U.S. Constitution, Article IV; U.S. Constitution, Thirteenth Amendment

F

Federal Courts

The judicial branch of the U.S. government.

Some of the Framers of the Constitution felt that federal courts were not necessary because the state courts were perfectly capable of judging matters. As a compromise, Article III, section 1, gives Congress permission to set up federal courts but does not require that it be done. Currently there are ninety-one district courts that try federal cases, and eleven courts of appeal that may be asked to review lower-court decisions. The Supreme Court is the only federal court specifically mentioned in the Constitution, in Article III, section 1. It is the highest court in the land.

According to Article III, section 2, federal courts try disputes in law and equity as well as disagreements about the Constitution, the laws of the United States, the law of the seas, and treaties. These courts also hear cases affecting ambassadors, public ministers, consuls, citizens of different states, and, in some circumstances, citizens of the same state. Finally, federal courts can decide lawsuits where the national government or two or more states are involved. The Eleventh Amendment prevents federal courts from settling disputes between a state and citizens of another state.

Ambassadors; Congress; Consuls; Equity; Framers; Judicial Branch; States; Supreme Court; Treaties; U.S. Constitution, Article III; U.S. Constitution, Eleventh Amendment

Federal Government

A term often used to refer to the national government of the United States.

It can also be used to refer to a system of government that follows the principle of federalism. The government of the United States is a federal government because power is distributed between the national government and the states. Both have important functions and govern the people directly. The national government and the states share concurrent powers. These include the right to tax and spend for the general well-being of the nation.

The national government has express, implied, and inherent powers of its own. Its express powers are listed in Articles I, II, and III of the Constitution. Implied powers are granted in the so-called elastic clause (or the necessary and proper clause) in Article I, section 8. Inherent powers, such as the president's right to conduct foreign relations, are not granted by any specific clause in the Constitution but rather included in other provisions, such as the power to negotiate treaties and receive ambassadors.

> "When the Federal Constitution was formed, there were already thirteen courts of justice in the United States which decided causes without appeal. That number has now increased. . . . [A government cannot] exist when its fundamental laws are subject to [many] different interpretations. . . . The American legislators therefore agreed to create a Federal judicial power to apply the laws of the Union."
>
> **Alexis de Tocqueville,**
> **Democracy in America, 1835**

Article VI makes the national government supreme. This means that the states must enforce the Constitution, national laws, and treaties. State and national officials have to take an oath to support the Constitution

The Tenth Amendment reserves to the states or to the people all powers not granted to the national government or forbidden by the Constitution in Article I, section 10. For example, states may not coin money or make treaties with foreign governments. Without the permission of Congress, they may not tax imports and exports, engage in war, or form compacts with other states. During debates over ratification of the Constitution, Antifederalists feared that the states would be swallowed up by the national government and demanded a reserved-powers amendment. Federalists argued that the national government could exercise only limited, express powers. Since passage of the amendment in 1791, the balance between the powers of national government and the states has constantly shifted. From the 1930s through the 1970s, the balance tilted in favor of the national government. Since the 1980s, it has been moving back toward the states.

Antifederalists; Concurrent Powers; Elastic Clause; Export Taxes; Express Powers; Federalism; Federalists; Imports; Inherent Powers; Ratification; States; Supremacy Clause; U.S. Constitution, Article I; U.S. Constitution, Article II; U.S. Constitution, Article III; U.S. Constitution, Tenth Amendment

"[F]ederalism is one of the most basic principles of our Constitution. By allowing the states sovereignty sufficient to govern we better secure our ultimate goal of political liberty through decentralized government."
Attorney General Edwin S. Meese III, Speech before the American Bar Association, July 9, 1985

Federalism

A system of government distributing power between a central government and other geographically divided political units of a nation, which are sometimes called states, provinces, or cantons.

Both the central government and the other geographic units have direct power over the people. The Framers of the Constitution of the United States decided to create a federal government. The states would never have consented to be dissolved and entirely replaced by a single, or unitary, government; on the other hand, their Confederation, giving almost all governmental powers to the states, had been unsuccessful. This is why federalism offered a promising solution.

Confederation; Federal Government; Framers

Federalist Papers

A series of eighty-five newspaper articles printed between 1787 and 1788, urging ratification of the U.S. Constitution.

John Jay was a very important political figure of the late colonial period and early years of the American republic.

Having served in the Continental Congress, Jay was later the main author of the New York state constitution—an important model for delegates to the Constitutional Convention. As the War for Independence came to a close, Jay joined the team of negotiators who hammered out the terms of peace. By the time he returned from Europe, the Confederation Congress had named him secretary of foreign affairs.

Although Jay did not attend the Constitutional Convention, he was a forceful supporter of the new plan of government and one of the leading Federalists. He wrote five of the essays later known as the Federalist Papers, but he fell ill and had to stop work.

After ratification of the Constitution, Jay became chief justice of the United States. (He is shown here in his judicial robes.) While serving as chief justice, he undertook a diplomatic mission abroad that resulted in a fiercely partisan fight at home. He resigned from the Court almost immediately.

They were written under the pen name "Publius" by John Jay, the secretary for foreign affairs of the Confederation Congress, and Framers Alexander Hamilton and James Madison. The articles were published in book form in 1788 as *The Federalist*. It offers a careful analysis of the Constitution and the Framers' principles of government. It was written to overcome the objections of the Antifederalists, a group that claimed the Constitution was drawn up illegally. The opponents also feared that the national government was too strong and would weaken states' rights and individuals' freedoms. They wanted changes to be made before they would approve the Constitution.

Jay, Hamilton, and Madison presented a series of arguments to deny the Antifederalists' claims. The three men explained that the Articles of Confederation had too many defects to be corrected simply by amendments. In addition, the amendment process required all the states to agree to changes, and this was impossible to achieve. By not sending any delegates to the Constitutional Convention, Rhode Island had shown how just one small state could prevent reforms the others wanted.

The authors of *The Federalist* tried to calm Antifederalists' fears that the national government would be too powerful. According to the three men, the Confederation was already falling apart. The states often took too long to decide to cooperate. What was needed was a national government capable of taking action. This government would not oppress the states or the citizens because its powers were delegated, clearly defined, and limited. The principles of separation of powers and checks and balances further restricted the government by dividing power among different branches and giving them shared responsibilities. This would prevent them from abusing their powers. To govern, they would have to cooperate and make compromises. Such compromises would help reconcile the various economic and political interests of the nation.

The Federalist is one of the most important documents for understanding the ideas of the people who wrote the Constitution and won ratification of it. Supreme Court justices often quote from it in their decisions.

Antifederalists; Articles of Confederation; Checks and Balances; Constitutional Convention; Convention; Express Powers; Federalists; Framers; Ratification; Separation of Powers; States' Rights

Federalists

The name given to those who supported the ratification of the U.S. Constitution.

Among them were Alexander Hamilton, John Jay, James Madison, Edmund Randolph, and George Washington. The Federalist Papers are the best-known presentation of their views. The name was later applied to members of the Federalist Party, led by Hamilton. They favored efforts to further strengthen the national government and to develop American commerce and manufacturing.

Antifederalists; Federalist Papers; Ratification

Felonies

Serious crimes, including murder, treason, robbery, and arson.

The term can be traced to English common law. Article I, section 6, of the Constitution grants immunity from prosecution to members of Congress while they are in a meeting of Congress or going to or coming from one. The protections of the Fifth, Sixth, and Eighth amendments to the Constitution apply to people accused of felonies.

Accused, Rights of the; Breach of the Peace; Common Law; Congress; Immunity; Treason;
U.S. Constitution, Article I; U.S. Constitution, Eighth Amendment; U.S. Constitution, Fifth
Amendment; U.S. Constitution, Sixth Amendment

Fines

Money paid as punishment, in a decision by a court of law.

The Eighth Amendment to the Constitution prohibits "excessive fines." Its roots can be traced to thirteenth-century England.

U.S. Constitution, Eighth Amendment

Foreign Affairs

Relations with other nations and with international organizations.

The conduct of American foreign relations is one of the inherent powers of the president. It is based on other grants of power mentioned in the Constitution. Article II, section 2, of the Constitution allows the president to make treaties and appoint ambassadors and consuls, with the advice and consent of the Senate. The section also makes the president commander in chief of the armed services. Section 3 allows the president to receive foreign ambassadors and other public officials.

In 1789, Congress created the Department of State to help manage American foreign relations. The secretary of state supervises U.S. diplomats, advises the president, and helps shape foreign policy. Gradually other departments of government became involved in foreign affairs: Defense,

Abraham Baldwin, Georgia, signer
Richard Bassett, Delaware, signer
Gunning Bedford Jr., Delaware, signer
John Blair, Virginia, signer
William Blount, North Carolina, signer
David Brearly, New Jersey, signer
Jacob Broom, Delaware, signer
Pierce Butler, South Carolina, signer
Daniel Carroll, Maryland, signer
George Clymer, Pennsylvania, signer
William Richardson Davie, North Carolina
Jonathan Dayton, New Jersey, signer
John Dickinson, Delaware, signer
Oliver Ellsworth, Connecticut
William Few, Georgia, signer
Thomas Fitzsimons, Pennsylvania, signer
Benjamin Franklin, Pennsylvania, signer
Elbridge Gerry, Massachusetts
Nicholas Gilman, New Hampshire, signer
Nathaniel Gorham, Massachusetts, signer
Alexander Hamilton, New York, signer
William Churchill Houston, New Jersey
William Houstoun, Georgia
Jared Ingersoll, Pennsylvania, signer
Daniel of St. Thomas Jenifer, Maryland,
    signer
William Samuel Johnson, Connecticut,
    signer
Rufus King, Massachusetts, signer
John Langdon, New Hampshire, signer
John Lansing Jr., New York
William Livingston, New Jersey, signer
James McClurg, Virginia
James McHenry, Maryland, signer
James Madison, Virginia, signer
Alexander Martin, North Carolina
Luther Martin, Maryland
George Mason, Virginia
John Francis Mercer, Maryland
Thomas Mifflin, Pennsylvania, signer
Gouverneur Morris, Pennsylvania, signer
Robert Morris, Pennsylvania, signer
William Paterson, New Jersey, signer
William Pierce, Georgia
Charles Pinckney, South Carolina, signer
Charles Cotesworth Pinckney,
    South Carolina, signer
Edmund Randolph, Virginia
George Read, Delaware, signer
John Rutledge, South Carolina, signer
Roger Sherman, Connecticut, signer
Richard Dobbs Spaight, North Carolina,
    signer
Caleb Strong, Massachusetts
George Washington, Virginia, signer
Hugh Williamson, North Carolina, signer
James Wilson, Pennsylvania, signer
George Wythe, Virginia
Robert Yates, New York

the Treasury, Agriculture, Commerce, Labor, and Energy. In addition, the Central Intelligence Agency was formed in 1947 to obtain information about other nations' secret plans. In the same year, Congress created the National Security Council. It helps the president coordinate military and economic policies with foreign policy. It also evaluates possible threats to the United States. A national security affairs adviser has joined the president's White House staff. It is that person's job to keep the president informed about developments overseas.

In foreign affairs, the president is influenced by many factors. For example, at the end of World War I, Americans in general did not want to join the League of Nations, an international organization created in 1919 to keep the peace. President Woodrow Wilson could not convince the public to change its mind. Many special-interest groups appeal to the president for help on matters of foreign policy. For example, Amnesty International wants support for human rights all over the world; the AFL-CIO, the biggest labor union in the United States, may ask for protection of its members' jobs through limits on cheap imports made by underpaid foreign workers. In the two centuries since the Constitution was written, the United States has become a major world power. Managing the foreign affairs of the nation has become a more difficult and complicated job.

Advice and Consent; Ambassadors; Appointment to Office; Commander in Chief; Congress; Consuls; Defense; Executive Departments; Executive Powers; Imports; Inherent Powers; President; Senate; Treaties; U.S. Constitution, Article II; War Powers

Framers

The men who helped to write the Constitution of the United States.

They met at the Constitutional Convention in Philadelphia from May 25 to September 17, 1787. The Framers of the Constitution were remarkable men, and the document they wrote in such a short time has lasted for well over two hundred years. The youngest participant, Jonathan Dayton, was twenty-seven years old. The oldest, Benjamin Franklin, was eighty-one. All of the fifty-five Framers were familiar with the problems of government. Among them were seven state governors, eight signers of the Declaration of Independence, and twenty-one veterans of the War for Independence. Many had helped to write their state constitutions. Almost three-fourths of them had served in the Continental Congress. They were farmers, lawyers, merchants, soldiers, doctors, and clergymen. Most of them were fairly wealthy, and at least twenty-five of them owned slaves.

They brought their different experiences and opinions to the Constitutional Convention. Some, like Luther Martin, William Paterson, Charles Cotesworth Pinckney, and John Lansing Jr., were committed to protect the interests of the states. Some others, like James Wilson, James Madison, and Alexander Hamilton, became spokesmen for a strong national government. Still others, like Jacob Broom, James McHenry, and John Blair, worked quietly behind the scenes to arrange compromises. Among the leading political figures who were absent were John Adams and Thomas Jefferson, who were serving as diplomats in London and Paris, respectively, and John Jay, who was secretary for foreign affairs for the Confederation in New York. Thirty-nine of the delegates signed the Constitution. The remaining sixteen went home before it was finished or refused to sign because they were dissatisfied with it.

Articles of Confederation; Constitutional Convention

Freedom

See: names of individual freedoms

Free Exercise Clause

See: Religion, Freedom of

Full Faith and Credit

The requirement that each state recognize as legal all public acts, records, and court decisions of other states.

This means that certificates of birth, marriage, divorce, and death are valid in every state. Wills that distribute a dead person's property and charters that set up corporations must also receive full faith and credit. This obligation is found in Article IV, section 1, of the Constitution. Judgments in one state are frequently disputed by another state, but for the most part, states recognize their constitutional duty.

States; U.S. Constitution, Article IV

Grand Jury

A group of between twelve and twenty-three citizens that determines whether a crime has been committed and whether a suspect should be charged with that crime.

The grand jury does not decide whether a suspect is innocent or guilty. In England, the grand jury was first used in 1166 when groups of twelve men were asked to report wrongdoing in their communities. According to the Fifth Amendment to the Constitution, civilians (as opposed to military personnel) can be tried for murder or other serious crimes only after they have been formally accused of the crime by a grand jury.

Jury Trial, Right to; U.S. Constitution, Fifth Amendment

Habeas Corpus, Writ of

A court order demanding that an arresting officer bring a prisoner before a judicial officer and explain why that person is being held in custody.

It is used to release suspects from unlawful imprisonment after they have proved that they were denied due process of law. The writ is a very basic right. It can be traced to the Magna Carta in 1215. It became part of the common law brought to the English colonies in North America. Most early state constitutions guaranteed this writ, to protect citizens from unlawful arrest. As the Constitutional Convention was coming to an end, Charles Cotesworth Pinckney proposed to include a similar guarantee in the Constitution.

In Article I, section 9, Congress is prevented from suspending the writ of habeas corpus unless there is a rebellion or invasion. In *Ex parte Merryman* (1861), Chief Justice Roger B. Taney condemned President Abraham Lincoln's orders to suspend the writ of habeas corpus and arrest disloyal civilians at the onset of the Civil War. Taney declared that the president lacked the power to issue such orders, although he said Congress could do so. Lincoln did not accept Taney's argument, but the person involved in that case was soon released anyway. In 1863, Congress satisfied Lincoln by passing a law suspending the writ. It was not until after the Civil War had ended that the entire Supreme Court ruled, in *Ex parte Milligan* (1866), that the president did not have the authority to suspend the writ. In fact, the Court ruled that neither the president nor Congress had the authority to approve the military trial of a civilian so long as the civil courts were functioning properly.

Another important case rejecting a suspension of the writ of habeas corpus came before the Court in 1946. Five years earlier, in response to a Japanese surprise attack on the American naval base at Pearl Harbor, Hawaii, Congress declared war on Japan. The governor of Hawaii suspended the writ of habeas corpus and declared martial law. As a result, the military closed all civilian courts. Later a civilian shipfitter named Duncan was tried and convicted for embezzlement under military law. Duncan

"[I]t is the birthright of every American citizen when charged with crime, to be tried and punished according to law."
Justice David Davis,
Ex parte Milligan, 1866

filed a petition for a writ of habeas corpus. The case reached the Supreme Court in 1946. In *Duncan v. Kahanamoku* (1946), the Court ordered his release from prison because it said the military had no right to try or punish him. The Court held that the act allowing martial law in Hawaii did not include the power to shut down civilian courts; the military was always subject to civilian control. Today the writ of habeas corpus remains an important safeguard, protecting those accused of crimes.

Common Law; Constitutional Convention; Due Process of Law; Magna Carta; Supreme Court; U.S. Constitution, Article I

House of Representatives

One of the two chambers of Congress, the legislative branch of the United States.

Originally, the House of Representatives was the only part of the national government directly elected by the people. As a result of the Connecticut Compromise, the Framers of the Constitution distributed seats in the House among the states according to their population. As a concession to the South, every five slaves were counted as three free persons in determining the number of people in each state. This Three-Fifths Compromise was eliminated by the Thirteenth and Fourteenth amendments to the Constitution.

The number of seats in the House of Representatives increased as more states entered the Union and the population grew. Finally, in 1910, Congress set a limit of 435 seats to keep the House from becoming unmanageable. As the Constitution requires, a census is conducted every ten years to apportion representatives, or readjust the number of seats given to each state. Every state is entitled to at least one representative.

According to Article I, section 2, of the Constitution, members of the House are elected for two-year terms. They must be at least twenty-five years old, citizens of the United States for seven years, and residents in the state that elects them. Article I, section 4, permits the states to regulate the "times, places, and manner" of holding elections. (Congress set a uniform date for elections, the Tuesday after the first Monday in November of even-numbered years, but this date is not in the Constitution.) The Twentieth Amendment to the Constitution set January 3 as the date when newly elected members of the House take office.

Members of the House manage their own affairs. According to Article I, section 2, members of the House choose their Speaker, other presiding officers, and such officials as a chaplain and clerk. Article I, section 5, gives them the right to judge their own election results, handle questions about members' qualifications, keep a record of their proceedings, and punish members for inappropriate behavior. Representatives may be expelled by a vote of the membership, although the courts have ruled that this can be done only for violation of internal House rules.

Members of the House have certain privileges. Article I, section 6, grants them immunity from arrest during sessions of Congress, except in cases of treason, felony, or a breach of the peace. This set of protections can be traced to seventeenth-century England.

The representatives are also subject to general restrictions placed on Congress. They may not hold any other public office while they are serving in the legislature, because this would violate the separation of powers. In Article I, section 9, Congress is denied certain specified powers. For example, the lawmakers may not grant titles of nobility or pass bills of attainder or ex post facto laws.

The House has its own special duties besides the express powers that Congress is given in Article I, section 8. According to Article I, section 2, the House has the sole power over impeachments; it may formally charge the president, or another public official, with misconduct.

The House also has the exclusive right to introduce all revenue bills, according to Article I, section 7. This is a great responsibility, because the government cannot function without money. Since the House receives requests for funds, its members know what is going on in the other branches of government, an example of checks and balances. The Framers expected that the House would be more careful about raising and spending money than the Senate. They knew that representatives would be up for election more frequently than senators and would not want to offend the voters.

Despite all the varied and complicated issues that modern lawmakers must handle, the House of Representatives does not differ all that much from the blueprint the Framers sketched in 1787.

Apportionment; Bill; Bill of Attainder; Breach of the Peace; Census; Checks and Balances; Congress; Connecticut Compromise; Denied Powers; Ex Post Facto Laws; Express Powers; Felonies; Framers; Immunity; Impeachment; Law; Legislative Branch; Nobility; Revenue; Senate; Separation of Powers; Speaker of the House of Representatives; Supreme Court; Three-Fifths Compromise; Treason; U.S. Constitution, Article I; U.S. Constitution, Thirteenth Amendment; U.S. Constitution, Fourteenth Amendment; U.S. Constitution, Twentieth Amendment

Immunity

Legal protection from penalties and imprisonment.

According to Article I, section 6, of the Constitution, members of Congress are immune from arrest for treason, felonies, or breaches of the peace. Representatives and senators enjoy immunity only while they are attending a meeting of Congress or going to or coming from a meeting. However, they are also immune from prosecution for any speech they may make in performance of their duties. This protection from arrest during a legislative session was introduced in Virginia in 1623. The freedom of debate that protects members of Congress for what they may say can be traced in the United States to a Connecticut law of 1639.

Breach of the Peace; Felonies; House of Representatives; Self-Incrimination; Senate; Treason; U.S. Constitution, Article I

Impairing the Obligation of Contracts

See: Contract Clause

Impeachment

The process of removing the president or another public official from office as a penalty for misconduct.

As early as 1386, English lawmakers impeached one of the king's ministers because he did not keep his promises to them. Article II, section 4, of the Constitution states that the president, vice president, federal court judges, and other public officials may be removed from office if they have committed treason, bribery, or other high crimes and misdemeanors. Members of the House of Representatives and the Senate are not subject to this penalty. Article I, section 5, states that they can be expelled only by the members of their own chamber.

According to Article I, section 2, the House of Representatives may charge an official with misconduct. Section 3 lets the Senate determine that person's guilt or innocence. In other words, the House indicts and the Senate acts as a trial court. Usually, the House Judiciary Committee investigates accusations against an official and makes a recommendation to the other representatives. The committee may draw up articles of impeachment, listing the charges against an official. If the House votes to accept these articles, the case is turned over to the Senate. When the Senate tries a president, Article I, section 3, requires the chief justice to preside instead of the vice president. A vote of two-thirds of the senators is needed for a

Representative Barbara C. Jordan of Texas served on the House Judiciary Committee that recommended articles of impeachment against President Richard M. Nixon in 1974.

On July 25, in a statement before the committee, Jordan called the charges against Nixon so serious and the evidence of his guilt so convincing that they surely were impeachable offenses. Otherwise, she said, the Constitution itself was worthless.

Jordan addressed her personal stake in the Constitution and in seeing it upheld. "'We, the people,'" she said. "It is a very eloquent beginning. But when that document was completed on the seventeenth of September in 1787 I was not included in that 'We, the people.' I felt somehow for many years that George Washington and Alexander Hamilton just left me out by mistake. But through the process of amendment, interpretation, and court decision I have finally been included in 'We, the people.'"

Jordan wanted her listeners to remember that blacks—like all Americans—depend on the Constitution as a guarantee of their liberties, and to have a president of the United States debase the Constitution was a threat to everyone's freedom.

conviction. If removed from office, an official may then be tried in a court of law.

To date, the House has investigated charges against sixty-seven officials. It voted formal charges against seventeen of them, including Presidents Andrew Johnson and Bill Clinton and Supreme Court Justice Samuel Chase. The Senate convicted just seven of them; all were federal judges. In 1989, one judge was impeached and removed from office on charges of accepting a $150,000 bribe. That same year another federal judge was removed while he was already serving a prison sentence for perjury, lying while under an oath to tell the truth.

Attempts to impeach U.S. presidents are dramatic examples of checks and balances in action. In 1868, President Andrew Johnson was almost removed from office. The president and Congress were competing for control over the reconstruction of the South after the Civil War. Johnson refused to obey the Tenure of Office Act of 1867. This law required him to seek Senate approval before he could fire heads of executive departments. He deliberately violated the act by firing his secretary of war, Edwin M. Stanton, who sided with Congress. The House voted to impeach Johnson. The Senate voted thirty-five to nineteen to convict him, but this was one vote short of the two-thirds needed to remove him from office.

In 1974, the House Judiciary Committee prepared three articles of impeachment against President Richard M. Nixon, a Republican. Members of his staff had supported a plan for burglars to break into Democratic Party headquarters in the Watergate complex in Washington, D.C., and plant eavesdropping equipment. Then the president and his staff publicly denied any involvement in the incident, covered up their knowledge of the crime, secretly paid large sums of money to the burglars and others in return for their silence in court, and tried to block government agencies from conducting a complete investigation. The Judiciary Committee accused Nixon of obstructing justice, by concealing evidence of a crime; abusing his power, by using the FBI and the Internal Revenue Service to go after people considered political "enemies"; and failing to cooperate with formal legal demands from Congress to turn over evidence. Before the House could vote on the charges, Nixon decided to avoid what by then appeared to be the certainty of impeachment and conviction. On August 9, 1974, he became the first president to resign from office.

Almost twenty-five years later, on December 19, 1998, President Bill Clinton, a Democrat, became the first elected president to be impeached by the House of Representatives. (Andrew Johnson was not an elected president. Instead, while serving as vice president, he succeeded to the presidency when Abraham Lincoln was assassinated.) The House voted two articles of impeachment against Clinton. They accused him of perjury, or lying under oath, about his relationship with a young woman working at the White House. They also charged him with obstruction of justice by concealing evidence and encouraging others to lie or withhold information. Selected members of the House argued the case against Clinton before the Senate. The president's lawyers insisted that he had not committed high crimes and misdemeanors, impeachable offenses. After the public presentation of arguments and some days of closed-door debate, the Senate voted, on February 12, 1999, not to remove the president from office for actions charged in the articles of impeachment.

Bribery; Checks and Balances; Chief Justice; Crimes and Misdemeanors; Executive Departments; Federal Courts; House of Representatives; Indictment; Parties, Political; President; Treason; U.S. Constitution, Article I; U.S. Constitution, Article II; Vice President

Implied Powers

See: Elastic Clause

Imports

Items purchased in one country that have been made in another.

During the Confederation, states often treated products made in another state as imports and placed tariffs on them. This hurt the free flow of trade among the states. The national government was not allowed to regulate these activities. The Constitution reversed this situation. Article I, section 8, of the Constitution gave Congress the power to set uniform taxes on imports, and section 10 made this one of the powers specifically denied to states. This arrangement primarily benefited the northern manufacturing states. As a compromise with the southern states, section 9 prevented Congress from taxing exports. This helped the southern economy, which depended on sales of farm products overseas.

Confederation; Congress; Denied Powers; Export Taxes; Tariffs; U.S. Constitution, Article I

Income Taxes

Revenue collected by the government from the earnings of individuals and businesses.

These clerks are processing some of the millions of income-tax returns that are filed each year with the Internal Revenue Service (IRS)—an increasing number of them filed electronically via the Internet.

The Bureau of Internal Revenue was established in 1862 to collect the personal income taxes levied during and just after the Civil War. (The bureau was reorganized as the IRS in 1953.) When the income tax was phased out, the bureau collected excise taxes and import duties. After ratification of the Sixteenth Amendment, the bureau again collected income taxes.

At first, few people were affected. For example, the 1913 tax rate began at 1 percent for an individual with an income above $3,000, yet the average personal income at the time was much less than $3,000 per year.

By 1939, still only 4 million people were required to file income-tax returns, out of a population of 86 million above the age of twenty. The cost of fighting World War II changed that. By 1945, almost 43 million people were required to file tax returns.

In the 1990s, 45 percent of federal revenues were raised from personal income taxes and 12 percent from business taxes. The rest came mostly from Social Security taxes.

The national government first taxed incomes in 1861 to help pay the costs of the Civil War. In *Springer v. United States* (1881), the Supreme Court ruled this was an indirect tax. The Court reasoned that the only direct taxes mentioned in the Constitution in Article I, section 9, were capitation taxes and taxes on property. As a result, income taxes did not have to be collected in proportion to the number of people living in each state, the requirement for direct taxes found in section 2.

The income tax had lapsed in 1872, but it was revived in 1894. Congress required individuals making over $4,000 a year and businesses to pay 2 percent of their earnings to the national government. A bank shareholder, named Pollock, opposed the tax. He sued his bank to keep it from paying the tax, and he won the case. In *Pollock v. Farmers' Loan and Trust Co.* (1895), the Supreme Court decided that the income tax was a direct tax after all and should be collected from the states on that basis. Given two different interpretations of the tax, Congress decided to add the Sixteenth Amendment to the Constitution. It gave Congress the power to collect income taxes from individuals and corporations regardless of the population of the states. Many Americans were pleased when the amendment was ratified in 1913, because they felt it was fairer than other taxes. For example, the rich and the poor alike had paid the same amount of excise taxes on the things they bought. In contrast, the income tax took differences in earnings into consideration. Over time, people have found *loopholes*, ways to claim that some of the money they earned was not taxable. Recent Congresses have attempted to find ways to plug up some of these loopholes.

Capitation Tax; Congress; Excise Taxes; Ratification; Revenue; Supreme Court; Taxation, Power of; U.S. Constitution, Article I; U.S. Constitution, Sixteenth Amendment

Incorporation of the Bill of Rights

Applying the freedoms and protections U.S. citizens enjoy at the national level (rights guaranteed under the Bill of Rights) to state and local circumstances and actions.

The Fourteenth Amendment to the Constitution bars states from denying the "privileges and immunites" of U.S. citizens or depriving them of "due process of law" or the "equal protection of the laws." The Supreme Court has gradually interpreted this amendment to incorporate, or include, many of the guarantees found in the Bill of Rights. These guarantees—freedom of speech and religion, for instance, or the right to a speedy and public trial in criminal cases—were once held not to apply to the states, but only to the federal government. Since the 1890s, and especially since the 1930s, the Supreme Court has increasingly insisted that for citizens to be treated fairly, states had to accept the limitations on government written into the Bill of Rights. However, not all guarantees outlined in the Bill of Rights have been incorporated into the Fourteenth Amendment. The states do not have to grant their citizens jury trials in civil cases, for example, something the Seventh Amendment guarantees for most civil cases in the federal courts.

Originally, in *Barron v. Baltimore* (1833), the Supreme Court ruled that the Bill of Rights restricted the national government but not the states. Soon afterward, southern states began passing laws making it a crime to attack slavery in speech or in print. After the Civil War, many of these same states passed Black Codes, which limited former slaves' freedom of speech and other freedoms. The Fourteenth Amendment was supposed by those who drafted it to remedy these wrongs. However, the Supreme Court soon began to construct, or interpret, the Fourteenth Amendment so strictly that it offered few safeguards to newly freed slaves.

When it came to interpreting the Fourteenth Amendment in cases not touching on former slaves, the Court was even narrower in its construction. In the *Slaughter-House Cases* (1873), the Court held onto the old distinction between state and national citizenship and refused to accept the argument that the Fourteenth Amendment could protect a group of butchers who claimed a state law violated guarantees outlined in the Bill of Rights.

Starting with *Chicago, Burlington and Quincy Railroad Co. v. Chicago* (1897), the Court began slowly to apply the Bill of Rights to the states, one by one, a process known as *selective incorporation*. In *Palko v. Connecticut* (1937), the justices concluded that some freedoms protected by the Bill of Rights were so important that states had to respect them. Others, however, were not of such fundamental importance. By the early 1970s, the Court had gradually incorporated most of the Bill of Rights into the Fourteenth Amendment, identifying, one by one, which freedoms applied to the states. Today, the protections offered by the First, Fourth,

> "It is my belief that there are 'absolutes' in our Bill of Rights, and that they were put there on purpose by men who knew what words meant and meant their prohibitions to be 'absolutes.'"
> Justice Hugo L. Black, Interview, American Jewish Congress, April 1962

Fifth, Sixth, and Eighth amendments apply throughout the United States, at both the federal and state levels.

Bill of Rights; Civil Law; Construction; Due Process of Law; Equal Protection of the Laws; Jury Trial, Right to; Privileges and Immunities; Religion, Freedom of; Slavery; Speech, Freedom of; Supreme Court; U.S. Constitution, First Amendment; U.S. Constitution, Fourth Amendment; U.S. Constitution, Fifth Amendment; U.S. Constitution, Sixth Amendment; U.S. Constitution, Seventh Amendment; U.S. Constitution, Eighth Amendment; U.S. Constitution, Fourteenth Amendment

Indictment

A formal written statement of the charges against a person suspected of committing a crime.

An indictment is issued by a grand jury, based on information provided by a legal prosecutor and others who are summoned to give testimony. An indictment is not evidence that the crime was committed or that the suspect was actually involved. Its only purpose is to accuse a person of a violation of the laws. It is required by the Fifth Amendment to the Constitution, part of the Bill of Rights, and it protects only civilians, not members of the armed services.

Bill of Rights; Grand Jury; Jury Trial, Right to; U.S. Constitution, Fifth Amendment

Inherent Powers

Powers available to the national government that are not specifically mentioned in the Constitution.

Article I gives Congress all legislative power, and Article II gives the president executive powers. Each article then lists specific duties and powers. However, supporters of inherent powers claim these lists were not intended to cover every possibility. They believe the government can exercise implied but unstated powers. Because Article I, section 10, denies certain powers to the states, the national government can claim them, including control over foreign affairs, war, and trade. In *United States v. Curtiss-Wright Export Corp.* (1936), the Supreme Court ruled that the powers of the federal government were delegated in internal affairs but inherent in foreign affairs, and that the president, or chief executive, is usually the official spokesperson for the national government in foreign relations.

Opponents of inherent powers claim that the Constitution makes no such distinction. In Article II, section 3, it simply requires the president to see that "the laws be faithfully executed." They also point to the Ninth and Tenth amendments to the Constitution, part of the Bill of Rights. These amendments reserve to the states and the people those powers not delegated to the national government in the Constitution.

The Supreme Court does not let the president do everything he wishes because of his inherent powers. In 1952, President Harry S. Truman seized the nation's steel mills during a strike. As commander in chief of the armed services, he wanted to continue steel production for weapons and ammunition needed during the Korean War. In *Youngstown Sheet and Tube Co. v. Sawyer* (1952), however, the Supreme Court ruled that he had exceeded his power because Congress had not given him authority to act.

Bill of Rights; Commander in Chief; Executive Powers; Foreign Affairs; Reserved Powers; Supreme Court; U.S. Constitution, Article I; U.S. Constitution, Article II; U.S. Constitution, Ninth Amendment; U.S. Constitution, Tenth Amendment

Integration

See: Segregation and Desegregation

Interstate and Intrastate Commerce

See: Commerce Clause

Involuntary Servitude

Compelling people to work for others against their will.

Slavery is a form of involuntary servitude. People who are being punished for crimes may also be compelled to work against their will—in prisons. The Thirteenth Amendment to the Constitution eliminated slavery and involuntary servitude within the United States, except for prisoners. The authors of the amendment copied the wording of the Northwest Ordinance of 1787, passed by the Confederation Congress.

The ban on slavery and involuntary servitude wiped out the openly racist sections of the Constitution: the Three-Fifths Compromise in Article I, section 2, which declared every five slaves equal to three free persons for purposes of counting the population; the continuation of the international slave trade until at least 1808—by then no longer in force anyway—in Article I, section 9; and the required return of fugitive slaves to their owners in Article IV, section 2. It also overturned the Supreme Court's decision in *Scott v. Sandford* (1857) that a slave was legally property, not a person. Finally, it canceled congressional laws, such as the Fugitive Slave Act of 1850, enforcing the requirement that runaway slaves be returned to their owners. The Thirteenth Amendment did not, however, give former slaves their civil rights. That required further amendments to the Constitution, and additional legislation a century later.

Civil Rights; Confederation Congress; Slavery; Supreme Court; Three-Fifths Compromise; U.S. Constitution, Article I; U.S. Constitution, Article IV; U.S. Constitution, Thirteenth Amendment

J

Journals

Records of the actions that take place in Congress.

Article I, section 5, of the Constitution requires the Senate and the House of Representatives each to keep and publish journals of its proceedings. Only matters that need to be kept secret, such as discussions of national security, do not have to be made public. Votes are recorded if a fifth of the members present demand it. The *Senate Journal* and the *House Journal* are published after each congressional session. While Congress is meeting, the *Congressional Record* is published daily. It contains the members' speeches (which they are permitted to alter or add to for the published record), votes (which they may not change), and an account of the day's activities.

Congress; House of Representatives; Senate; U.S. Constitution, Article I

Judicial Activism

"We . . . read the Constitution in the only way that we can: as Americans [of our era]. . . . We look to the history of the time of the framing and to the intervening history of interpretation. But the ultimate question must be, what do the words of the text mean in our time?"
Justice William J. Brennan Jr., Speech, Georgetown University, October 1985

Using the power of judicial review and a loose construction, or broader interpretation, of the Constitution to give it new meanings.

Unlike judicial restraint, judicial activism is less concerned with the original purposes of the Framers, and activist judges are more likely to reinterpret the words of the Constitution and the amendments in order to adapt them to the needs of their own times. For example, conservative activists developed the idea of substantive due process to block economic reforms such as child-labor laws. Liberal activists came up with the right to privacy as a way to let women decide whether to end their pregnancies. In a way, these judges take over the duties given to lawmakers because they make new law by interpreting old laws. Their decisions often help keep the Constitution up-to-date.

Construction; Due Process of Law; Framers; Judicial Branch; Judicial Restraint; Judicial Review; Original Intent; Privacy; Supreme Court

Judicial Branch

One of three major divisions of government, also known as the judiciary.

It has responsibility for settling legal disputes arising under federal laws. The judicial branch is made up of ninety-one district courts that hear cases and twelve courts of appeal that review lower-court decisions. In addition, there are special courts, such as the Court of Veterans' Appeals. The Supreme Court is the highest court of appeals. It is the only court specifically mentioned in the Constitution (in Article III, sections 1 and 2). Some of the Framers of the Constitution did not think additional federal courts were necessary. They argued that state courts could handle the nation's legal disputes, subject to review by the Supreme Court when necessary. As a compromise, Article III, section 1, gives Congress the power to set up additional federal courts but does not require them.

The Framers followed the principle of separation of powers by giving the courts their own functions to perform. According to Article III, section 2, federal courts try disputes in law and equity and disagreements about the Constitution, the laws of the United States, the law of the seas, and treaties. They have jurisdiction over cases affecting ambassadors, public ministers, consuls, citizens of different states, and citizens of the same state who own lands granted by different states. Finally, they can decide lawsuits in which the United States government or two or more states are involved. The Eleventh Amendment prevents federal courts from settling disputes between a state and citizens of another state.

The federal judiciary is an example of how checks and balances work. Federal judges are appointed by the president with the advice and consent of the Senate. They usually hold office for life. If they are found guilty of wrongdoing, they may be removed by the impeachment process, involving both houses of Congress. Through the power of judicial review, federal judges make sure that state governments and the other branches of the national government do not abuse their powers.

Advice and Consent; Ambassadors; Appointment to Office; Checks and Balances; Consuls; Equity; Federal Courts; Framers; Impeachment; Judicial Review; Jurisdiction; Law; President; Senate; Separation of Powers; Supreme Court; Treaties; U.S. Constitution, Article III; U.S. Constitution, Eleventh Amendment

> **"[T]he meaning of the Constitution does not change with the ebb and flow of economic events. . . . The judicial function is that of interpretation; it does not include the power of amendment under the guise of interpretation."**
> Justice George Sutherland, Dissent, *West Coast Hotel v. Parrish,* 1937

Judicial Restraint

A reluctance to use judicial review to declare laws unconstitutional.

Unlike judicial activism, judicial restraint keeps a judge from giving new meanings to the Constitution, the amendments, or laws. Instead, the judges follow a strict construction, or narrow interpretation, of the exact wording in the Constitution. Self-restraining judges believe that a court's judgment about a law generally should yield to the judgment of the legislature that created the law. Such judges prefer to trust the legislature's decisions because the lawmakers, unlike judges, are elected by and responsible to the people.

Construction; Judicial Activism; Judicial Review; Law; Separation of Powers; Supreme Court

Judicial Review

The power to interpret the meaning of the words and phrases of the Constitution and to decide whether actions of the states and the national government violate its requirements.

Between 1789 and 1987, the Supreme Court declared 135 acts of Congress wholly or partially in violation of the Constitution. During the same time span, nearly 1,000 state laws and parts of state constitutions were also struck down.

The Constitution does not specifically give federal courts the power of judicial review. In fact, it took a long time for this idea to be accepted, and the Supreme Court overturned an act of Congress only once before 1857. Such important Framers of the Constitution as James Wilson, James Madison, Gouverneur Morris, Oliver Ellsworth, Rufus King, and Alexander Hamilton assumed that the courts would have the power to interpret the Constitution. In number 78 of the Federalist Papers, a series of newspaper articles supporting ratification of the Constitution, Hamilton claimed this authority for judges based on their special training. However, he was discussing the fine points of legal interpretation, and it is not clear that he understood judicial review as we know it today.

In the landmark case of *Marbury v. Madison* (1803), Chief Justice John Marshall claimed the power of judicial review for the Supreme Court. When Marshall was secretary of state for a few months in early 1801, he had failed to deliver papers appointing William Marbury as a justice of the peace. Marbury sued in the Supreme Court to demand those papers from the new secretary of state, James Madison. He cited the Judiciary Act of 1789, in which Congress let the Supreme Court act as a trial court to force officeholders to perform their official duties. Now on the Supreme Court, Marshall decided that this section of the Judiciary Act violated the Constitution. He reasoned that Article III of the Constitution had already determined what the Court's jurisdiction was; Congress could not give it extra duties. So Marshall told Marbury to look elsewhere for a remedy to his problem. In *Marbury v. Madison* the Court declared an act of Congress unconstitutional for the first time. It did not do so again until *Scott v.*

Sandford (1857), which struck down the Missouri Compromise of 1820, a law barring slavery from the northern part of the Louisiana Purchase.

Judicial review is not limited to acts of Congress. The Court first ruled an act of a state legislature unconstitutional in *Fletcher v. Peck* (1810). It decided that the Georgia legislature could not repeal public-land grants that corrupt state lawmakers had made. Under the repeal, individuals would have lost the property they had bought, and their sales contract would have been broken. The Court reasoned that this would violate Article I, section 10, of the Constitution, which forbids states from impairing the obligation of contracts. The Court has often used judicial review to limit or overturn state laws regulating business or working conditions.

The Supreme Court has also reviewed presidents' decisions. In *Ex parte Merryman* (1861), Chief Justice Roger B. Taney condemned President Abraham Lincoln's orders to suspend the writ of habeas corpus and arrest disloyal civilians at the beginning of the Civil War. Taney declared that only Congress could issue such orders, and it did in 1863 (though Lincoln never acknowledged Taney's order, and the entire Supreme Court did not rule against Lincoln's actions until 1866, after the Civil War was over and Lincoln was dead). Nearly a century later, the Court overturned President Harry S. Truman's seizure of the nation's steel mills during a strike in 1952. The president had ordered the government to run the mills to guarantee a supply of equipment and ammunition to American soldiers fighting in the Korean War. The Court ruled that the president's action was illegal because Congress had not given him authority to act. In 1974 the Supreme Court required President Richard M. Nixon to provide officials with unedited tapes of his conversations, containing evidence needed in criminal trials. On the tapes, Nixon and his top aides could be heard discussing ways of blocking investigations into a break-in at the Democratic Party's national headquarters and of covering up their involvement in this incident. Within a few days of the release of the tapes, Nixon resigned in the face of apparently certain impeachment and conviction.

The Court's use of judicial review is an example of checks and balances, although it is one the Framers did not discuss at the Constitutional Convention. It ensures that the other branches of national government and the states stay within the limits of their powers, as defined by the Constitution. However, Court decisions themselves can be modified by amendments to the Constitution. The Sixteenth Amendment, allowing income taxes, is one such example.

"[I]t is very difficult for me to believe that [the Framers] did not expect some form of judicial review in cases involving constitutional questions. At any rate, . . . [t]he matter seems to be settled by long usage, and without it I think we would have to look about for some substitute as far as holding the balance between rival claims of powers of the state and national governments."
Justice Harlan Fiske Stone,
Letter to Edward S. Corwin,
March 6, 1939

How judges feel about the Constitution affects judicial review. Some judges prefer to follow the exact wording of the articles and amendments. They try to find out what the Framers had in mind and what the original meanings of sections of the Constitution might have been. To do this, they may consult primary sources and early legal opinions. We say they give the Constitution a *strict construction*. (The legal term *construction* means interpretation, making sense of complex or unclear words and phrases.) Other judges refuse to be bound by the past and give the Constitution a *loose construction*. They realize that the Framers sometimes used general expressions to allow for future developments. One example is the phrase "necessary and proper" found in the elastic clause (Article I, section 8). Even the meaning of very specific phrases, such as impairing the obligation of contracts, may have to be changed over time to fit new circumstances.

In the early days of the nation, the Supreme Court used judicial review to expand the powers of the national government. After the Civil War, it helped the growth of private businesses by overturning federal and state laws that limited workers' hours, set minimum wages, and banned child labor, among other restrictions. Since the 1920s, the Supreme Court has used judicial review more frequently to rule on freedom of assembly, freedom of association, freedom of religion, freedom of speech, freedom of the press, civil rights, the right to privacy, and other individual rights. In doing so, the Court is passing judgment on the activities of Congress, the states, and local governments. Overall, judicial review has adapted an eighteenth-century document to modern times.

Appointment to Office; Assembly, Freedom of; Association, Freedom of; Checks and Balances; Chief Justice; Civil Rights; Construction; Contract Clause; Elastic Clause; Federal Courts; Framers; Habeas Corpus, Writ of; Impeachment; Inherent Powers; Jurisdiction; Law; Press, Freedom of the; Privacy; Religion, Freedom of; Slavery; Speech, Freedom of; Supreme Court; U.S. Constitution, Article I; U.S. Constitution, Article III; U.S. Constitution, Sixteenth Amendment

Judicial Tenure

The length of time judges serve on the bench.

In many states, judges are elected to office for a fixed term. They can be voted out of office at the time of regular elections. However, Article III, section 1, of the Constitution stipulates that federal judges are to hold office "during good behavior." They are appointed by the president, subject to the advice and consent of the Senate. Giving these judges lifetime tenure helps make them more impartial and independent. They can be free to criticize the actions of the other branches of government and act as a check to the legislative and executive branches.

Article II, section 4, explains that as officials of the U.S. government, federal judges can be removed from office for "conviction of treason, bribery, or other high crimes and misdemeanors." In such cases of impeachment, federal judges must be accused by vote of the House of Representatives and tried by the Senate, as outlined in Article I, section 3. Since 1804, seven federal judges have been removed from office. Four others have been acquitted of the charges brought against them.

Advice and Consent; Appointment to Office; Bribery; Checks and Balances; Crimes and Misdemeanors; Executive Branch; Federal Courts; House of Representatives; Impeachment; Legislative Branch; President; Senate; Treason; U.S. Constitution, Article I; U.S. Constitution, Article II; U.S. Constitution, Article III

Federal Judges Removed from Office
John Pickering, March 12, 1804
West H. Humphreys, June 26, 1862
Robert W. Archbald, January 13, 1913
Halsted L. Ritter, April 17, 1936
Harry E. Claiborne, October 9, 1986
Alcee L. Hastings, October 20, 1989
Walter L. Nixon, November 3, 1989

Jurisdiction

The authority that each court has to settle specific kinds of disputes.

Article III, section 2, of the Constitution gives federal courts the power to try disputes in law and equity, as well as disagreements about the Constitution, the laws of the United States, the law of the seas, and treaties. These courts also hear cases affecting ambassadors, public ministers, consuls, citizens of different states, and citizens of the same state who own lands granted by different states. Finally, the courts can decide lawsuits in which the U.S. government or two or more states are involved. The Eleventh Amendment prevents federal courts from settling disputes between a state and citizens of another state.

Appellate jurisdiction is the power to hear appeals from lower-court decisions. Congress has set up eleven circuit courts to hear appeals from trial courts. Circuit-court decisions may be reviewed by the Supreme Court, the highest court of appeals in the United States. It has appellate jurisdiction over all the disputes and cases listed in Article III, section 2.

Original jurisdiction is the power of a trial court to decide a case before any other court can settle it. Congress created ninety-one district courts with original jurisdiction. They try cases in which federal laws have been violated, in addition to the disputes listed in Article III, section 2. The Supreme Court has original jurisdiction only in cases involving ambassadors, consuls, and other public ministers, or a state. In the landmark case *Marbury v. Madison* (1803), Chief Justice John Marshall struck down section 13 of the Judiciary Act of 1789. It let the Supreme Court act as a trial court in cases where officeholders failed to perform their official duties. Marshall reasoned that Congress did not have the power to change the Constitution by adding to the original jurisdiction of the Court. In reaching his decision, he used judicial review to overturn part of an act of Congress for the first time in American history.

Ambassadors; Chief Justice; Consuls; Debts; Equity; Federal Courts; Judicial Review; Laws;
Supreme Court; Treaties; U.S. Constitution, Article III; U.S. Constitution, Eleventh Amendment

Jury Trial, Right to

The guarantee that a person accused of committing certain crimes or actions can be judged in court by a group of citizens (usually twelve).

Such jurors do not reach a verdict, or decide whether the accused person is guilty, until they have heard evidence and other arguments for and against that person in relation to the accusations.

The tradition of being tried for a crime by a jury of one's equals can be traced back to twelfth-century England. In the Declaration of Independence, American colonists complained that they were being denied their right to a trial by jury under British law. They wanted jury trials because they felt that royal judges could not be trusted to handle colonial disputes impartially. After the War for Independence, the former colonists wanted jury trials in civil cases, those involving money, to make it more difficult for British merchants to win lawsuits against them, especially in cases involving debts that arose during the war.

Guarantees of trial by an impartial jury can be found in Article III, section 2, of the Constitution and in the Sixth, Seventh, and Fourteenth amendments. (At the time the Constitution was written, trial by jury was perhaps the most democratic feature of the new government.) Both Article III, section 2, and the Sixth Amendment require that in criminal cases, the jury trial be held in the local community where the crime was committed. The Framers and members of the first Congress could remember that colonists were sometimes sent to Canadian or English courts. Away from home, they were more likely to be convicted and given harsh sentences. The Seventh Amendment extends jury trials to all but the most minor civil-law disputes. In *Duncan v. Louisiana* (1968), the Supreme Court used the Fourteenth Amendment as well as the Sixth Amendment to rule that states, not just federal courts, must hold jury trials in criminal cases.

Jury trials have often helped protect citizens from abuses of power by judges and prosecutors. Juries sometimes also bend the law in the interests

"Freedom of religion; freedom of the press, and freedom of person under the protection of . . . trial by juries impartially selected. These principles . . . should be the creed of our political faith."
Thomas Jefferson,
First Inaugural Address,
March 1801

of mercy. Civil trials by jury are valued in part because juries are sometimes sympathetic to a victim's pain and suffering.

Accused, Rights of the; Civil Law; Congress; Debts; Framers; Supreme Court;

U.S. Constitution, Article III; U.S. Constitution, Sixth Amendment; U.S. Constitution,

Seventh Amendment; U.S. Constitution, Fourteenth Amendment

L

Lame Ducks

Officeholders who are serving out the remainder of their term before leaving office.

These officeholders have been defeated for reelection, are not allowed to run again for the same office, or have decided not to remain in that office. They are often less effective in using their power to achieve their desired goals. Because of their often reduced power, politicians who were soon going to leave office were compared to lame ducks whose wings had been clipped. Although these elected officials' terms have a known end, they can nonetheless continue to pass or enforce laws and appoint people to government jobs. Article I, section 4, of the Constitution helped create this situation. Originally, a new Congress elected in November of an even-numbered year did not necessarily meet until thirteen months later, while the old Congress had a session beginning a month after the election. Meanwhile, according to the Twelfth Amendment, a new president elected in November had to wait until March to begin the term; until then, the departing president remained in power. In 1933, the Twentieth Amendment set January 3 as the date when new members of Congress take office and January 20 as the date when newly elected presidents are sworn in. This reduced the amount of time lame ducks serve.

Congress; Oaths of Office; President; Term Limits; U.S. Constitution, Article I; U.S. Constitution,

Twelfth Amendment; U.S. Constitution, Twentieth Amendment

Law

"Laws are a dead letter without courts to expound and define their true meaning."
Alexander Hamilton,
The Federalist No. 22

A bill passed by Congress that must be obeyed and can be enforced.

The types of law that apply to federal-court trials are listed in Article III, section 2, of the Constitution. They include law and equity, arising under the Constitution, treaties, and the laws of the United States. According to Article I, section 7, laws of the United States are made by acts of Congress that are signed by the president or passed again after a president's veto.

Bill; Congress; Equity; Federal Courts; House of Representatives; Senate; President; Treaties;

U.S. Constitution, Article I; U.S. Constitution, Article III; Veto

Legislative Branch

One of three major divisions of government, known as the Congress. Its main duty is to make laws.

Congress is divided into two chambers: the House of Representatives and the Senate. Membership in the two chambers of Congress was fixed by the Connecticut Compromise, which settled differences between the large and small states at the Constitutional Convention. The House of Representatives is based on the size of the population in each state, with each state having at least one member. In the Senate, each state is treated equally by having two members apiece. Originally, Article I, section 2, of the Constitution counted every five slaves as three free people for purposes of representation. The Fourteenth Amendment specified that "the whole number of persons in each state," except untaxed Indians, are to be counted to determine representation.

The legislative branch is accountable to the people. Members of the House are elected for two-year terms. Senators serve for six-year terms, with one-third of them facing reelection every two years. Until passage of the Seventeenth Amendment, senators were chosen by state legislatures. Since then, they have been elected directly by the people living in each state. Under Article I, section 6, the lawmakers are forbidden to hold another office in the government while serving in Congress. This ban guarantees separation of powers.

The lawmaking process is described in Article I, section 7. It requires the cooperation of both houses of Congress as well as the president. After the House and the Senate pass a bill, it is sent to the president for approval. If the president disapproves and both houses are in session, the bill can become law if two-thirds of the members of each house vote for it.

The subjects on which Congress can pass laws are listed in Article I, section 8. These include taxes, duties and imposts, commerce, bankruptcy, coining money, borrowing money, weights and measures, counterfeiting, the post office, copyrights, patents, and military regulations. Congress also has the power to declare war and to make rules for governing the District of Columbia, the nation's capital. Most importantly, the elastic clause in section 8 gives the legislative branch the power to make all laws that are "necessary and proper" for carrying out its duties.

The Constitution limits Congress's lawmaking powers in Article I, section 9. For example, lawmakers could not ban the slave trade until 1808. They may not suspend the writ of habeas corpus unless there is a war or

How a Bill Becomes a Law

1. The Senate or House of Representatives passes a bill. (Bills to raise or spend revenue must start in the House.)

2. The other chamber passes the same bill. If there are any changes, the revised bill must go back to the originating chamber for approval.

3. Once an identical bill has passed both houses, it is called an act of Congress and is sent to the president.

4. If the president signs the act, it becomes a law. If the president vetoes the act, it does not become law.

5. However, if two-thirds of each house of Congress approve the act again after the president has vetoed it, then it still becomes a law.

rebellion. They cannot pass bills of attainder, ex post facto laws, or export taxes. Among their other denied powers, members of Congress may not grant titles of nobility.

In addition to making laws, Congress has other responsibilities. Under Article I, sections 2 and 3, it may impeach the president, members of the judicial branch, and other public officials. Article IV, section 3, gives the legislative branch control over territories and other properties belonging to the United States. It also allows Congress to admit new states. Under Article V, the lawmakers may propose amendments to the Constitution. In addition, the Senate approves presidential appointments, such as heads of executive departments and judges of federal courts. It must also consent to treaties. These are examples of checks and balances. Although the legislative branch is powerful, its decisions can be overturned by the Supreme Court. Members of Congress can also be voted out of office.

Amendment Process; Appointment to Office; Bankruptcy; Bill; Bill of Attainder; Checks and Balances; Commerce Clause; Congress; Connecticut Compromise; Constitutional Convention; Copyright; Counterfeiting; Denied Powers; District of Columbia; Duties and Imposts; Elastic Clause; Elections; Executive Departments; Export Taxes; Ex Post Facto Laws; Federal Courts; Habeas Corpus, Writ of; House of Representatives; Impeachment; Judicial Branch; Law; Nobility; Patents; President; Senate; Separation of Powers; Supreme Court; Taxation, Power of; Treaties; U.S. Constitution, Article I; U.S. Constitution, Article IV; U.S. Constitution, Article V; U.S. Constitution, Thirteenth Amendment; U.S. Constitution, Seventeenth Amendment

Letters of Marque and Reprisal

Permission for privately owned ships to be armed and to capture enemy ships during wartime.

Article I, section 8, of the Constitution gives Congress the power to issue letters of marque and reprisal. People who had letters of marque and reprisal were called *privateers*, to distinguish them from lawless pirates who robbed and seized ships without any governmental authorization. Two of the Framers, Elbridge Gerry and Nathaniel Gorham, were briefly involved in privateering before they attended the Constitutional Convention.

Congress; Constitutional Convention; U.S. Constitution, Article I

Limited Government

A political system in which laws restrict rulers from abusing their powers.

For example, the Magna Carta and the English Bill of Rights required monarchs to uphold the laws and respect their subjects' rights. Under limited governments, constitutions distribute power and set conditions for its use. The Constitution of the United States divides power among the executive, legislative, and judicial branches. This principle of separation of powers helps to keep any individual or group from claiming too much power. The Constitution also lets each branch take part in the duties of the other branches. This principle of checks and balances encourages them to keep any other branch from becoming too powerful. The principle of federalism further divides power, between states and the national government. The states do not exist merely to carry out orders from the federal government. For example, they set the times, place, and manner of national elections. They also may propose amendments to the Constitution, which take effect only when three-fourths of the states ratify them.

The Constitution of the United States contains express powers, such as the power to make treaties, and implied powers, such as the power to do what is necessary and proper to carry out laws. These describe which actions are permissible. The Constitution also includes denied powers, which prohibit certain activities, such as the right to tax exports. Finally, the Supreme Court can help limit the power of state and national governments through the process of judicial review. It can strike down government activities that violate the Constitution.

Amendment Process; Bill of Rights; Checks and Balances; Constitution; Denied Powers;

Executive Branch; Export Taxes; Express Powers; Federalism; Judicial Branch; Judicial Review;

Legislative Branch; Magna Carta; Ratification; Separation of Powers; Supreme Court; Treaties

> "No freeman shall be taken or imprisoned, or diseased, or out-lawed, or banished, or in any way destroyed, nor will we pass [sentence] upon him, unless by the lawful judgment of his peers, or by the law of the land."
> Magna Carta, 1215

M

Magna Carta

The Great Charter, a document written in 1215 to restrain an English monarch who abused his powers.

Many of its clauses dealt with the king's specific duties to his knights. Nevertheless, the Magna Carta also guaranteed the personal liberty and property of the king's subjects and put limits on taxation. For example, it provided that no person can be imprisoned without a trial by jury before a judge. The Magna Carta became a symbol of freedom for generations of English subjects and, much later, for American colonists.

Jury Trial, Right to; Limited Government; Property Rights

Militia

A military organization of citizen volunteers with limited training who usually serve during emergencies.

At the Constitutional Convention, some delegates, like Elbridge Gerry and Luther Martin, feared the creation of a standing army under the control of a national government. They demanded that the militias be kept under state control. Other delegates, like Charles Cotesworth Pinckney, remembered how difficult it was to get the states to contribute fighting units and supplies to the Continental Army during the War for Independence. They had little faith in state militias and wanted to set up a national military force.

The Constitution contains a series of compromises that preserved the militias but allowed the national government to direct and deploy them. Article II, section 2, makes the president the commander in chief of the militias when they are called up to serve the United States. Article I, section 8, gives Congress the power to call up the militias to carry out the laws of the nation and to put down insurrections. Congress is also in charge of arming, organizing, and disciplining the militias to provide uniformity among the states. The states retain the right to appoint officers and to train the militia, according to rules set by Congress.

After the Civil War, the state militias were mostly made up of wealthy men who could afford to buy their own uniforms. Militia units frequently served as honor guards, though they occasionally broke up strikes. By the 1880s, their name was changed to the National Guard. During the twentieth century, the National Guard served in World War I and World War II and is still used in emergencies. National Guard troops have restored order during natural disasters, like major hurricanes. They have also enforced federal laws. For example, their presence in Little Rock, Arkansas, in 1957 made it possible for black students to enter the all-white Central High School for the first time, despite protests of white citizens and state officials.

Arms, Rights to Bear; Constitutional Convention; Delegates; Domestic Violence; U.S. Constitution, Article I; U.S. Constitution, Article II; U.S. Constitution, Second Amendment

In late September 1957, twenty days after the school year started, the Little Rock Nine—the first nine black students to attend the previously all-white Central High School in Little Rock, Arkansas—were finally escorted through an angry and sometimes violent mob of white residents opposed to integration. Their escorts included the U.S. Army and Arkansas National Guard units federalized by President Dwight D. Eisenhower. Interestingly enough, before Eisenhower exercised his power to federalize the militia, Governor Orval Faubus of Arkansas employed the same guardsmen to block the black students from entering the school.

Money and Coinage

A means of payment for purchases.

Under the Articles of Confederation, there was no standard currency. The Spanish dollar was widely used, but its value varied from state to state. In New York, it was equivalent to eight shillings (a British unit of currency); in South Carolina, thirty-two shillings and six pence. Other coins circulated through the United States as well. These included French crowns, doubloons, and ducats. Counterfeiting was widespread, so merchants often weighed coins to make sure they contained the proper amount of gold or silver. Besides this, some states began to print their own paper money, whose value quickly declined. For these reasons, the Framers of the Constitution decided that a standard national currency was needed. In Article I, section 10, they forbade states from issuing money, and in section 8 they gave Congress the power to coin and regulate money.

The Constitution, however, did not forbid citizens from issuing money in their local communities. In the 1990s, more than sixty local communities in the United States began issuing their own paper currency. This was done to keep money within economically troubled communities and to encourage local businesses. The money can be spent only within the local area and is used to buy goods and services. Local currencies are legal as long as they are converted to U.S. dollars when it is time to pay taxes.

Articles of Confederation; Counterfeiting; Debts; Express Powers; Framers; Taxation, Power of; U.S. Constitution, Article I

Native Americans

The earliest peoples to arrive in North America, originally known to Europeans as American Indians.

Indians are the only people mentioned by name in the Constitution. To the colonists, they could be friendly helpers, allies against the British, or hostile raiders, depending on the tribe and the circumstances of a given moment. Before long, the Indians realized that the colonists wanted to take over their lands, sometimes by using force and sometimes simply by moving into an area and building houses or a settlement. During the Confederation, some states negotiated treaties with local tribes to obtain land.

The Framers of the Constitution gave the national government the responsibility for dealing with Native Americans. They wanted Congress to create and carry out a uniform policy for dealing with peoples they considered uncivilized, failing to recognize the Indians' own centuries-old cultures. The Constitution mentions Indians in three places. In Article I,

These five Navajos registered to vote in New Mexico in September 1948. The state had denied them the right to vote because, as residents of a reservation, they paid no state income tax. A federal court decision handed down shortly before this photograph was taken ruled the provision unconstitutional and said that these people could vote if they met residence requirements set for other citizens.

This period saw a great expansion in voting rights for minorities. Only four years earlier, in *Smith v. Allwright* (1944), the Supreme Court had ruled that the Texas Democratic Party could not limit its membership to whites. Subsequent legislation (the Voting Rights Act of 1965, for instance), Supreme Court decisions (*Baker v. Carr*, 1962), and constitutional amendments (the Twenty-fourth Amendment, ratified in 1964) established the right of all citizens to vote, given that they are properly registered.

Today, voting requirements differ from state to state, but they are all based on a number of days either in residence or registered to vote before the election. A good rule of thumb (although not one that applies to every state) is that a voter should be registered at least thirty days before an election.

section 2, it states that they are not to be counted for purposes of taxation or representation. This is repeated in the Fourteenth Amendment. In Article I, section 8, Congress is given the authority to regulate commerce with the tribes.

Government policy toward Indians has not been consistent. Until the 1830s, Native American tribes were officially treated as dependent nations within the United States. Congress simply regulated trade with them. However, the federal government did little to discourage white settlers from occupying Indian lands. Then, under the Indian Removal Act of 1830, it began to force the tribes to relocate. For example, once gold was found in Cherokee territory, the Georgia legislature passed a law to seize the Indian lands within that state. In *Worcester v. Georgia* (1832), the Supreme Court overturned the Georgia law because it violated a treaty with the tribe. However, President Andrew Jackson refused to enforce the Court's decision. Under the Indian Removal Act, the Cherokee marched on foot to territory in what is now Oklahoma, under military escort. Along this "Trail of Tears," approximately 4,000 members of the tribe died. The survivors were confined to a reservation. Throughout the nineteenth century, as settlers moved farther west, the government repeatedly violated earlier treaties and the U.S. Army attacked and killed or imprisoned any tribes that tried to protect their hunting grounds and traditional lands. Many Indians were relocated to reservations. There they lived in poverty and neglect, at the mercy of greedy traders. Once Indians were confined to reservations, the government accepted responsibility for them and created the Bureau of Indian Affairs to manage their affairs. In *Elk v. Wilkins* (1884), the Supreme Court declared that Indians were not citizens.

Since then, government policy has seesawed between discouraging and supporting the tribal way of life. In the 1880s, the government tried to break up tribes. The Dawes Severalty Act of 1887 encouraged Native Americans to subdivide their commonly held land, distribute plots to individual Indians, and sell off any surplus. Unscrupulous buyers swindled many Indians out of their new holdings and bought up the surplus land at very low prices. In 1924, the Indian Citizenship Act gave citizenship to Native Americans who chose to leave the reservation and to Indian women

William Paterson served in the New Jersey state government during the War for Independence, but he turned down an offer to attend the Continental Congress.

He was forty-two years old when he arrived in Philadelphia for the Constitutional Convention. There, he was among those who spoke for state interests, as did, for differing reasons, John Lansing Jr. and Robert Yates of New York, Luther Martin of Maryland, and Charles Cotesworth Pinckney of South Carolina. Paterson's interest was in protecting the small states, and in that role he was one of the authors of the New Jersey Plan. He presented it to the Convention in June and only reluctantly accepted the Connecticut Compromise, hammered out in July. At the end of July, Paterson went home, having managed to protect the interests of small states. He kept notes on the debates until he left. He returned to sign the Constitution and helped secure its ratification.

He later served in the Senate, as governor of New Jersey, and, from 1793 until his death in 1806, on the United States Supreme Court.

While on the Court, Paterson, like all Supreme Court justices of his day, "rode the circuit." That is, he literally rode from town to town to preside in federal circuit courts where there were no other judges.

who married non-Indians. In 1934, with passage of the Indian Reorganization Act, the government reversed itself and began to revive Native American organizations again. This law allowed tribes on reservations to adopt their own constitutions and set up tribal governments to deal with the states and the national government. Then, in 1953, the government began to stop services to and relations with Indian tribes. In 1968, a law gave Indians their own Bill of Rights to protect them from tribal decisions that interfered with their liberties. During the 1960s, Native Americans began to hold demonstrations to protest their mistreatment by the U.S. government. Through lawsuits, they successfully reclaimed some of their rights under old treaties with the United States. They recovered some lands and fishing, hunting, and mineral rights.

Citizenship; Commerce Clause; Confederation; Framers; Supreme Court; Taxation, Power of; Treaties; U.S. Constitution, Article I; U.S. Constitution, Fourteenth Amendment

Naturalization

See: Citizenship

Necessary and Proper Clause

See: Elastic Clause

New Jersey Plan

Nine resolutions for creating a national government, drawn up by delegates from the small states to the Constitutional Convention.

The New Jersey Plan was prepared as a response to the Virginia Plan, supported by the large states. William Paterson presented the New Jersey Plan to the delegates. David Brearly, John Lansing, Alexander Martin, and Roger Sherman argued in favor of it. James Madison, Edmund Randolph, and James Wilson were its main opponents. The Connecticut Compromise settled differences between the small and large states by combining parts of the New Jersey Plan and the Virginia Plan.

The New Jersey Plan provided for a one-chamber legislature, called Congress. Each state would be equally represented. Congress could raise revenue by taxing imports, by requiring stamps on documents, and by charging for postage. Revenues collected from states would be based on the states' population, and free people of every age, sex, and condition would be counted except for Indians. Every five slaves would be counted as three free people. Congress could make laws to regulate trade and commerce. State courts, however, would punish any violations of these laws. Appeals from their judgments would be decided by a national court.

The Congress would elect an executive, who would be ineligible to serve a second term. No pay increase or decrease could take effect while the executive was holding office. The executive would carry out federal laws, appoint federal officials, and direct military actions.

The plan also recommended that a Supreme Court be created, with judges appointed by the executive. It would hear impeachment charges against federal officials, appeals from decisions of state courts, cases affecting ambassadors, and disputes about the law of the seas, treaties, trade regulations, or the collection of federal revenues. All national laws and treaties would be the supreme law of the land. Arrangements would be made to admit new states to the Union and to create the same law for naturalization in every state. Citizens committing crimes in another state would be treated as if they lived in that state.

Ambassadors; Citizenship; Commerce Clause; Compensation; Congress; Connecticut Compromise; Constitutional Convention; Delegates; Impeachment; Imports; President; Revenue; States; Supreme Court; Three-Fifths Compromise; Unicameral Legislature; Virginia Plan

Nobility

People who receive land and aristocratic titles from a monarch. Such titles and lands are usually passed down from generation to generation.

In Article I of the Constitution, sections 9 and 10 forbid Congress and the states from granting titles of nobility. This was similar to a clause in the Articles of Confederation. The Framers did not want to create a permanent upper class based solely on the benefits of birth. The Declaration of Independence stated that all men are created equal. Although the American people were in fact unequal in wealth and possessions, they did have equality of opportunity to improve themselves—except for slaves, women, and Indians, but their time would come.

Amendments, Unratified; Articles of Confederation; Congress; Framers; U.S. Constitution, Article I

O

Oaths of Office

Pledges to carry out official duties and responsibilities to the public and to support the nation's basic laws.

Article II, section 1, of the Constitution requires incoming presidents to take the following oath: "I do solemnly swear (or affirm) that I will faithfully execute the Office of President of the United States, and will to

Abraham Lincoln (on the left) is shown here being sworn in for a second term as president of the United States on March 4, 1865. In a tradition that began with George Washington and continues to this day, Lincoln placed his hand on a Bible as he repeated the constitutionally prescribed words of the oath of office. Another custom, only rarely broken, is for the chief justice of the Unites States to administer the oath. Chief Justice Salmon P. Chase (on the right) is doing so here.

Lincoln's second inauguration was much like the inauguration of any president, but the circumstances surrounding it were highly extraordinary.

The United States was fighting the Civil War, a crisis of such urgency that some people had privately suggested to Lincoln that he cancel the election of 1864 and remain in office under declaration of martial law. Lincoln thought this was out of the question, and at the end of a difficult campaign he was reelected by a wide margin. His greatest support came from soldiers in the field, who cast absentee ballots—that is, voted in their districts back home by mailing in their ballots. Absentee ballots are now used frequently for people, such as military personnel, students, and tourists, who cannot be in their home towns at election time.

the best of my ability, preserve, protect and defend the Constitution of the United States." Article VI requires senators, representatives, members of state legislatures, and all national and state executives and judges to swear to support the Constitution. During the debates at the Constitution Convention, Elbridge Gerry convinced the other delegates to add state officials to the list of officials in Article VI. He wanted these officers of the states to feel they were part of one national system. The oaths help make the Constitution, federal laws, and treaties the supreme law of the land.

Constitutional Convention; Delegates; President; Religious Tests; Supremacy Clause; Treaties; U.S. Constitution, Article II; U.S. Constitution, Article VI

One-Person, One-Vote Rule

The idea that every person's vote should be counted the same as everyone else's, regardless of race, gender, wealth, or neighborhood.

This guarantee has been read into the Constitution. Article I, section 4, and Article II, section 1, gives the states the power to create election districts to allow voters to choose their lawmakers. When these districts were first laid out, rural populations were often given more representatives to state and national government than city dwellers. This meant that a vote cast in a city counted less than a vote cast in the countryside. Similarly, many states later drew district lines to discourage minority candidates. They would, for instance, create oddly shaped districts that split up the African-American voting population so that black votes could never effectively elect a candidate.

In *Baker v. Carr* (1962), the Supreme Court ruled that people had the right to challenge the way state lawmakers drew up election districts. In this case, the Tennessee state legislature had not changed the boundaries of election districts since 1901. As a result, city dwellers did not have their fair share of representatives in state government. In the past, federal and state judges had argued that cases involving election districts were political questions outside their jurisdiction. In *Baker v. Carr*, the Court reasoned that the people of Tennessee had been denied the equal protection of the laws and had the right to appeal to the courts. Two years later, in

Wesberry v. Sanders (1964), the Court required that members of Congress be elected from districts of roughly equal size so that one person's vote counted as much as another's. In *Reynolds v. Sims* (1964), this principle was applied to both houses of state legislatures.

Apportionment; Congress; Elections; Equal Protection of the Laws; Jurisdiction; Popular Vote; States; Supreme Court; U.S. Constitution, Article I; U.S. Constitution, Article II; Voting Rights

Original Intent

The meaning and purpose of laws, the Constitution, or other public documents at the time they were written.

When judges decide cases, they often look at the original intent of lawmakers and the Framers. They may reread debates in Congress or at the Constitutional Convention as well as letters and diaries. Such research may help them with their construction, or interpretation, of the law.

Congress; Constitutional Convention; Construction; Framers; Judicial Restraint; Law

P

Pardons and Reprieves

Setting aside punishment for a crime (permanently, for a pardon, or temporarily, for a reprieve).

Traditionally, the English monarch sometimes granted mercy for offenses against the Crown. In the United States, offenses were committed against the people, not the Crown. Because they represent the people, some states' legislatures make the final decisions about pardons and reprieves. Most states also let their executives set aside punishments. During debates at the Constitutional Convention, James Wilson wanted to use pardons to get suspects to testify against their accomplices. Most of the other Framers agreed. In number 74 of the Federalist Papers, a series of newspaper articles supporting ratification of the Constitution, Alexander Hamilton argued that pardons could also be granted in cases of treason.

Article II, section 2, of the Constitution gives the president the power to grant pardons and reprieves for all offenses against the United States, except in cases of impeachment. Presidents have used this power from George Washington's day to the present. In 1974, President Gerald R. Ford made a very controversial decision to pardon the previous president, Richard M. Nixon, for any offenses he may have committed against the United States. Nixon had resigned from office because he did not want to be impeached for abusing his powers. As president, he had tried to prevent the government from properly investigating a break-in at Democratic

Party headquarters in the Watergate complex, masterminded by his aides at the White House. He had also lied to the public and to Congress to protect his aides. Because the news media had covered the Watergate scandal in great detail for two years, Ford felt it would be difficult for the former president to receive a fair trial anywhere in the United States. He also believed that leaving office in disgrace was sufficient punishment for Nixon. The pardon put an end to the Watergate scandal and let the nation get on with its other business.

Constitutional Convention; Executive Powers; Framers; Impeachment; President; Treason; U.S. Constitution, Article II

Parties, Political

Major and Significant Minor Political Parties in U.S. History
Federalist Party, 1790s–1810s
Democratic-Republican Party, 1790s–1820s
Democratic Party, 1820s–
National Republican Party, 1828–1832
Anti-Masonic Party, 1832
Whig Party, 1834–1850s
Liberty Party, 1840–1847
Free Soil Party, 1848–1854
American (Know-Nothing) Party, 1850s
Republican Party, 1854–
Constitutional Union Party, 1860
Greenback Party, 1876–1884
Prohibition Party, 1884–1920
People's (Populist) Party, 1890s
Socialist Party, 1901–1940s
Progressive (Bull Moose) Party, 1912
Farmer-Labor Party, 1920
Progressive Party, 1924
Communist Party, 1932
Union Party, 1936
States' Rights Democrats (Dixiecrats), 1948
Progressive Party, 1948
American Independent Party, 1968–1972
Libertarian Party, 1976–
Reform Party, 1992–

Organizations that choose candidates for public office and help them win elections.

Political parties are not mentioned in the Constitution. In fact, at the Constitutional Convention, the Framers had feared the rise of parties, or factions, as they called them. They felt that factions might undermine the stability of the government by creating groups with narrow interests. They wanted to keep parties from controlling the government and forcing their economic and social views on the rest of the nation. This is why the Framers established a federal system of government marked by separation of powers and checks and balances.

Despite the Framers' intentions, political parties developed when George Washington was president in the 1790s. (It can even be said that they developed during the debate over ratification of the Constitution.) Secretary of the Treasury Alexander Hamilton sought out lawmakers willing to help the nation become a commercial and manufacturing power, mostly by concentrating power in the national government. Secretary of State Thomas Jefferson, who wanted the republic to become a nation of independent farmers, sought to limit the powers of the national government. He was soon supported by lawmakers who shared his views. It was a small step from getting favorable laws passed to seeing that cooperative lawmakers were elected and reelected. In this way, the Federalist and Democratic-Republican parties emerged. After Washington left office, the two parties began contesting presidential elections.

For the most part, just two major political parties have continued to compete for votes up to the present. Minor parties sometimes win an important number of votes—and they may even replace one of the major parties (as the Republican Party replaced the Whigs after 1856)—but the nature of elective politics under the Constitution has so far generally prevented three major parties from competing at the same time. Today, the Democratic Party (the successor to the Democratic-Republicans) and the Republican Party are the two major parties.

Although political parties are not mentioned in the Constitution, they affected the way the Constitution developed. The original method of electing a president and vice president was for votes in the electoral college to be cast for two people, the winner being elected president and the runner-up vice president. This did not work very well, and in 1796 a Federalist president, John Adams, was elected with a Democratic-Republican vice president, Thomas Jefferson. Four years later, this system resulted in a tie between two Democratic-Republican candidates, Jefferson and Aaron Burr, which led to a constitutional crisis. As a result, the Twelfth Amendment was passed, changing the way the president was elected. Under the Twelfth Amendment, separate votes were cast in the electoral college for president and vice president. This ensured not only that the two winners would be from the same party but that there would be no confusion over which candidate was running for president and which one for vice president.

The existence of political parties had changed the electoral procedures outlined in the Constitution. However, the method of choosing a president, by the votes of state delegations to the electoral college, remained the same. This method, which requires a candidate to win a majority of the states' votes, not a simple majority of the popular vote, encourages broad national parties rather than parties that can command all of the votes in just one region. In this way, despite what the Framers intended when they drafted the Constitution, the American political system encourages a two-party system of government.

Antifederalists; Checks and Balances; Congress; Constitutional Convention; Elections;
Electoral College; Executive Departments; Federalism; Federalists; Framers; Popular Vote;
President; Ratification; Separation of Powers; U.S. Constitution, Twelfth Amendment

Patents

Sole rights to produce and sell inventions.

Article I, section 8, of the Constitution lets Congress provide for patents to inventors to protect their discoveries in order to promote progress in science and the "useful arts."

Congress; U.S. Constitution, Article I

Petition the Government for a Redress of Grievances, Right to

The right of people to ask the government to correct wrongs.

It is found in the First Amendment to the Constitution, part of the Bill of Rights. Freedom to petition was first recognized in tenth-century England. It was protected in the Magna Carta and mentioned again in the English Bill of Rights. When he wrote the Declaration of Independence in 1776, Thomas Jefferson accused King George III of, among other things, ignoring colonists' petitions to right wrongs. Thus, it is not surprising that the freedom to petition was placed in many state constitutions and in the American Bill of Rights.

In the United States, most Americans take for granted their right to request action from their government to solve a problem. In addition, they routinely circulate and sign petitions sponsored by groups favoring or opposing certain government programs. Few cases have come before the Supreme Court to challenge their right to do so (though some cases have examined the extent to which petitions may be circulated on private property that has come to have a public function, such as shopping malls). In 1836, however, the House of Representatives passed a rule to refuse to hear petitions from people opposed to slavery. In 1844, under the leadership of John Quincy Adams, this "gag rule" was finally repealed.

Assembly, Freedom of; Bill of Rights; House of Representatives; Magna Carta; Slavery; Supreme Court; U.S. Constitution, First Amendment

> "[I]t is the right of subjects to petition the king, and all commitments [to prison] and prosecution for such petitioning are illegal."
> **English Bill of Rights, 1689**

Police Powers

Government measures intended to provide for the safety and general well-being of the public.

Police powers extend to such areas as health, prosperity, morals, and public order. They permit governments to pass laws for the public good that may limit personal freedom and property rights. Police powers are implied but not identified in the Preamble to the Constitution and in the Tenth Amendment to the Constitution. They are concurrent powers of the national and state governments.

The Supreme Court has often served as a referee deciding when national and state police powers should be used. Until the Civil War, the Court used the commerce clause and the supremacy clause, among others, to broaden federal power at the expense of the states. In the 1880s, the Court used the due process clause of the Fourteenth Amendment to the Constitution to further limit state police powers and keep them from regulating businesses. During the 1930s, when the nation's economy collapsed, the Court gradually expanded both state and federal police powers. Officials needed these powers to deal with widespread business failures, unemployment, homelessness, and starvation during this national emergency. More recently, the Court has had to decide when and how police powers apply to such issues as privacy, civil rights, and the basic freedoms guaranteed by the Bill of Rights.

Bill of Rights; Civil Rights; Commerce Clause; Concurrent Powers; Due Process of Law; Preamble; Privacy; Speech, Freedom of; Supremacy Clause; Supreme Court; U.S. Constitution, Tenth Amendment; U.S. Constitution, Fourteenth Amendment

This photograph was taken in Texas in 1939. The poster was a reminder to local citizens to pay their poll taxes, a requirement in many states, particularly in the South. After passage of the Fifteenth Amendment in 1870, blacks in the former slave states generally were able to vote and exercise their political rights. Gradually, however, and especially in the 1890s and afterward, many states imposed restrictions on voting. While supposedly not racially motivated or biased, these restrictions—poll taxes as well as literacy and property requirements—in fact were designed to keep blacks and poor whites from voting. For decades after the Constitution promised them the right to vote, the vast majority of blacks were denied access to the ballot box in much of the United States.

It was not until 1964, with ratification of the Twenty-fourth Amendment and passage of the Civil Rights Act, that blacks were given the opportunity to vote everywhere in the country in numbers proportional to the population.

Poll Taxes

Payments required in order to vote, and often applied in a racially discriminatory way in some parts of the country.

Poll taxes were banned by the Twenty-fourth Amendment to the Constitution.

Capitation Tax; U.S. Constitution, Twenty-fourth Amendment; Voting Rights

Popular Sovereignty

The belief that all power in government comes from the people.

This view is found in the writings of the English political philosopher John Locke and accepted by the Framers of the Constitution. In the Preamble, they wrote that the people of the United States intended to form a "more perfect Union."

Popular sovereignty was raised during the debate over ratification at the Constitutional Convention. James Madison and James Wilson insisted that the Constitution be submitted directly to the people for their approval. The two Framers also argued that if the Constitution were submitted to state legislatures, the work of the Convention might easily be undone.

The Framers believed in the power of the people in theory but not in practice. They did not entirely trust the people's judgment, claiming that ordinary citizens were too easily swayed by their emotions. Nevertheless, the Framers were practical as well as principled men. They decided to submit the Constitution to special conventions of delegates elected by the people in each state. These delegates, rather than state legislatures or the people themselves, decided the fate of the Constitution.

Constitutional Convention; Convention; Delegates; Framers; Preamble; Ratification; Second Treatise on Government

Popular Vote

Election by the people.

At the Constitutional Convention, the Framers debated whether to let the people vote directly for members of the House of Representatives and the Senate, and for the president. Opponents of the popular vote argued that the public was easily misled and lacked the necessary information to judge candidates. These Framers wanted the states to select members of the national government. That way, they said, the states would then be less likely to lose influence or power to the national government. Supporters of the popular vote argued that the only way for people to have confidence in the government was if they helped to elect it. They said the national government should know and represent every part of the community and its different interests. Among the most outspoken opponents of popular election of the House were Luther Martin, Charles Cotesworth Pinckney, and John Rutledge. James Wilson and James Madison were among its strongest supporters.

In the original Constitution, only the House was directly elected by the people. The delegates debated how seats in the House should be distributed among the states. Some argued for wealth (how much the people in a state owned or earned) while others preferred numbers (how many people lived in a state). James Wilson convinced the delegates that distributing seats by either method produced approximately the same results. A compromise was reached by permitting each state's share of representation in the House and taxes owed to the national government to be based on population, with every five slaves counted as three free people. The delegates also required that a census be held every ten years to determine population changes in each state so that seats in the House could be redistributed. Until 1913, with the ratification of the Seventeenth Amendment to the Constitution, state legislatures elected members of the Senate. Now the people in each state are entitled to vote for the two senators who represent the state. The president is still formally elected by the electoral college, not the popular vote. At best, it can be said that the president is indirectly elected by the popular vote, since the votes cast by the people determine electors to the electoral college. A number of problems have occurred as a result of this.

Apportionment; Census; Constitutional Convention; Electoral College; Framers; House of Representatives; President; Ratification; Senate; Three-Fifths Compromise; U.S. Constitution, Seventeenth Amendment

This 1887 cover of *Harper's Weekly* depicts a lonely frontiersman mailing a letter. In 1862, after only two years of carrying mail across the continent, the Pony Express was replaced by the telegraph. Twenty-five years later, the whole country was connected by regular mail service.

Postal Service

A government-operated system for delivering letters and packages.

Article I, section 8, of the Constitution gives Congress the power to set up post offices nationwide. Before the Constitution went into effect, seventy-six post offices were already delivering mail. The president appointed a postmaster general to take charge of the system. Presidents usually used this government post to reward politicians who helped them get elected. The postmaster general became a member of the president's cabinet in 1829. The federal Post Office itself was made an executive department in 1872. In 1970 the department was turned into a government agency, called the United States Postal Service, and dropped from the cabinet. Today it is run by an eleven-member board of governors that chooses the postmaster general.

During the nineteenth century, private companies successfully competed with the Post Office until postal rates were lowered in 1845. By 1864, postal money orders had been introduced. They allowed people to send money safely and easily. The Post Office signed contracts for mail to travel across oceans in 1845, by railroads in 1865, and by airplane in 1918. Now some private companies are luring away postal customers by offering faster, more efficient service.

Cabinet; Congress; Executive Departments; President; U.S. Constitution, Article I

President Franklin D. Roosevelt meant children like these when he said, in 1937, "I see one-third of a nation . . . ill-nourished." Whether their well-being and the "general Welfare" of the Preamble were the same thing was—and remains—a debated question.

Preamble

An introductory statement.

The Preamble to the Constitution explains why the Constitution was created—to "form a more perfect Union" (than the Articles of Confederation). To achieve this goal, it must "establish Justice," by setting up laws that treat everyone fairly; "insure domestic Tranquility," by keeping the peace and suppressing local uprisings; "provide for the common defense," by protecting the nation from invasions and other threats to its security; "promote the general Welfare," by encouraging trade, the arts, and scientific discoveries to improve the well-being of citizens; and "secure the Blessings of Liberty to ourselves and our Posterity," by respecting and protecting individual freedoms for generations to come.

Articles of Confederation; Constitution; Defense; Domestic Violence; Equal Protection of the Laws

Presidents of the United States

President

The chief executive and head of state of the United States.

The president is in charge of the executive branch of the national government. After their experiences without an executive, under the Articles of Confederation, the delegates to the Constitutional Convention decided to create one. They wanted to make sure that the laws Congress passed were carried out. The delegates had little experience with executives other than the powerful King George III of Great Britain and his royal governors, or weak state governors after independence was won.

Early on, the Framers debated whether to have an executive of one person or several. James Wilson, Elbridge Gerry, Pierce Butler, and John Rutledge supported a single person. Edmund Randolph and Hugh Williamson preferred three, from different parts of the country. They feared that a monarchy would develop if one person were president. Alexander Hamilton did not think that would be such a bad idea. Once the Committee on Postponed Matters worked out a compromise about choosing the president, the idea of a multiple executive was dropped.

Originally the Framers considered two main methods for selecting a president. The first allowed Congress to make the choice. Some Framers objected that this would make a president too dependent on the legislative branch. It would violate the principle of separation of powers. The second method left the choice of a president up to the people. Most of the delegates, however, did not believe that ordinary people had the knowledge to make informed judgments. In addition, this method favored states with large populations. The Convention's Committee on Postponed Matters came up with a compromise solution: the electoral college, written into Article II, section 1, of the Constitution. In the same article, the Framers required the president to be at least thirty-five years old, to be a natural-born (not a naturalized) citizen, and to have lived in the United States for fourteen years.

Roger Sherman wanted to limit the power of the president by simply requiring the chief executive to put laws into effect. This might have violated separation of powers by making the president merely the law-enforcement arm of Congress. Instead, Article II created a strong official with more powers than any state governor had. According to the principle of checks and balances, some of these powers are shared with Congress. For example, according to Article II, section 2, the Senate approves or rejects presidential appointments of judges, ambassadors, and heads of

This photograph shows a crew laying a sidewalk in Faribault, Minnesota, in summer 1936. The workers were part of the Works Progress Administration, or WPA, one of many government programs launched during the Great Depression as part of President Franklin D. Roosevelt's New Deal.

The depression of the 1930s was by far the most crippling economic crisis ever faced by the United States. Fully 25 percent of the labor force was out of work, and people everywhere had too little to eat and no place to live. Immediately upon taking office in March 1933, Roosevelt began pushing programs to create work and get the economy moving, partly by controlling the way it functioned (through wage and price guidelines that were later ruled unconstitutional).

Ultimately, however, the greater part of Roosevelt's program was allowed to stand. It greatly expanded the reach of the federal government and increased the number of Americans who had direct contact with their government. The effects of these changes were still apparent long afterward, from the Social Security program to the regulation of public utilities to, most obviously, the generally increased power of the executive branch of government and of the president.

executive departments. The president also must obtain its advice and consent to any treaties signed in the name of the United States. Furthermore, Article II, section 4, gives Congress the threat of impeachment to keep a president from abusing presidential powers.

Several amendments to the Constitution concern the presidency. The Twelfth Amendment corrects a flaw in the electoral college that resulted in a crisis following the election of 1800. The Twentieth Amendment moves the start of the president's term from March to January after the presidential election and provides rules for succession to the presidency. The Twenty-second Amendment limits a president to two full terms in office. (If a vice president succeeds to the presidency and serves more than two years of the previous chief executive's term, then the limitation is reduced to one full term in addition to the two-plus years.) The Twenty-fifth Amendment clarifies the matter of succession to the presidency in cases of death or disability.

The president has become a powerful figure in American government. National crises, such as major wars, widespread business failures, and threats to the nation's security, have demanded strong leadership. The president has been able to provide it, using the powers of the office to the fullest. Article II, section 2, makes the president commander in chief of the military. By stretching this power, presidents have sent troops to serve at overseas bases, to settle other nations' problems, and even to fight, all without having Congress declare war as required by Article I, section 8. Of course, Congress has to provide the funds for such military missions.

Under Article II, section 3, presidents may recommend laws to Congress. Now Congress expects presidents to outline a full program of government activities. President Franklin D. Roosevelt's New Deal programs greatly expanded the federal government's role in helping private individuals who needed work, food, and housing during the economic crisis of the 1930s. During the 1980s, President Ronald Reagan thought government was doing far too much, and he gave Congress a series of proposals to cut back activities. He wanted private businesses and individuals to do more for themselves. Presidents also use their powers to prepare a budget. This determines how much money can be spent on government programs. Roosevelt increased government spending, and Reagan tried (unsuccessfully) to reduce it.

Article II, section 3, also requires the president to give Congress a report on the current "State of the Union." With all the information available to him from his advisers in the executive branch, the president has the opportunity to become the best-informed individual in the nation. The nation's first two presidents appeared before Congress to give their speeches, but President Thomas Jefferson abandoned the practice. He thought it was too monarchical. More than a hundred years later, President Woodrow Wilson decided to address Congress in person, and modern presidents have followed his example. The annual State of the Union speech has become increasingly important. A popular president, like Roosevelt or Reagan, can use it to give Congress guidance and direction in passing laws.

Modern media have made the president a familiar figure to most Americans. This has also increased presidential power. President Franklin D. Roosevelt started the trend by talking informally to Americans over the radio in "fireside chats." Now television shows the president at work, overseas, and even relaxing. The Internet is providing another means for the president to reach the public and convince them to support certain programs. It also gives Americans an increased opportunity to talk back, using computer e-mail.

Ambassadors; Articles of Confederation; Checks and Balances; Commander in Chief; Congress; Constitutional Convention; Delegates; Electoral College; Executive Branch; Executive Departments; Executive Powers; Federal Government; Framers; Impeachment; Legislative Branch; Presidential Disability; Presidential Succession; Separation of Powers; Term Limits; Treaties; U.S. Constitution, Article I; U.S. Constitution, Article II; U.S. Constitution, Twelfth Amendment; U.S. Constitution, Twentieth Amendment; U.S. Constitution, Twenty-second Amendment; U.S. Constitution, Twenty-fifth Amendment; Vice President

President Bill Clinton is shown here with his wife, Hillary. Many people ranked Clinton among the most media-savvy presidents, together with Franklin D. Roosevelt (whose mastery of radio helped advance his political agenda in the 1930s and 1940s) and Ronald Reagan (whose use of television in the 1980s was similarly successful). Both supporters and detractors of Clinton marveled at his ability to turn political disaster into success, at least as measured by public opinion polls. For some, this reflected Clinton's relatively good use of the presidency, especially in times of political difficulty, as a platform from which to address the American public directly. To others, less taken with the Clinton style, his successes were those of a scandalous politician who knew how to play the public better than most. What most everyone agreed on, however, was that in the 1990s, under Clinton, the president of the United States came under an unprecedented scrutiny and public investigation. What people disagreed about was whether Clinton had brought that investigation upon himself (as some think he did, both by unprincipled or illegal actions and by revealing personal details about himself), or whether he was the victim of attacks out of proportion to any errors he had committed.

Presidential Disability

An illness or accident that prevents a president from performing official duties, temporarily or permanently.

The Constitution does not outline procedures to be followed if an ailing president insists on remaining in office but cannot function. It also fails to provide for circumstances when a seriously ill president recovers and wants to go back to work. In late 1919, for example, President Woodrow Wilson suffered a stroke and was left barely able to fulfill the duties of his office until the end of his term, more than a year later. With much less media attention on the presidency than there is today, his doctors, wife, vice president, top aides, and other officials were able to hide the extent of his disability, which did not become widely known until long after his death. The Twenty-fifth Amendment to the Constitution deals with the issue of presidential disability.

President; U.S. Constitution, Twenty-fifth Amendment; Vice President

Order of Presidential Succession
Vice President
Speaker of the House
President Pro Tempore of the Senate
Secretary of State
Secretary of the Treasury
Secretary of Defense
Attorney General
Secretary of the Interior
Secretary of Agriculture
Secretary of Commerce
Secretary of Labor
Secretary of Health and Human Services
Secretary of Housing and Urban Development
Secretary of Transportation
Secretary of Energy
Secretary of Education
Secretary of Veterans' Affairs

Presidential Succession

The procedure for replacing a president who resigns, is disabled, or dies in office.

When the office of president is vacant, Article II, section 1, of the Constitution does not make clear whether the vice president becomes president or serves as a caretaker until a new president can be elected. At the Constitutional Convention, the Committee on Style accidentally created this confusion.

The Framers had agreed that the vice president would serve as a temporary substitute for the president, until a proper replacement could be elected. The Committee on Style failed to include this in Article II, section 1, of the final version of the Constitution. Nor did the Framers specifically write that the vice president becomes president. At the time, none of the Framers were aware that this created a problem. Then, in 1841, when President William Henry Harrison died, Vice President John Tyler refused to act merely as a caretaker and was sworn in as president. Other vice presidents who became president followed his example. The Twenty-fifth Amendment to the Constitution finally made this tradition the law of the land. It stated that the vice president becomes president if the office of president is vacant.

The Twentieth Amendment solved other problems with presidential succession. If an incoming president dies before being able to take office, the vice president becomes president. (In 1933, a month before he was to be sworn in, President Franklin D. Roosevelt was almost assassinated.) If a president does not qualify by January 20, the date of the presidential inauguration, the vice president temporarily acts as president. (This can happen if the House of Representatives must decide a presidential election and delays in choosing the winner.) If neither the new president nor the vice president qualifies, Congress may pass a law to solve the problem. Finally, if the House has to choose a president, or the Senate a vice president, and that person dies, Congress must find other candidates. The Presidential Succession Act of 1947 lists the order of replacement if, for any reason, the president and vice president cannot serve. They are the Speaker of the House, president pro tempore of the Senate, and heads of executive departments, according to the date each department was established.

Constitutional Convention; Framers; President; U.S. Constitution, Article II; U.S. Constitution, Twentieth Amendment; U.S. Constitution, Twenty-fifth Amendment; Vice President

President Pro Tempore of the Senate

The official who temporarily presides over the Senate when the vice president is absent.

As the presiding officer, the president pro tempore (meaning "for the time being") recognizes members who wish to speak during debates. That official may also have to rule on questions of Senate procedure. The president pro tempore is usually the most senior (longest-serving) senator from the majority party, the party that controls the most seats in the chamber. Because presiding over the Senate is time-consuming and often boring, other senators usually take over this chore for the president pro tempore. Although this position is a ceremonial one for the most part, under the Presidential Succession Act of 1947 the president pro tempore is third in line to the presidency, after the vice president and the Speaker of the House of Representatives, in case the president dies or is disabled.

Presidential Succession; Senate; Speaker of the House of Representatives; Vice President

Press, Freedom of the

The guarantee that Congress will not prevent books, magazines, newspapers, or other printed matter from being published.

It is found in the First Amendment to the Constitution, part of the Bill of Rights. Freedom of the press is vital to democracy. The press supplies news stories about political issues and the conduct of public officials. With

The United States had recently entered World War II when this newspaper vendor was photographed in 1942. Judging from the headline, the Allied Expeditionary Force (AEF) had had some success.

During wartime, liberty of expression is often severely tested. The U.S. government has put limits on the press in wartime. In the 1860s, during the Civil War, newpapers were impounded for revealing troop movements (or for being antigovernment publications). In World War I, the Sedition Act of 1918 was used to close publications critical of the government. In the 1970s, the government tried to block publication of secret Defense Department documents on the Vietnam War.

In 1919, in *Schenck v. United States*, Justice Oliver Wendell Holmes wrote that in "war, many things that might be said in time of peace . . . will not be endured." Yet Holmes himself qualified this comment—and he did so the same year, noting that spoken or published speech should not be limited, even in wartime, unless the words pose a real danger.

freedom of the press, people are better able to study, learn, and make discoveries and well-informed decisions. In the 1730s, John Peter Zenger had printed criticism of New York's royal governor, William Cosby, and was then arrested. The colonial jury found Zenger innocent of the libel charges against him because what he said was true. Even after the First Amendment was ratified, however, Americans were still punished for criticizing officials even though what they said might be true. What the First Amendment accomplished was to let writers and printers publish without first getting approval from government officials.

In 1798 the federal government passed the Sedition Act, making it a crime to print, write, or publish any false or malicious criticism of the government. It was feared that Thomas Jefferson's opposition Democratic-Republican Party would spread radical ideas from the French Revolution in America and overturn the government. As a result of the Sedition Act, three newspapers were forced to stop publishing, and ten people were convicted. The act did allow the truth to be used as a defense. It also let juries decide the lawsuits. These requirements survived.

Writers and journalists are no longer punished for what they have published. In *New York Times Co. v. Sullivan* (1964), the Supreme Court required public officials and public figures to prove that reporters knowingly and maliciously printed lies about them. In this case, the Court recognized that in the heat of an argument, people might say things that were not true. Nevertheless, this could be printed because it was part of a public debate and vital to the free expression of ideas. The Court has even ruled, in *Florida Star v. B.J.F.* (1989), that the media may reveal embarrassing information about a person's *private* life, if they legally obtain the information through governmental sources. The Supreme Court also has struck down government attempts to censor the press before an article is published. The Court first forbade such prior government censorship in *Near v. Minnesota* (1931). The decision in *New York Times Co. v. United States* (1971) even held that the officials could not stop publication of articles about a secret government report on Vietnam, because the government had failed to prove that release of the so-called Pentagon Papers would seriously damage the security of the United States.

Although the Supreme Court has supported the press's right to publish, it has not always protected the right to gather news. Starting with *Richmond Newspapers, Inc. v. Virginia* (1980), however, the Court has allowed the press to attend criminal trials. This helps give the public more confidence in the court system. According to *Chandler v. Florida* (1981), cameras and tape recordings are allowed in court as long as they do not interfere with a suspect's right to a fair trial. The Internet provides a new arena for concern about freedom of the press and the protection of the First Amendment.

Bill of Rights; Congress; Speech, Freedom of; Supreme Court; U.S. Constitution, First Amendment

> **"Only a free and unrestrained press can effectively expose deception in government."**
> Justice Hugo L. Black,
> *New York Times Co. v. United States*, 1971

Privacy

The right to be free from government interference in personal matters.

The right to privacy is not specifically mentioned in the Constitution. However, many parts of the Bill of Rights have been used to protect people's freedom to be left alone. The Supreme Court has also used the contract clause of the Constitution and the due process clause of the Fourteenth Amendment to prevent state regulations from intruding on people's personal lives. In a landmark case about privacy, *Griswold v. Connecticut* (1965), the Court ruled that a state could not ban instruction about or use of birth-control devices. Connecticut's ban was illegal because it invaded the privacy of marriage. In this case, the Court found that privacy was one of a number of penumbras—bodies of implied rights, or rights not specifically mentioned but understood to exist—in the Constitution. The Fourteenth Amendment protects the "privileges" of U.S. citizens, and the Court found that privacy was reflected in the "privileges" of the First Amendment (the guarantee of a right of association), the Third Amendment (the protection against quartering of troops), the Fourth Amendment (the safeguard against unreasonable searches), and the Fifth Amendment (the protection against self-incrimination). In a concurring, or agreeing, opinion, one justice singled out the Ninth Amendment for special attention because it reserves to the people certain rights not listed in the Constitution.

Public opinion has been widely divided about another right-to-privacy issue: abortion. In *Roe v. Wade* (1973), the Supreme Court effectively

In *Roe v. Wade* (1973), the Supreme Court ruled that women have a constitutional right to abortion. The pro- and anti-abortion demonstrations shown above were reactions to that decision.

Abortion—ending a pregnancy by removing the embryo or fetus, normally before a legally prescribed point in its development—is one of the most hotly debated issues in the United States today. Although the debate began in the mid-1800s as a medical question, it is now wrapped up in many other issues, including the right to privacy as well as economic opportunity and religious and moral beliefs.

Supporters of legalized abortion (or pro-choice advocates) say that criminalizing the procedure again would force many women to obtain "back-alley" abortions—unsanitary and dangerous procedures performed in secret. They say that many of the mothers who have their babies but are not ready for them will end up in poverty.

Opponents of abortion (or pro-life advocates) say abortion is killing an unborn baby. They say a fetus has constitutional rights, even if it is not yet born.

overturned laws in forty-six states that prevented women from ending unwanted pregnancies. The Court ruled that during the first twelve to fourteen weeks of a pregnancy, states could not interfere with a woman's right to choose whether to have a child; once a baby could survive outside its mother's body, the states could reasonably pass laws to protect it. The Court based its decision on the right to personal freedom found in the Fourteenth Amendment and on the Ninth Amendment.

Since the *Roe* decision, the Court has struck down a number of state abortion rules. For example, women do not have to wait a certain period of time before having an abortion; husbands do not have a right to prevent their wives from ending pregnancies; doctors do not have to give women detailed information about the risks of abortion that do not apply to their personal circumstances; abortions after the first twelve to fourteen weeks do not have to be performed in hospitals.

On the other hand, the Court has upheld state laws requiring that parents become involved in abortion decisions when their daughters are underage. States have also been allowed to prevent public funds from being used to pay for abortions. In *Webster v. Reproductive Health Services* (1989), the Court widened the range of state restrictions on abortions. It allowed the states to protect developing human life before a baby can exist outside its mother's body. As a result, some states have banned abortions at an earlier stage of a woman's pregnancy than previously permitted.

The issue of privacy has also created controversy about the rights of gay individuals and couples. In *Bowers v. Hardwick* (1986), the Supreme Court ruled that the right to privacy did not protect gay people from state laws banning homosexual conduct. However, in other cases, the Court did protect their rights, citing freedom of speech instead of privacy. Many gay people face problems getting housing, gaining custody of children, and being treated fairly in the workplace. Yet the Court refused to hear cases involving teachers who were fired because they were gay. In 1998, on the other hand, a lower federal court ruled that the Navy could not discharge a sailor who was suspected of being gay, because of information improperly obtained about him from an Internet service provider.

Bill of Rights; Contract Clause; Due Process of Law; Federal Courts; Supreme Court; U.S. Constitution, Third Amendment; U.S. Constitution, Fourth Amendment; U.S. Constitution, Fifth Amendment; U.S. Constitution, Ninth Amendment; U.S. Constitution, Fourteenth Amendment

Privileges and Immunities

The requirement that each state must treat citizens from other states and its own citizens equally.

This guarantee can be found in Article IV, section 2, of the Constitution and in the Fourteenth Amendment. It includes equal protection of the laws, the right to be a member of a profession, the ability to use the courts, and freedom from special taxes on "outsiders." States may, however, require newcomers to live in the state for a period of time before they can vote, apply for a driver's license, qualify for welfare payments, or pay the lower tuition fees that residents often enjoy at state-supported colleges and universities.

Equal Protection of the Laws; U.S. Constitution, Article IV; U.S. Constitution, Fourteenth Amendment

Probable Cause

Reasonable grounds for taking legal action.

Like an educated guess, it lies somewhere between certainty and suspicion. The Fourth Amendment to the Constitution is intended to prevent the government from unduly investigating people. For a place to be searched, for evidence to be seized, or for a person to be arrested, there must be probable cause. The available information and the situation must lead a reasonable individual to believe that a crime has been committed.

Privacy; Searches and Seizures; U.S. Constitution, Fourth Amendment

Prohibition

A ban on the sale, manufacture, and transportation of liquor and other alcoholic beverages.

Los Angeles authorities are shown here emptying barrels of rum in the street in 1931. The Eighteenth Amendment, the so-called Prohibition Amendment, outlawed (prohibited) the "manufacture, sale, or transportation of intoxicating liquors" in the United States. The Volstead Act, passed by Congress in 1919 and signed by President Woodrow Wilson, implemented the amendment by specifying penalties for criminals and establishing a law-enforcement apparatus for the amendment.

The Eighteenth Amendment was the only one to be repealed (canceled) by another amendment, the Twenty-first.

However, one decision of the Supreme Court involving the Eighteenth Amendment—*Dillon v. Gloss* (1921)—has determined the language of three amendments since that time. The last section of the Eighteenth Amendment says that it will not take effect unless ratified by the states "within seven years." The challenge to the amendment brought in the 1921 case was on the constitutional grounds that Congress had no right to impose a limit on the time allowed for ratification. The Court disagreed, deciding that nothing in the Constitution prevented Congress from imposing a limit for ratification of an amendment.

By 1920, in response to moral condemnation of drinking and the effects of alcoholism, many states had passed Prohibition laws. The Eighteenth Amendment to the Constitution gave Congress the power to pass such a law nationwide, the Volstead Act (1919). However, Prohibition was a failure. Many Americans disobeyed the unpopular act. Often they turned to gangsters to supply them with alcoholic beverages. Prohibition set off a crime wave when these gangsters fought each other for control of the illegal-liquor industry. Finally, in 1933, the Twenty-first Amendment ended Prohibition.

Congress; U.S. Constitution, Eighteenth Amendment; U.S. Constitution, Twenty-first Amendment

Property Rights

Guarantees of private ownership of land, buildings, and other valuables, as well as of owners' freedom to operate and manage their property without governmental interference.

The delegates to the Constitutional Convention were farmers, plantation owners, merchants, and professional men, who wanted to protect their possessions. They were influenced by the writings of the English philosopher John Locke, who claimed that the right to own property existed even before any governments were set up. The delegates believed that owning private property preserved people's liberty, because it made them independent; landowners did not have to rely on other people or a government to survive. Property also made people responsible citizens, interested in preserving what they owned. This is why the delegates wanted to limit voting rights to property owners. They decided, however, to leave such decisions to the states.

The Framers of the Constitution protected private property by restricting the powers of Congress and the states. For example, in Article I of the Constitution, sections 9 and 10 prevent government from taking away people's property by passing bills of attainder. Since southerners treated slaves as property, Article I, section 9, bars Congress from taxing slaves and banned regulation of the slave trade until 1808. States were prevented from impairing the obligation of contracts, or interfering with property rights established by contract.

The Fifth Amendment, part of the Bill of Rights, also contains important measures to protect private property. It requires a government to pay property owners a fair price when it takes away their land for a public purpose under eminent domain. In the late 1800s and early 1900s, industries grew and more people moved to cities. As a result, states and the national government tried to regulate the way land was used. For example, they divided areas into zones for manufacturing or for homes. For the most part, the Supreme Court upheld these and later land-use laws. It has also taken property values into account. In *Causby v. United States* (1946), the Court banned military flights over a farm because these reduced the value of the land. Yet in *Penn Central Transportation Co. v. City of New York* (1978), it upheld a law making Grand Central Station a landmark. That reduced the value of the owner's property, because he could not make changes without the permission of the city.

From the 1880s to the 1930s, the Court also used the Fifth Amendment to protect the way businesses and corporations operate and manage their property. The Court defined business corporations as "persons" and gave them all of the protections people enjoy under the Constitution. Under the Fifth Amendment, no person can be deprived of life, liberty, or property without due process of law. The Court used the due process clause to strike down national and state regulations affecting the way corporations were run. For example, laws setting maximum hours for workers and minimum pay rates were overturned because they interfered with property rights. During the widespread national economic crisis of the 1930s, however, the Court began to uphold such laws. The crisis required massive government intervention in the economy to keep more businesses from shutting down, to provide jobs for unemployed workers, and to offer shelter to the homeless and food to the hungry.

For decades afterward, the Court did not prevent governments from regulating the way businesses operated. Many new laws were passed to make workplaces safer and to protect the environment. In the 1970s, the Court briefly began to expand the notion of property rights to include welfare benefits and social security. By the end of the decade, however, the Court retreated from this position. It even let governments end some benefits, a process that continued into the 1990s.

Bill of Attainder; Congress; Constitutional Convention; Contract Clause; Debts; Delegates;
Due Process of Law; Eminent Domain; Framers; Second Treatise on Government; Supreme Court;
U.S. Constitution, Article I; U.S. Constitution, Fifth Amendment

"The great and chief end . . . of Men['] s uniting into Commonwealths, and putting themselves under Governments, is the Preservation of their Property."
John Locke, *Second Treatise on Government,* 1690

Quartering of Troops

The practice of housing soldiers in private homes.

The Quartering Act of 1765 forced colonists to feed and house British troops in peacetime. These soldiers had been sent to defend the colonies. Previously, colonists had relied on their own militias. They resented having to contribute to the cost of keeping the British soldiers in North America. To make sure this would never happen again, the Third Amendment was added to the Constitution. It is part of the Bill of Rights and guarantees that in peacetime, troops will be quartered only with a homeowner's consent, and in wartime, only according to law.

Bill of Rights; Militia; U.S. Constitution, Third Amendment

Quorum

The minimum number of people required to be present in order to conduct official business.

Article I, section 5, of the Constitution states that a majority of the members of each house of Congress serve as its quorum. Today, that means 218 representatives and 51 senators. On the Supreme Court, six of the nine justices serve as a quorum.

Congress; House of Representatives; Senate; Supreme Court; U.S. Constitution, Article I

Ratification

Formal approval of an amendment or a constitution.

Procedures for ratifying amendments are found in Article V of the Constitution; for ratifying the Constitution, in Article VII. The Framers had to decide how many state ratifications would be needed for an amendment to take effect. They wanted to avoid the requirement of the Articles of Confederation that all thirteen states agree to proposed major changes, since that had proved impossible. Therefore, another solution was needed. Serious debate on amendments did not take place until the last week of the Constitutional Convention. By then the delegates were tired. They spent very little time discussing Article V. The Committee of Detail had already suggested that Congress call for a national convention to propose amendments at the request of two-thirds of the states. No mention was made of ratification. Elbridge Gerry warned that such a convention could destroy state constitutions, and Roger Sherman insisted that ratification by the states was necessary. The delegates wanted to protect their own states' interests from changes other states might propose.

This woodcut appeared in the Boston newspaper *The Centinel* on August 2, 1788, one week after New York narrowly ratified the Constitution. The cartoon suggests that the ratifying states were columns in a great new structure. The dates of ratification and votes cast in conventions were as follows:

	yes	no
Delaware		
December 7, 1787	30	0
Pennsylvania		
December 12, 1787	46	23
New Jersey		
December 18, 1787	38	0
Georgia		
January 2, 1788	26	0
Connecticut		
January 9, 1788	128	40
Massachusetts		
February 6, 1788	187	168
Maryland		
April 28, 1788	63	11
South Carolina		
May 23, 1788	149	73
New Hampshire		
June 21, 1788	57	47
Virginia		
June 25, 1788	89	79
New York		
July 26, 1788	30	27
North Carolina		
November 27, 1789	194	77
Rhode Island		
May 29, 1790	34	32

James Madison and James Wilson suggested that three-fourths of the state legislatures or conventions in three-fourths of the states ratify amendments. They dropped the plan for a national convention. This was acceptable to most delegates. Article V also protects the small states by banning amendments to change the states' equal representation in the Senate (unless the states deprived of equal representation agree to it). In addition, it prevented interference with the slave trade until 1808. At present, twenty-seven amendments to the Constitution have been ratified.

During the debate over ratifying the Constitution itself, Oliver Ellsworth proposed to let state legislatures approve the new government. Nathaniel Gorham pointed out that state officials were unlikely to accept the Constitution, because they would lose power under the national government. Further, ratification would be dragged out and delayed because state legislatures were divided into two houses. George Mason opposed ratification by state legislatures because they would treat the Constitution like ordinary law, easily repealed. He reminded the delegates that the Constitution was a framework of government, not an ordinary law.

Along with Mason, James Madison, Rufus King, and James Wilson argued for popular sovereignty, the notion that the people were the source of all power in government. They convinced the other delegates that the people should give their consent by electing special conventions in each state to ratify the Constitution. If conventions were held in the states, the Constitution would be treated as a basic law, not easily altered. It could also be claimed that the new national government received its powers from the people, not from the states. Although neither women, blacks, nor the poor took part in the ratification process, it can still be argued that the Constitution was put into effect by the consent of the people—or at least the people qualified to vote at the time.

The delegates did not want to set aside the Articles of Confederation without the consent of the member states, but they did not want to wait for ratification by all

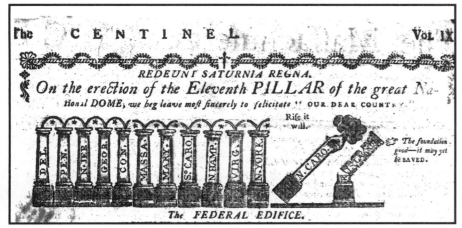

REDEUNT SATURNIA REGNA.

On the erection of the Eleventh PILLAR of the great National DOME, we beg leave most sincerely to felicitate OUR DEAR COUNTRY.

Rise it will.

The foundation good—it may yet be SAVED.

The FEDERAL EDIFICE.

thirteen states, as required under the Articles of Confederation. In Article VII of the Constitution, they required ratification by conventions in nine states, three-quarters of the thirteen then in existence, before the new government could be established.

The Confederation Congress tried to change the delegates' proposals before sending them to the states for ratification. However, Federalists and a number of Framers of the Constitution managed to win a majority in Congress for passing the Constitution on to the states without a recommendation one way or the other about whether it should be ratified.

Delaware was the first state to ratify the Constitution, on December 7, 1787; New Hampshire was the ninth, on June 21, 1788, putting the Constitution into effect; Rhode Island, which had refused to send any delegates to the Constitutional Convention, was the thirteenth and last of the original states to ratify the Constitution, on May 29, 1790.

Amendment Process; Articles of Confederation; Confederation Congress; Constitutional Convention; Delegates; Framers; Law; Popular Sovereignty; U.S. Constitution, Article V; U.S. Constitution, Article VII

Religion, Freedom of

The guarantee that Congress shall not establish an official religion in the United States or prevent people from worshiping as they please.

> **"Neither a state nor the federal government can set up a church. Neither can pass laws which aid one religion, aid all religions, or prefer one religion over another."**
> Justice Hugo L. Black, *Everson v. Board of Education of Ewing Township,* 1947

It is found in the First Amendment to the Constitution, part of the Bill of Rights. Many colonists had come to North America to escape religious persecution. The English had an official religion and required believers and nonbelievers alike to support the Church of England or be punished. Although the early colonists sought freedom to practice their own religion, they were often intolerant of people who did not share their beliefs. They even made religious tests a requirement to hold office. After the War for Independence, however, religious toleration became widespread. Most state constitutions or laws protected freedom of religion. A famous example is the Virginia Statute for Religious Freedom, written by Thomas Jefferson. It expressed many ideas of the English philosopher John Locke. In 1791, Congress extended this right to all Americans.

The First Amendment guarantee of freedom of religion has two parts. The first part is called the *establishment clause*. It says that "Congress shall make no law respecting an establishment of religion." In its broadest sense, this means that Congress cannot establish an official religion. The second part of the guarantee is called the *free-exercise clause*. It says that

In 1962, in the case of *Engel v. Vitale,* the Supreme Court declared unconstitutional a New York law requiring a morning prayer in the public schools. The response to this decision was striking. Many people criticized it. In school districts around the country, no change was even considered to make school policy conform to the Court's ruling. In fact, this photograph of first graders praying in a South Carolina public school was taken in 1966, fully four years after the Court ruled that such activities were a violation of the First Amendment. The decision still provokes debate. Supporters of school prayer have tried on several occasions to pass an amendment to the Constitution that would allow it. In 1984, one such amendment came to a vote on the floor of the Senate, where it was backed by a majority of the senators but not by the two-thirds vote that would have been necessary to send it on to the House of Representatives and then to the states for ratification. That proposed amendment read, in part, "Nothing in this Constitution shall be construed to prohibit . . . prayers in the public schools or other public institutions. . . . No person shall be required . . . to participate in prayer."

"Congress shall make no law . . . prohibiting the free exercise" of religion. In its largest sense, this means that Congress cannot prevent people from practicing their religion.

In essence, then, the First Amendment forbids an official state religion and guarantees freedom of worship. Yet in the nineteenth century, most Americans felt they were part of the Protestant tradition. Teachers read prayers, Christmas and Easter became official holidays, and states closed businesses on Sundays. Little effort was made to extend the First Amendment requirements about religion to the states. By the 1940s, however, society became more secular, more worldly and concerned with material things. A number of cases concerning the relationship between church and state in schools reached the Supreme Court. In *Everson v. Board of Education of Ewing Township* (1947), for example, the Court ruled that a city could pay to bus children to religious as well as public schools. Nevertheless, in this decision the Court also borrowed a famous phrase from the writings of Jefferson and stated that it would build "a wall of separation" between church and state. This proved difficult to do.

In *Lemon v. Kurtzman* (1972), the Court developed a test to make sure that government was neutral toward religion. To avoid charges that it was supporting an official religion, government actions had to have a secular purpose that did not favor or oppose religion; could not have an effect that favored or opposed religion; and could not let either religion or government become involved in each other's affairs. The *Lemon* test proved difficult to apply. It produced many contradictory results. Under Court rulings, government financial aid to private religious elementary and high schools was forbidden, but free bus transportation and textbooks were permitted. Free testing and counseling services were also allowed if these took place away from the religious school.

The Supreme Court has ruled that public school officials may not sponsor prayers or encourage children to pray in schools. The Court made this controversial ruling in *Engel v. Vitale* (1962), refusing to let New York students recite a nonsectarian prayer (one not linked to any specific religion) written by school officials. The school district argued that it was favoring all religions equally by having such a nondenominational prayer. However, the Court reasoned that state sponsorship of all religions together was as much a violation of the Constitution as sponsorship of one religion alone. The Court cited the First Amendment prohibition against any law "respecting an establishment of religion." On similar grounds, the Court has also overturned state laws setting aside a moment of silence for voluntary prayer or meditatation.

In *Board of Education v. Mergens* (1990), the Court upheld a law allowing student groups to discuss the Bible and pray together on school property as long as their activities were not part of the school program. The Court also ordered that for the law to be constitutional, non-Christian students had to be able to form their own groups and meet on school property. The Court decided that these were private actions, not sponsored by government, and thus permissible under the Constitution. In all likelihood, the Court will make further rulings on this issue, since it is one that has divided many communities.

On the whole, the Supreme Court has been more lenient toward government activities involving religion outside of schools, provided no one religion or religious view is favored. For the most part, it has also allowed Christian Nativity scenes and Jewish menorahs to be displayed at holiday times on city property.

The right to worship as one pleases has raised questions about laws that violate people's religious beliefs. In *Reynolds v. United States* (1879), the Supreme Court upheld laws forbidding Mormons from taking more than

This photograph, taken in 1970, shows an Ohio second-grade class pledging allegiance to the American flag. Although to many people the Pledge of Allegiance is an act of patriotism—or perhaps of civic duty—to some it goes against their religious beliefs. In the 1940 case of *Minersville School District v. Gobitis,* the Supreme Court was called upon to rule decide whether William and Lillian Gobitis, two Jehovah's Witness children, could be expelled from school for refusing to say the Pledge of Allegiance. The Gobitises believed that saying the Pledge of Allegiance was the same thing as bowing down before an idol, something their religion forbade. The Supreme Court disagreed, saying that the flag was "the symbol of our national unity" and that it was permissible to require public schoolchildren to say the pledge. Just three years later, however, in *West Virginia State Board of Education v. Barnett* (1943), the Court reversed itself, ruling that the national unity it had spoken of earlier could not be achieved by "compulsion" but only "by persuasion and example." The Pledge of Allegiance, the Court concluded, amounts to a religious test or a forced profession of faith to anyone who sees it that way.

one wife at a time, a practice accepted by their religion then. On the other hand, in *United States v. Ballard* (1944), the Court upheld a not-guilty verdict in the case of religious cult members accused of using the mails to defraud people of their money. The group claimed that donations to their cult would cure disease. If a group of doctors had said that in a mailing, they would probably have been held accountable for mail fraud. However, the Court ruled that if the cult members truly believed in this practice, then it was not fraud. Similarly, in *Sherbert v. Verner* (1963), a state was ordered to pay unemployment benefits to a Seventh-Day Adventist who refused to work on Saturdays, the religious holy day for followers of that religion. In *Wisconsin v. Yoder* (1972), the Court permitted the Amish to keep their children out of school after eighth grade.

In the 1980s and 1990s, the Court became more willing to allow states to limit religious practices considered unacceptable. For example, in *Employment Division v. Smith* (1990), it supported a state decision to deny unemployment benefits to two Native Americans who had been fired for smoking peyote on the job. They claimed they were practicing a religious ritual. The state argued successfully that they were violating a criminal law by smoking a banned substance.

Bill of Rights; Congress; Religious Tests; Second Treatise on Government; Supreme Court; U.S. Constitution, First Amendment; Virginia Statute for Religious Freedom

"If there is any fixed star in our constitutional constellation, it is that no official, high or petty, can prescribe what shall be orthodox in politics, nationalism, religion, or other matters of opinion or force citizens to confess by word or act their faith therein."
Justice Robert H. Jackson,
West Virginia State Board of Education v. Barnette, 1943

Religious Tests

Requirements that people swear they hold certain religious beliefs or that they do not belong to certain undesirable religious groups.

England used Test Acts to keep nonmembers of the Church of England from holding public office, including members of many Protestant sects. Catholics could not hold office in Great Britain until 1828. Test Acts were finally repealed in the 1870s and 1880s.

Many of Britain's American colonies were founded to protect religious freedom. Yet on the eve of the War for Independence, every colonial government made religious tests a requirement for holding office. Eight colonies even had official religions. After the Revolution, however, the new states gradually removed these restrictions. For example, the Virginia Statute for Religious Freedom of 1786 separated church and state and banned religious tests. As the Constitutional Convention drew to a close, Charles Pinckney suggested that a ban on religious tests for holding public office be added to Article VI of the Constitution. It was one of several rights that was included in the Constitution despite a lack of earlier debate.

Constitutional Convention; Oaths of Office; U.S. Constitution, Article VI; Virginia Statute for Religious Freedom

Representative Democracy

A political system in which the rulers are regularly elected by the people to govern them and are responsible to them.

James Wilson was born in Scotland and came to Philadelphia in 1765. He was elected to the Continental Congress from Pennsylvania and was a signer of the Declaration of Independence.

At the Constitutional Convention, he was an extremely influential leader, second only to James Madison in importance. While he was determined to create a stronger national government, he recognized that the government must draw its power from the people. In his judgment, the people had to elect the president and both houses of Congress.

He favored yearly elections to the House of Representatives. He also wanted senators' terms in office to be staggered to keep them in touch with public opinion. This is why he supported the proposal to have one-third of members of the Senate elected every two years. He also opposed requiring that people own property in order to be able to vote. Later, he supported a plan to have the House, rather than the Senate, elect the president if a candidate did not receive a majority of votes in the electoral college.

Wilson signed the Constitution and led the campaign for its ratification in Pennsylvania. In 1789, President George Washington appointed him to the Supreme Court. Meanwhile he made unwise investments in land and lost large sums of money. To avoid arrest for debt, he fled to New Jersey in 1797. A year later, he died.

By contrast, in a *direct democracy*, like a New England town meeting, all the people get together from time to time in order to make all the rules for themselves. In 1781, when the independent states at last joined together under the Articles of Confederation, they sent delegates to represent their views in the Confederation Congress. This was not representative democracy either. The delegates were spokesmen for their states, not for the people. The sovereign states' governments gave the delegates instructions on how to vote. Therefore, they were more like ambassadors, officials serving separate nations.

The idea of representative democracy spread slowly. In the eighteenth century, people were more concerned with representation than with democracy. Traditionally, representative legislatures were seen as checks on a monarch, to keep him from abusing his powers. Parliament protected the liberties of British citizens, and colonial assemblies kept royal governors from oppressing American colonists. This was the view the Framers accepted at the Constitutional Convention. However, during the debates, James Madison, George Mason, and James Wilson argued for limited democracy. They insisted that the people had to take part in the new government so that they would have confidence in it. They convinced the other delegates to let the people elect the House of Representatives.

However, the Framers did not want the representatives to become merely instructed delegates, because they did not entirely trust public opinion. The Framers expected members of Congress to use their own judgment. They wanted capable leaders to decide what was best for the nation, and not just focus on the needs of their local communities. This is why, in Article I, section 2, of the Constitution, they recommended large election districts with one representative for every 30,000 people. They expected these districts to reduce the influence of local interests and to produce skilled lawmakers. In Article I, sections 2 and 3, the Framers also set qualifications for election to get the best leaders. Frequent elections, mentioned in Article I, section 2, would ensure, however, that the representatives were accountable to the people for their actions.

What the Framers created was not truly a representative democracy in the modern sense of the word. Only one part of the national government, the House of Representatives, was directly elected by the people. (This was not true of the Senate until ratification of the Seventeenth Amendment. Until then, state legislatures elected members of the Senate.) What's more, blacks, women, Indians, older teenagers, and even those without property could not yet vote for representatives. At the time, however, compared to Britain, the new American system of representation gave the people more power over their government. With the passage of the Fifteenth, Seventeenth, Nineteenth, Twenty-third, Twenty-fourth, and Twenty-sixth amendments, the United States became a more representative democracy.

Ambassadors; Articles of Confederation; Confederation Congress; Congress; Constitutional
Convention; Delegates; Framers; House of Representatives; Law; U.S. Constitution, Article I;
U.S. Constitution, Fifteenth Amendment; U.S. Constitution, Seventeenth Amendment;
U.S. Constitution, Nineteenth Amendment; U.S. Constitution, Twenty-third Amendment;
U.S. Constitution, Twenty-fourth Amendment; U.S. Constitution, Twenty-sixth Amendment

Republican Form of Government

A term used to describe self-government, in which power comes from the people, and there is no monarch to rule them with absolute power.

During the eighteenth century, republics were usually seen as small, self-sufficient communities made up of people with similar backgrounds. James Madison, however, applied the term to the United States, a large nation with a diverse population.

Article IV, section 4, of the Constitution requires the national government to guarantee a republican form of government to each state. As originally written, this section would have also guaranteed a state's existing laws. During the debates at the Constitutional Convention, Gouverneur Morris objected to this provision. He did not want the national government to have to protect Rhode Island's laws easing the payment of debts. James Wilson reassured him that the guarantee was really meant only to protect states from domestic insurrections. George Mason and Luther Martin, however, felt the national government had no right to interfere in such uprisings. Nathaniel Gorham thought it would be strange if some state decided to have a monarchy, and the national government stood by helplessly. Daniel Carroll, Edmund Randolph, James Madison, and James Wilson agreed with Gorham. The guarantee was reworded to overcome Morris's objections and became part of the Constitution.

Constitution; Debts; Domestic Violence; Representative Democracy; States; U.S. Constitution,
Article IV

Reserved Powers

Powers not specifically mentioned in the Constitution or implied in other powers.

The Tenth Amendment to the Constitution reserves to the states or the people all powers that are not delegated to the national government or denied to any state government. One of the Framers of the Constitution, Alexander Hamilton, thought this amendment was unnecessary because the national government had only limited powers, those enumerated in the Constitution. Nevertheless, Antifederalists insisted, and the Tenth Amendment was added to the Constitution in 1791.

From 1800 to 1861, states used their reserved powers to defy federal laws. They maintained that the national government could not use its powers to interfere with activities reserved to the states. For example, the Virginia and Kentucky Resolutions rejected the Sedition Act of 1798. This act made it a crime to criticize national officials or government activities. The authors of the resolutions, Thomas Jefferson and James Madison, claimed that the states did not have to obey the act because it violated the Constitution. According to them, the Constitution was a compact among sovereign states (like the Articles of Confederation). The states had the reserved power to decide whether federal laws violated the Constitution and to "nullify," or cancel, them. Similar arguments were advanced by Vice President John C. Calhoun to protest high tariff rates in 1828 and 1832. In 1861, eleven southern states left the Union to protect what they said were their reserved powers. In each instance, however, the federal government triumphed—the last time, only by fighting the Civil War.

Since the Civil War, the Supreme Court has had to decide a number of cases involving the reserved powers of states, with some inconsistency depending in part on who was sitting on the Court. In the *Civil Rights Cases* (1883), the Court upheld the Tenth Amendment and let states deny certain rights to freed blacks. On the other hand, in the early twentieth century, the Court allowed the national government to regulate state lotteries, as well as the food, drug, and meat industries. In the 1920s and 1930s, however, the Court interpreted the Tenth Amendment to block federal laws regulating child labor in the states. During the 1930s, the Court also used it to reject a number of federal laws setting standards for workers' wages and hours. However, by the end of the decade, the Court reversed these earlier rulings on the Tenth Amendment and upheld federal social and economic laws designed to help the nation recover from a widespread and long-lasting economic crisis.

In recent times, two major cases involved the reserved powers of states. In *National League of Cities v. Usery* (1976), the Court rejected the fed-

"The power to locate its own seat of government and to determine when and how it shall be changed from one place to another . . . are essentially and peculiarly state powers."
Justice William H. Rehnquist,
National League of Cities v. Usery, 1976

eral government's attempt to apply national wage and hour standards to state and local government workers. That decision was reversed in *Garcia v. San Antonio Metropolitan Transit Authority* (1985).

Antifederalists; Articles of Confederation; Denied Powers; Express Powers; Federalists; Framers; Law; States' Rights; Supreme Court; Tariffs; U.S. Constitution, Tenth Amendment

Resolutions

Expressions of congressional opinion, single-purpose laws, or interpretations of rules.

Joint resolutions are simple laws, passed by both houses of Congress. They require the president's signature to take effect. A joint resolution was used, for example, to admit Texas to the Union. *Continuing resolutions* are laws that renew resolutions that would otherwise end, continuing to fund a program at its current levels, for instance. They must be passed by both houses of Congress and signed by the president. *Concurrent resolutions*, passed by Congress, and *simple resolutions*, passed by one chamber, offer praise or sympathy or deal with procedures. They are not sent to the president for approval, and they do not have the force of law. Resolutions are mentioned in Article I, section 7, of the Constitution.

Bill; Congress; Law; U.S. Constitution, Article I

Revenue

Public monies that the government receives.

They are collected from income taxes, excise taxes, tariffs, customs and imposts, license fees, and other sources. This money is used to pay government expenses. "No taxation without representation" was a major reason that Americans had fought the War for Independence. As a result of the colonists' experience with Great Britain, Article I, section 7, of the Constitution requires that all revenue bills must first be introduced in the House of Representatives. When the Constitution was written, this was the only part of the government directly elected by the people.

The Framers of the Constitution realized that giving control over revenues to representatives of the people would also let the representatives limit the activities of the other branches of government. This is an example of checks and balances. The Framers knew that Parliament was able to restrain the British monarch by withholding funds. It is unlikely, however, that they expected the government to shut down if Congress and the president disagreed about how federal money should be spent.

With a portrait of Thomas Jefferson peering over his shoulder, President Bill Clinton is shown here (center) with Speaker of the House Newt Gingrich (right) and Senator Robert Dole (left) during negotiations over the federal budget in late 1995. The three were meeting in the White House, the office and residence of the president, in Washington, D.C.

Gingrich and Dole, both Republicans, had assumed increased responsibilities in 1995, following an electoral victory by the Republican Party in November 1994. The win gave their party control of the House of Representatives and the Senate. As leader of the Republican majority, Dole took charge of managing the Senate's business. As leader of the House Republicans, Gingrich became Speaker of the House.

Clinton was a Democrat, and this meant that different parties controlled the executive and legislative branches. This sort of division has been common, especially since about 1946, with one party controlling Congress (or at least one chamber of it) and the other party controlling the White House.

Nevertheless, over two hundred years later, on November 14, 1995, that is what happened. The president and Congress were deadlocked over funding programs for education, the environment, and medical care for the aged and the needy. Hoping to force the president to give in to their demands, the representatives refused to vote money to keep the government running. All but essential services were suspended, and 777,000 government workers were sent home. They returned to work on November 20, after the president and Congress settled their dispute. This was a unique event up to then. Normally, the government continues to function (with continuing resolutions providing appropriations at previously approved levels of spending) when presidents and Congress differ over how much revenue the government should collect, for what purpose, and who should pay.

Appropriations; Bill; Checks and Balances; Congress; Duties and Imposts; Excise Taxes; Framers; House of Representatives; Income Taxes; Money and Coinage; President; Resolutions; Tariffs; Taxation, Power of; U.S. Constitution, Article I

Rights

See: names of individual rights

Rights Retained by the People

Freedoms not listed in the Bill of Rights that are protected from government actions.

Sharing the beliefs of John Locke and other philosophers, the Framers of the Constitution thought that people had certain basic rights, such as the rights to life, liberty, and property. These existed before governments were created. When governments were set up, citizens kept these basic freedoms. The Bill of Rights lists only those rights that are most likely to be threatened by governments. It does not list everything. This fact is specifically stated in the Ninth Amendment to the Constitution, which is itself part of the Bill of Rights. Among the other rights retained by the people, as determined in part by decisions of the Supreme Court, are the rights to travel and to privacy.

Bill of Rights; Framers; Privacy; Second Treatise on Government; *U.S. Constitution, Ninth Amendment*

S

Searches and Seizures

Inspecting citizens' homes, possessions, and persons in order to get evidence against them.

Before the War for Independence, British officials searched colonists' homes in order to catch smugglers. Smugglers were violating trade laws by bringing in and selling non-British products. The officials abused their powers and often failed to obtain permission from courts for their searches and seizures. Alternatively, they got vaguely worded general permits to ransack colonists' places of business and homes. The Fourth Amendment to the Constitution, part of the Bill of Rights, was intended to make sure such abuses would not occur again.

Today, judges require probable cause before granting permission to search. Under certain circumstances, however, police may look for evidence and take it away without first going to court. Such circumstances exist if evidence is in plain view, if a suspect attempts to destroy it, or if a building is on fire. Usually, if evidence is taken illegally, it is excluded and cannot be used in trials. The Supreme Court announced this exclusionary rule in *Weeks v. United States* (1914) and extended it to the states in *Mapp v. Ohio* (1961). This helps to prevent police misconduct. However, in *United States v. Leon* (1984), the Court allowed evidence that was taken without permission when the police acted in "good faith." Because of the war on illegal drugs, the Court has often used "reasonable suspicion," a looser standard than "probable cause," to allow the police to carry out searches and seizures. It has let law-enforcement officials conduct aerial surveillance of a home, search garbage bags left out on the street, and eavesdrop over the telephone. Now the courts are beginning to hear cases setting standards for information transmitted over the Internet.

Accused, Rights of the; Bill of Rights; Probable Cause; Supreme Court; U.S. Constitution, Fourth Amendment

Second Treatise on Government

A book published in 1690 and written by John Locke, an English philosopher whose writings greatly influenced the Framers of the Constitution.

In Locke's time, the English king and Parliament had fought a bitter civil war. Then, in 1688, one line of monarchs was replaced by another without bloodshed; Parliament had finally triumphed. Locke's *Second Treatise on Government* celebrated this event. It contains his most important ideas about government and politics.

"[T]he Legislative
Power, . . . in the
utmost Bounds of it,
is limited to the pub-
lick good of the
Society. It is a Power,
that hath no other
end but preservation,
and therefore can
never have a right to
destroy, enslave, or
designedly to impov-
erish the Subjects."
**John Locke, *Second Treatise
on Government*, 1690**

In this work, Locke reasoned that people were naturally cooperative and peaceful. They respected each other's basic rights to life, liberty, and property. Nevertheless, they chose to create societies to protect themselves from the inconveniences of living on their own. Later, they decided to form governments to make rules for them, but they still kept their basic rights. Government was set up by majority vote of the people. Its main function was to make laws by consent of the majority. Through elections, government continued to be accountable to the people. He argued that the people could rebel against an abusive government and form a new one. Meanwhile, however, their society would continue to exist.

Locke's writings strongly influenced Thomas Jefferson, who shared the view that governments that violated basic rights should be overthrown. Jefferson used many of Locke's ideas when he wrote the Declaration of Independence (1776). He was also impressed by Locke's *Letter Concerning Toleration* (1689), which defended freedom of religion. Jefferson's Virginia Statute for Religious Freedom (written in 1777; enacted in 1786) expresses many of Locke's thoughts.

The Framers were also familiar with Locke's writings. They admired his statements about basic rights. Like Locke, they believed that no lawful government could deny people their rights to life, liberty, and property. They accepted his argument that all government is based on popular consent. However, the Framers did not completely accept Locke's proposals on majority rule. They feared that majority rule would destroy minorities' rights. One minority that the Framers especially wanted to protect was wealthy property owners, like themselves. So they made it more difficult for majorities to control the national government.

Framers; Property Rights; Religion, Freedom of; Separation of Powers; Virginia Statute for Religious Freedom

Segregation and Desegregation

The separation of people based on race or other factors, and the removal of barriers separating people of different races.

The removal of the barriers helps to promote equality. Laws, housing, schooling, and job opportunities, to name a few examples, may be used to keep people apart or to bring them together.

In the North, free blacks had been denied voting rights in the mid-1800s, but they did generally have personal liberties. In the South, most blacks were slaves. After the Civil War, former slaves were subjected to

Black Codes, laws that set up curfews and denied them the right to serve on juries, have firearms, or appear in certain public places.

Passage of the Fourteenth and Fifteenth amendments to the Constitution was supposed to guarantee blacks equal treatment under the laws. The Civil Rights Act of 1875 was designed to strengthen the Fourteenth Amendment. It gave blacks equality in housing, public buildings and parks, various places of entertainment, restaurants, and transportation. In the *Civil Rights Cases* (1883), however, the Supreme Court ruled that the Civil Rights Act protected social, not civil, rights. The Court decided that Congress had no power to regulate social conduct. The final blow came in *Plessy v. Ferguson* (1896), when the Court upheld a law separating whites and blacks on railroad trains. From that decision came the doctrine of "separate but equal": the two races could legally be kept apart, provided the same arrangements were available for each race. In actuality, however, schools, housing, hotels, and transportation for blacks were very inferior to what was available for whites.

Beginning with *Missouri ex rel. Gaines v. Canada* (1938), the Supreme Court took the first steps toward removing racial barriers to education. In that case, the Court struck down Missouri's higher out-of-state tuition for black law students. Then, in 1950, the Court integrated interstate-railroad dining cars. This paved the way for the landmark case of *Brown v. Board of Education of Topeka* (1954), which required public schools to admit black and white students together. After this decision, Congress passed laws to secure voting rights for blacks. Then the Twenty-fourth Amendment banned poll taxes, which had been used to keep many racial and ethnic minorities from voting. The landmark Civil Rights Act of 1964 desegregated transportation, hotels, restaurants, movie theaters, parks, and other public areas. This act also forbade governments, employers, or trade unions to turn away job seekers because of their race. It set up the Equal Employment Opportunity Commission to enforce this section of the law.

The races were still separated, but not by law. Instead, patterns of housing, teacher assignments, and school construction kept them apart. To overcome such economic and social segregation, the Civil Rights Act of 1968 made it illegal to refuse to rent or sell homes to people because of their race. Laws were also passed to require children to be bused out of their neighborhoods to integrate schools. Local residents sometimes opposed such measures. In *Swann v. Charlotte-Mecklenburg Board of Education* (1971), however, the Supreme Court upheld such school-

The photograph above, taken in 1935, shows attorney Thurgood Marshall (left) arguing for a client, Donald Gaines Murray (center). Murray, a graduate of Amherst College, had been denied admission to the University of Maryland school of law because he was black. Representing Murray in a civil suit, Marshall was trying his first case since graduating from the law school of Howard University.

Also seated at the table (right) is Charles Hamilton Houston, dean of the Howard University law school and one of his generation's great civil-rights leaders. Marshall had followed his example by becoming counsel to the National Association for the Advancement of Colored People (NAACP), a black civil-rights organization. In almost thirty years with the NAACP, Marshall argued thirty-two cases before the Supreme Court, winning all but three. In 1967, President Lyndon B. Johnson named Marshall to the Court. He was the first black justice.

Johnson can be seen in the photograph at right. The occasion was the signing, at the White House, of the Civil Rights Act of 1964. Johnson, seated, is turning to shake the hand of the civil-rights leader Martin Luther King Jr. Standing between them is Senator Jacob Javits of New York, instrumental in getting the legislation passed.

desegregation laws. Since then, the Court has ruled that courts cannot remedy economic and social patterns of segregation by race unless these are the result of government policies.

Affirmative action offered another way to encourage desegregation. Such laws, designed to make up for decades of past mistreatment in hiring and admissions policies, required that applicants' race and sex be taken into consideration and, in the case of racial minorities and women, given some degree of preference for jobs, government contracts, and college and graduation admissions. In some cases, a specific number or percentage of acceptances was set aside for these applicants. In *Regents of the University of California v. Allan Bakke* (1978), the Supreme Court struck down "fixed quotas" but allowed the consideration of race as a factor in hiring and college admissions practices. Nevertheless, affirmative-action programs came under attack in the 1980s and 1990s. Opponents saw them merely as quotas, creating unfair distinctions among people and sometimes resulting in preferential treatment for unqualified applicants. California voters eliminated such programs in 1997. As a result, fewer members of racial minorities attended the state's colleges and universities. The future of affirmative action is uncertain.

Civil Rights; Congress; Discrimination; Poll Taxes; Separate but Equal Doctrine; Supreme Court; U.S. Constitution, Fourteenth Amendment; U.S. Constitution, Fifteenth Amendment; U.S. Constitution, Twenty-fourth Amendment

Self-Incrimination

Testifying against oneself.

Centuries ago, in England and other European countries, people suspected of crimes were often tortured to get them to confess, whether or not they were guilty. In the late 1700s, the British banned the use of such confessions as evidence in trials. Americans followed their example by passing the Fifth Amendment to the Constitution, part of the Bill of Rights. The Supreme Court strengthened this guarantee against self-incrimination in *Miranda v. Arizona* (1966). People arrested for crimes must be advised of their right to remain silent during questioning. At times, a government may need people to give information about themselves or others. To protect them from self-incrimination, they may be offered grants of immunity. These guarantee that what they say will not be used against them in the future and that they will not go to trial as a result of their statements.

Accused, Rights of the; Bill of Rights; Confession Immunity; Supreme Court; U.S. Constitution, Fifth Amendment

Senate

One of the two chambers of Congress, the legislative branch of the United States.

The Senate is composed of two members from each state. At the Constitutional Convention, the small states had prepared the New Jersey Plan. It gave them equality of representation with the larger states in a one-chamber legislature. Earlier, it had been argued that representatives should be elected by the people according to the population in each state. This would have given a great advantage to the larger states. In the Connecticut Compromise, the small states accepted equality in one chamber of the legislative branch, the Senate, while the members of the House of Representatives are elected on the basis of population. As a further guarantee, Article V specifies that no state may be deprived of its two Senate seats without its consent.

Once the Connecticut Compromise was accepted, the Framers of the Constitution agreed that senators would be chosen by state legislatures rather than directly by the people, as was the case with the House. By the turn of the twentieth century, the Senate was known as the "Millionaires' Club." Its wealthy members often served as spokespeople for business interests, an arrangement that struck many as corrupt. Reformers passed the Seventeenth Amendment to have senators elected by the people. The number of senators for each state, however, remained the same.

The Constitutional Convention's Committee of Compromise on Representation debated the terms that senators should serve. The Framers wanted this branch to be less dependent on public opinion than the House. They felt the lower house would reflect the ordinary citizens' selfish interests and uninformed views. The Senate was designed to counteract the democratic lower house and give stability to the national government. During the debate, William Pierce wanted three-year terms, to keep

"[T]he equal vote allowed to each State [in the Senate] is at once a constitutional recognition of the . . . sovereignty remaining in the individual States and an instrument for preserving that . . . sovereignty."
James Madison, *The Federalist* No. 62

senators accountable. James Wilson pointed out that longer terms would make the Senate more "respectable" to foreign governments.

Article I, section 3, gives senators six-year terms, with one-third of the members elected every two years. This way, the Senate is more responsive to fresh ideas and changing conditions. Yet there is also stability, since only one-third of the membership is up for reelection at one time, whereas the entire House faces the voters every two years. Article I, section 3, also sets the qualifications for senators: they have to be at least thirty years old, a citizen for nine years, and a resident of the state that elects them to office.

In accordance with section 5, the Senate, like the House, judges the qualifications of its members, determines its own rules, and keeps a journal of its activities. In section 6, senators, like representatives, are forbidden to hold any other government position while serving as senator; doing so would violate separation of powers. They are paid for their service.

The powers of the Senate reflect the Framers' concern with checks and balances. According to Article II, section 2, the votes of two-thirds of the members of the Senate are required for approval of treaties proposed by the president, and their advice and consent must be obtained for presidential appointments of the heads of executive departments, ambassadors, consuls, other government officials, and members of the Supreme Court. The Senate and House both take part in impeachment proceedings. The House issues an indictment, but the Senate holds the trial to determine whether an official should be removed from office. The other express powers that the Senate shares with the House are listed in Article I, section 8.

Article I, section 7, requires the Senate and the House to agree to pass a bill before it can be sent to the president for signature. If the president refuses to sign, two-thirds of the members of each house have to pass the bill again before it can become law. The Senate, however, is barred from introducing revenue bills. Today, with one hundred members, the Senate is much smaller than the House. As a result, it has more time to study and debate bills. This gives the senators the opportunity for more thoughtful consideration, much as the Framers intended.

Advice and Consent; Ambassadors; Bicameral Legislature; Bill; Breach of the Peace; Checks and Balances; Congress; Connecticut Compromise; Constitutional Convention; Consuls; Express Powers; Felonies; Framers; House of Representatives; Immunity; Impeachment; Journals; Law; Legislative Branch; New Jersey Plan; President; Separation of Powers; States; Supreme Court; Treason; Unicameral Legislature; U.S. Constitution, Article I; U.S. Constitution, Article II; U.S. Constitution, Article V; U.S. Constitution, Seventeenth Amendment

Separate but Equal Doctrine

The view that laws segregating people by race were legal as long as the public facilities for each race were more or less the same.

The Supreme Court announced the "separate but equal" doctrine in *Plessy v. Ferguson* (1896), a lawsuit challenging segregation by race on railroads. By this decision the Court declared legal the southern practice of keeping blacks and whites apart, and laws segregating the races only increased afterward. Beginning in the 1930s, African Americans brought new lawsuits seeking to end racial segregation. The Court began rolling back segregation, but only in very limited ways. Finally, in *Brown v. Board of Education of Topeka* (1954), the Supreme Court clearly reversed its 1896 decision and declared that segregation itself was a form of discrimination. Segregation, the Court said, violated the equal protection and due process clauses of the Fourteenth Amendment to the Constitution.

Civil Rights; Discrimination; Due Process of Law; Equal Protection of the Laws; Segregation and Desegregation; Supreme Court; U.S. Constitution, Fourteenth Amendment

Separation of Powers

Division of a government into branches, each with its own functions.

If power is divided, it is less likely that one part of the government can dominate the other parts or oppress the people. The Framers of the Constitution borrowed this idea from the French philosopher Montesquieu and the English philosopher John Locke. They had recommended separation of powers as a method of creating limited government. During the Constitutional Convention, the Framers separated the powers of government into three different divisions: the legislative branch, to make laws; the executive branch, to put laws into effect; and the judicial branch, to decide disputes involving the laws. The opening sentences of Articles I, II, and III of the Constitution clearly present this division of power.

Many of the Framers felt that the real threat to individuals' liberty was popularly elected legislatures. In the states, legislatures were taking on more and more powers and weakening the other branches of their government. They were also passing laws that benefited debtors and hurt property owners. The Framers feared the uninformed and changeable opinions of ordinary citizens. They did not want the people to control the national legislative branch. This is one reason that they made Congress a two-chamber legislature. The further division of power between a popularly elected House of Representatives and a state-selected Senate would

"[T]he preservation of liberty requires that the three great departments of power should be separate and distinct."
James Madison, *The Federalist* No. 47

keep the people's representatives from becoming too powerful. By limiting the power of popular majorities, the Framers hoped to preserve minority rights. By minority, they meant wealthy, landowning Americans.

As a result of separation of powers, the national government is often slow to take action on serious problems. For action to be taken, the three branches must cooperate to find a solution acceptable to all.

Bicameral Legislature; Checks and Balances; Congress; Constitutional Convention; Debts; Executive Branch; Framers; House of Representatives; Judicial Branch; Legislative Branch; Limited Government; President; Second Treatise on Government; *Senate;* Spirit of the Laws; *U.S. Constitution, Article I; U.S. Constitution, Article II; U.S. Constitution, Article III*

Slavery

The practice in which some people are held, against their will, under the complete control and legal ownership of other people.

Many countries and different cultures around the world have used slave labor, especially for difficult or unpleasant work. In the European colonies of the Americas, slavery quickly came to apply only to black people captured in Africa, as well as many generations of their descendants, during a period that lasted a total of nearly 250 years in North America.

The colonies passed laws establishing that the children of slaves were born into slavery. Owners could sell any of their slaves, even if it broke up a family, and they could also lease out their slaves' time and work. Slavery gradually declined in the English colonies in the North. By the time of the War for Independence, however, the economies of the southern colonies had come to depend on these unpaid, involuntary workers to grow cotton, indigo, tobacco, and other agricultural products shipped abroad for profit. The international slave trade also brought wealth to the region. Led by Charles Cotesworth Pinckney, most southern delegates at the Constitutional Convention negotiated compromises to preserve their way of life, despite the opposition of Virginians George Mason and James Madison, and a few northerners.

The Constitution referred to slaves as "other Persons." They were mentioned in three Articles, all of which involved concessions to southern states. Article I, section 2, required that every five slaves be counted as three "free Persons" for purposes of distributing seats in the House of Representatives and determining capitation taxes. Article I, section 9, limited the amount of tax Congress could charge on slaves imported from abroad and prohibited Congress from ending the African slave trade before 1808. Article IV, section 2, required states to return runaway slaves. Finally, Article V prevented any amendments affecting the international slave trade from being added to the Constitution before 1808. The requirement that three-fourths of the states had to ratify proposed amendments let the southern states block any attempts to interfere with slavery until the Civil War. In addition, other parts of the Constitution could be applied to enforce slavery. For example, Article I, section 8, gave Congress the power to call up troops to put down domestic insurrections, including slave rebellions. Article I, section 9, barred taxes on exports, and until 1808 slaves could be sold abroad.

The Supreme Court accepted the idea that the national government could not do anything about slavery in the states where it already existed. However, after 1808, the Court heard cases about the international slave trade. In the *Antelope* case (1825), it had to decide what to do with slaves on board a slave ship seized by American agents in American waters. Slaves judged to belong to a Spanish owner were turned over to the government of Spain. The rest of the captives were sent to western Africa. In *United States v. The Amistad* (1841), the Court dealt with newly captured slaves on a Spanish ship. They had mutinied and killed most of the crew. The Court refused to let them be tried for murder in either the United States or Spain. Since the slave trade (that is, not slavery itself but the importation of slaves) was by then illegal in Spain and in the United States, the Court freed the men and ordered that they be returned to Africa.

Another topic that came before the Court was the problem of runaway slaves. In 1793, Congress passed a Fugitive Slave Act. It allowed owners or their agents to capture slaves, bring them to a court, and request a certificate allowing them to be taken out of state to be returned to their owners. However, by that time most northern states were abolishing slavery. They also passed personal-liberty laws to protect free blacks from being kidnapped and taken to the South.

Such laws were tested in the case of *Prigg v. Pennsylvania* (1842). Edward Prigg, a slave catcher, captured Margaret Morgan, a runaway, and her children. He applied to a Pennsylvania court for a certificate and was turned down under Pennsylvania's personal-liberty law of 1826. Prigg took her away anyhow and was convicted of kidnapping under Pennsylvania's law. He appealed to the Supreme Court and won. The Court reasoned that the 1793 federal law was valid because it carried out requirements of Article IV, section 2, to return runaway slaves.

> "What, to the American slave, is your Fourth of July? . . . To him your celebration is a sham."
>
> Frederick Douglass, Speech at Rochester, N.Y., July 4, 1852

Born a slave, Dred Scott fought in the courts for almost ten years to win his freedom. His case was finally appealed to the Supreme Court, which decided against him. The Court then went on—going far beyond the basic issue—to say that no one "of the African race" could "become a member of the political community . . . formed . . . by the constitution."

Speakers of the House
Frederick A.C. Muhlenberg, Pa., 1789–1791
Jonathan Trumbull, Conn., 1791–1793
Frederick A.C. Muhlenberg, Pa., 1793–1795
Jonathan Dayton, N.J., 1795–1799
Theodore Sedgwick, Mass., 1799–1801
Nathaniel Macon, N.C., 1801–1807
Joseph B. Varnum, Mass., 1807–1811
Henry Clay, Ky., 1811–1814
Langdon Cheves, S.C., 1814–1815
Henry Clay, Ky., 1815–1820
John W. Taylor, N.Y., 1820–1821
Philip P. Barbour, Va., 1821–1823
Henry Clay, Ky., 1823–1825
John W. Taylor, N.Y., 1825–1827
Andrew Stevenson, Va., 1827–1834
John Bell, Tenn., 1834–1835
James K. Polk, Tenn., 1835–1839
Robert M.T. Hunter, Va., 1839–1841
John White, Ky., 1841–1843

Pennsylvania's law was unconstitutional because it interfered with enforcement of the Fugitive Slave Act.

The Court could not make states enforce the 1793 law, so Congress passed a tougher Fugitive Slave Act in 1850. It called for the appointment of federal commissioners to issue certificates to remove runaway slaves. Federal marshals would make sure the law was obeyed. However, opposition in the North made the law almost unenforceable.

The Supreme Court also had to decide cases concerning slavery in the territories and slaves taken into antislavery states. Congress had banned the spread of slavery to the Ohio River territory in the Northwest Ordinance of 1787. In the Missouri Compromise of 1820, slavery was banned north of a line drawn at 36 degrees 30 minutes latitude across the Louisiana Purchase territory. These boundaries were tested in the famous case of *Scott v. Sandford* (1857). Dred Scott was a slave who had lived in forts with his master in Illinois and in present-day Minnesota. Then he was returned to Missouri. He sued for his freedom because he had lived in free territory. The case eventually reached the Supreme Court.

In his landmark decision, Chief Justice Roger B. Taney ruled that blacks, whether free or slaves, had no right to sue in court because they were not citizens of the United States. He also held that Scott could not have become free by living north of the line at 36 degrees 30 minutes. He declared that the Missouri Compromise violated the Constitution because Congress had no power to ban slavery in the territories. The decision caused an uproar in the North. Only after the Civil War was it overturned, by the Thirteenth and Fourteenth amendments to the Constitution. They ended slavery and gave blacks the rights of citizenship.

Amendment Process; Apportionment; Capitation Tax; Chief Justice; Citizenship; Congress; Constitutional Convention; Delegates; Domestic Violence; Supreme Court; Territories; Three-Fifths Compromise; U.S. Constitution, Article I; U.S. Constitution, Article IV; U.S. Constitution, Article V; U.S. Constitution, Thirteenth Amendment; U.S. Constitution, Fourteenth Amendment

Speaker of the House of Representatives

The presiding officer of the House of Representatives, mentioned in Article I, section 2, of the Constitution.

The Speaker is usually chosen by the leaders of the political party with a majority of seats in the House. The Speaker's duties include recognizing representatives during debates, sending bills to committee for study, and ruling on House procedures. Until 1910, Speakers also had the power to appoint members to committees, to determine what matters would be discussed by the House, and to control debate. In 1910, Congress took away these powers because Speaker Joseph G. Cannon abused them and would not let those who disagreed with him be heard. Under the Presidential Succession Act of 1947, the Speaker of the House is second in line to the presidency, after the vice president, in case the president dies or is too disabled to continue to serve in that office.

Bill; Congress; House of Representatives; Presidential Succession; U.S. Constitution, Article I

Speech, Freedom of

The right to express written and spoken opinions in private or public.

The guarantee of free speech is found in the First Amendment to the Constitution, part of the Bill of Rights. In 1791, when it was adopted, most Americans agreed that the government had no right to prevent people from voicing their opinions. Like the British, however, many Americans felt that the government did have the right to punish individuals *after* they criticized government actions or officials. This had an effect on the development of opposition parties. For example, the Sedition Act of 1798 was passed to stop criticism of government officials or their programs. It was used to try to stop Thomas Jefferson's Democratic-Republicans from condemning President John Adams's Federalists, who controlled the national government. Some Democratic-Republican writers and editors were arrested for publishing unfavorable articles about the Adams government. The law expired in 1801, the same year Jefferson succeeded Adams as president.

In the first half of the twentieth century, the Supreme Court developed three historic tests to define the limits of free speech. The first was the "clear and present danger" test, stated in *Schenck v. United States* (1919). The United States was drafting men into the Army to fight in World War I. Charles Schenck published a pamphlet urging people to oppose the draft. In doing so, he violated the Espionage Act of 1917, which made it a crime to interfere with military recruitment. He was arrested, and his case was appealed to the Supreme Court. The Court upheld the Espionage Act. In his opinion, Associate Justice Oliver Wendell Holmes announced the "clear and present danger" test, which he said this case met because it was wartime. In general, he reasoned that words had to create a significant risk of "substantive evil" of a kind that Congress could prevent by law. The famous example Holmes cited was that the First Amendment would not allow someone to falsely shout "Fire!" in a crowded theater, creating a dangerous panic.

The "bad tendency" test was first declared in *Gitlow v. New York* (1925). In the 1920s, when Americans feared the spread of radical ideas, Benjamin Gitlow was arrested for violating a New York State law making it a crime to urge the violent overthrow of the government. His lawyer claimed that Gitlow was only expressing a philosophical idea, and that no one had acted on his urgings. The Court, however, ruled that speech could be banned if it had a *tendency* to produce dangerous results at some later time. Therefore, it upheld Gitlow's conviction. On the other hand, it was in this landmark case that the Court first applied the Fourteenth Amendment to prevent the states, as well as the federal government, from limiting free speech in most circumstances.

Some members of the Supreme Court briefly put forward what was called the "preferred position" doctrine in the 1940s. This idea, never fully accepted by the Court, said that speech should almost never be banned, because it is so important to a free society. In other words, speech is in a preferred position in society.

None of the historic tests defining the limits of free speech were satisfactory. The problem was the connection between speech and action. Shouldn't the government be able to protect the public from speech that might cause riots or other harmful activity? How much time was needed between a speech and an action? How much damage had to be caused?

Over time, the Supreme Court has developed a number of other tests to set limits for laws restricting free speech. These determine whether the laws are too vague or too broad or too biased. They also have narrowed the scope of the earlier historic tests of free speech. In *Brandenburg v. Ohio* (1969), for example, the Court allowed speech to be banned only if the government could show it would *immediately* encourage or produce lawless action. Clarence Brandenburg had spoken out on television in favor of racial conflict during a rally of the Ku Klux Klan, a white-supremacy organization. His hate-filled speech was condemned by numerous citizens. In fact, he even violated an Ohio law making it a crime to urge others to violence. However, the Court protected Brandenburg's right to express an unpopular opinion.

In addition to deciding cases in which a speaker urged illegal actions, the Supreme Court has ruled on lawsuits involving "symbolic speech." This type of speech expresses an idea through an action. In *Tinker v. Des*

Moines Independent Community School District (1969), the Court upheld the right of students to protest the Vietnam War by peacefully wearing armbands to school. They had been suspended because school officials disagreed with their antiwar message, not because the armbands had caused any disruption in school activities. In two cases in 1989 and 1990, the Court overturned state and federal laws that made it illegal to burn the American flag. Yet the Court previously allowed students to be punished for burning draft cards in defiance of the law. The line between symbolic speech and action has remained unclear.

The Court has refused to apply First Amendment protections to certain other forms of speech, such as "fighting words." In *Chaplinsky v. New Hampshire* (1942), the Court explained that these words make someone want to fight back, resulting in riots and disorder. They do not contribute to people's understanding of public issues. In *Miller v. California* (1973), the Court denied First Amendment protection to another category of speech, obscenity. Earlier Court decisions had defined something as obscene if it described sexual behavior in an offensive or disgusting way and lacked any serious literary, scientific, political, artistic, or social value. In the 1973 case, the Court allowed that local communities could label specific forms of speech obscene—and so ban them from their communities—if an average citizen, applying local community values, found that the material in question was designed solely to stimulate sexual feelings.

The Supreme Court also has handed down decisions about free speech in the media and in advertising. Congress has issued licenses to radio and television stations since 1927. In *FCC v. Pacifica Foundation* (1978), the Court allowed the Federal Communications Commission to regulate the broadcast of dirty words because children might hear them. The Court was willing to limit free speech in advertising because it is used to sell goods and services, rather than to inform. In *Central Hudson Gas & Electric Corporation v. Public Service Commission of New York* (1980), the

Student demonstrators are shown here on the campus of Columbia University in New York in April 1968. They had occupied Low Library, which houses the university's administrative offices. Their protest occurred against the backdrop of the Vietnam War and an increasingly agitated political atmosphere around the country. The year 1968 saw political assassinations (Martin Luther King Jr. had recently been killed; Senator Robert F. Kennedy would be assassinated five weeks later) and sometimes brutal police crackdowns (as in response to the demonstration at Columbia and, in the summer, at the Democratic National Convention in Chicago).

This was the larger context of the Columbia protest. The immediate cause was the university's plan to build an athletic facility in Morningside Park, the sort of no-man's-land that divided the privileged university community from the relatively impoverished local community in Harlem. The students saw the university's project as encroaching on the local community, not investing in its future. The university responded that the students had occupied private property and were not within their rights.

Court ruled that the First Amendment protects only truthful advertising about legal products.

The problems of free speech in a free society are never-ending. The Internet and cable television are two areas where new interpretations of the First Amendment guarantee are needed. In *Reno v. American Civil Liberties Union* (1997), the Supreme Court struck down the Communications Decency Act. This law was intended to prevent people from sending indecent messages to minors over the Internet. The Court ruled that it violated the First Amendment guarantee of free speech.

Bill of Rights; Congress; Incorporation of the Bill of Rights; Press, Freedom of the; Supreme Court; U.S. Constitution, First Amendment; U.S. Constitution, Fourteenth Amendment

Spirit of the Laws

A book written in 1748 by Charles-Louis de Secondat, Baron de La Brède et de Montesquieu—a French aristocrat better known simply as Montesquieu—in which the author investigated types of governments and the goals they pursued.

> "There can be no liberty where the legislative and executive powers are united in the same person."
> Montesquieu, *The Spirit of the Laws*, 1748

Montesquieu's writings were an important influence on the Framers of the Constitution. Born into a minor aristocratic family, Montesquieu devoted himself to legal and historical studies and to travel. In his writings he searched for ways to limit the king's power in order to restore individual liberty to France.

In *The Spirit of the Laws* (1748), his most important book, Montesquieu concluded that the British monarchy was the only government of his day that valued political liberty. Montesquieu argued that the political liberty of British citizens was protected because government power was equally divided into the legislative, executive, and judicial branches. Each branch shared some powers with the others so that they could keep each other from becoming too powerful.

The Framers were attracted to Montesquieu's writings because he favored separation of powers and checks and balances. They did not want to create an all-powerful government that would destroy the rights of individuals or the states. Nor did they want to keep the weak government of the Articles of Confederation. Montesquieu's writings offered a solution. Applying his ideas, they could create an effective national government and preserve freedom.

Articles of Confederation; Checks and Balances; Executive Branch; Framers; Judicial Branch; Legislative Branch; Separation of Powers

States

Self-governing parts of the federal system of the United States.

There are now fifty states, exercising limited sovereignty as permitted by the Constitution. Under the Articles of Confederation, the states had been independent republics, prepared to take joint action in matters of common concern. Some of the delegates to the Constitutional Convention were anxious to preserve the independent powers of the states. These included Gunning Bedford Jr., William Paterson, Luther Martin, and John Lansing Jr. Others, such as Elbridge Gerry, Roger Sherman, Charles Cotesworth Pinckney, and George Mason, did not wish to make the national government too strong at the expense of the states.

As a result of a series of compromises, the Constitution gives states a significant role in the federal system. Article I, section 3, grants the states equal representation in the Senate. Article V prevents constitutional amendments from altering this arrangement. Senators were even elected by state legislatures until the Seventeenth Amendment was ratified.

States are expected to conduct national elections. According to Article I, section 4, they determine the "times, places, and manner of holding elections for senators and representatives," subject to change by Congress. Under Article II, section 1, they choose members of the electoral college, which directly elects the president. If a presidential candidate fails to win a majority of electoral votes, an election is held in the House of Representatives, with states having one vote apiece.

States are also required to contribute to the nation's defense, and they must consent to any changes in the Constitution. Article I, section 8, lets states keep their militias, but these may be called up to join the national army when needed. The states can appoint officers and train troops, but Congress makes the rules for their discipline. Article V also gives the states an important role in the amending process. Two-thirds of the states can require Congress to call a convention to propose changes in the Constitution. No amendments can be adopted unless three-fourths of the states approve them.

To preserve the federal system and protect the liberties of the citizens, the Constitution prevents states from engaging in certain activities. Article I, section 10, lists their denied powers. For example, they cannot make treaties, coin money, pass bills of attainder or ex post facto laws, impair the obligations of contracts, tax imports or exports, or grant titles of nobility. They also have certain responsibilities to each other, described in Article

IV. These include giving full faith and credit to each other's public acts, granting equal privileges and immunities to citizens from other states, and returning escaped prisoners if requested to do so. Until passage of the Thirteenth and Fourteenth amendments, they also had to return runaway slaves. The Eleventh Amendment gives states protection from lawsuits brought by citizens of others states, by removing such suits from the jurisdiction of the federal courts.

Article IV also lists the federal government's commitments to the states. Congress governs new territories and admits new states, but no new states can be formed from existing states' lands without their consent. The national government also guarantees the states a republican form of government. Finally, the government must protect the states from domestic insurrection and foreign invasion. In return, state officials must take an oath to support the Constitution, a requirement found in Article VI.

Amendment Process; Articles of Confederation; Bill of Attainder; Concurrent Powers; Congress; Constitutional Convention; Contract Clause; Convention; Delegates; Denied Powers; Domestic Violence; Electoral College; Export Taxes; Ex Post Facto Laws; Federalism; Full Faith and Credit; House of Representatives; Imports; Jurisdiction; Nobility; Oaths of Office; President; Privileges and Immunities; Republican Form of Government; Senate; States' Rights; Supremacy Clause; Treaties; U.S. Constitution, Article I; U.S. Constitution, Article II; U.S. Constitution, Article IV; U.S. Constitution, Article V; U.S. Constitution, Article VI; U.S. Constitution, Eleventh Amendment; U.S. Constitution, Thirteenth Amendment; U.S. Constitution, Fourteenth Amendment; U.S. Constitution, Seventeenth Amendment

States' Rights

The political theory that the national government is merely an agent of the states and its powers are limited to the specific words of the Constitution.

According to this view, federal laws may not interfere with activities reserved to the states under the Tenth Amendment. *McCulloch v. Maryland* (1819) was one of the most famous states' rights cases to come before the Supreme Court. Congress had created a national bank. The state of Maryland taxed the bank, but the cashier of the bank, James McCulloch, refused to pay the tax. He argued that a state could not tax an agency of the national government. Luther Martin, one of the Framers of the Constitution, argued the case for the state of Maryland. He insisted that Article I, section 8, of the Constitution did not give the national government the express power to create a national bank. He said the elastic clause gave Congress the power to pass only laws that were essential to carrying out its express powers. A bank was not needed for Congress to be able to coin money. Maryland could tax the existing bank, because the power to tax was reserved to the states under the Tenth Amendment.

Maryland lost the case. Chief Justice John Marshall accepted the arguments presented by Daniel Webster, one of the lawyers for the national government. The Supreme Court held that Congress was properly exercising its implied powers under the elastic clause when it created a bank. No state could use its reserved powers to tax a national institution. States could destroy the entire national government by taxing it. This decision, a triumph over states' rights, enabled the national government to expand its powers to meet the needs of a growing nation.

States' rights supporters, however, continued to challenge the national government in the courts, mostly on matters of taxes and states' police powers. During the nineteenth century, the Supreme Court developed the doctrine of *dual sovereignty* to settle these disputes. This doctrine held that national and state governments were equal sovereigns, each operating in its own area. The Court's duty was to determine the boundary between the two. For example, in *Ableman v. Booth* (1859), the Court had to decide whether a state or the national government should punish a man who had violated the Fugitive Slave Act of 1850. The case involved a Wisconsin court's decision to free the man. He was being held by the national government for aiding a slave to escape. Chief Justice Roger B. Taney ruled that the state judges lacked jurisdiction to hear the case.

Though states' rights was, famously, one of the great causes of the Civil War in 1861, the doctrine of dual sovereignty continued to be applied after the war. Then, in the late 1930s, the Court began to uphold most federal regulations at the expense of states' rights. The Court reasoned that a strong national government was needed to solve the economic crisis that crippled the nation at that time. Under President Franklin D. Roosevelt, the federal government had taken on new responsibilities to provide citizens with the basic necessities of life. For the first time, for example, the national government provided public assistance for the needy and Social Security for the elderly and unemployed.

In the 1950s and the 1960s, states' righters took up another cause: segregation. They appealed to the Supreme Court to overturn federal laws ending segregation. However, *Heart of Atlanta Motel v. United States* (1964) and *Katzenbach v. McClung* (1964) upheld the Civil Rights Act of 1964, opening motels, restaurants, and other public accommodations to

Earl Warren was among the most important—and most controversial—chief
justices of the Supreme Court. Presiding
over the Court from 1953 to 1969, he
shepherded through a major reinterpre-
tation of the Constitution, extending the
protections of the Bill of Rights and
requiring that states take specific
actions to remedy injustice.

This represented a change in the
relationship between the federal government and the states, and many people
applauded. Critics, however, said the
Court was denying the states their
authority to act. The most serious
protests followed the Court's decision in
Brown v. Board of Education of Topeka
(1954), which declared segregation in
the public schools unconstitutional.
Conservative southerners began talking
about impeaching the chief justice.

What critics failed to note was that
the Court was not acting alone. For
instance, the Warren Court endorsed, in
South Carolina v. Katzenbach (1966),
federal intervention at the local level to
protect voting rights—a decision
attacked by states' rights advocates. Yet
it was only applying a law, the Voting
Rights Act of 1965, that allowed federal
examiners to investigate counties where
less than 50 percent of the population
was registered to vote. That law
expressed congressional resolve to protect voting rights. By its decision, the
Court merely reinforced that resolve.

blacks. In *South Carolina v. Katzenbach* (1966), the Court rejected states' requirements that voters prove they could read English before they were allowed to vote in elections.

Defeated on issues of civil rights, states' righters became more successful in limiting federal economic controls over the states. In *National League of Cities v. Usery* (1976), the Supreme Court decided that the national government could not apply federal wage and hour standards to state employees. The decision was reversed, however, in 1985. Nevertheless, in the 1980s, states' righters had cause to celebrate with the election of President Ronald Reagan; he shared their views. During his eight years in office, controls over how federal aid could be spent were relaxed. In the 1990s, under President Bill Clinton, federal welfare programs were gradually turned over to the states and even partly phased out. States and cities had to take responsibility for their own needy citizens. To some extent, states' rights had become acceptable once again. No doubt it would be challenged in the future, however.

Chief Justice; Civil Rights; Congress; Elastic Clause; Express Powers; Federal Government; Jurisdiction; Law; Police Powers; Reserved Powers; Segregation and Desegregation; States; Supremacy Clause; Supreme Court; Treaties; U.S. Constitution, Article I; U.S. Constitution, Tenth Amendment

Supremacy Clause

The statement in Article VI of the Constitution that the U.S. Constitution itself, all laws made to carry out the requirements of the Constitution, and all treaties signed by the United States are "the supreme Law of the Land," superior to any conflicting state law or constitution.

Luther Martin proposed the supremacy clause, which was backed by the military power of the government. It was designed to ensure that laws Congress passed were put into effect. The Confederation Congress had to depend on the states to voluntarily carry out its recommendations, and most of the time they refused to cooperate. Article VI also requires national and state officials to take an oath to support the Constitution.

Confederation Congress; Congress; Oaths of Office; States; States' Rights; Treaties; U.S. Constitution, Article V

Supreme Court

The highest court in the United States, created by Article III of the Constitution.

Its members are appointed for life and can be removed only for misconduct. Its jurisdiction is outlined in Article III, section 2. The Supreme Court has the right to hear appeals from lower courts about law and equity arising under the Constitution, treaties, federal law, and the law of the seas. It also decides disputes in which the United States or two or more states are involved, as well as lawsuits between citizens of two or more states, between citizens of the same state claiming lands under grants from different states, and between a state or its citizens and a foreign country. The Supreme Court acts like a trial court in cases involving ambassadors, consuls, and other public ministers, and where a state is involved. The Eleventh Amendment to the Constitution prevents the Court from hearing cases between states and citizens of other states.

The Framers of the Constitution did not specifically give the Court the power of judicial review. However, many of them assumed the Court would use this power to ensure that the actions of Congress, the president, other courts, and state officials did not violate the Constitution. In 1801, under Chief Justice John Marshall, the Supreme Court first exercised the power of judicial review, in the case of *Marbury v. Madison*. Between 1789 and 1987, the Court declared that 135 acts of Congress wholly or partially violated the Constitution. During the same time span, nearly 1,000 state laws and parts of state constitutions were also overturned.

The chief justice is the head of the Supreme Court, and the only judicial official mentioned in the Constitution. Article I, section 3, names the chief justice as the presiding officer in presidential impeachment trials. Decisions about other members of the Court were left to Congress. (Judges appointed to the Supreme Court are called *justices*.) The number of justices has varied over the years: from six in 1789 to seven in 1807, nine in 1837, and ten in 1863. Since 1869, the size of the Court has remained at nine. However, in 1937, after the Court had rejected many of the laws passed by Congress to solve the major national economic crisis known as the Great Depression, President Franklin D. Roosevelt threatened to have Congress increase the size of the Court, in order to include several justices appointed by him. The Court soon began upholding Roosevelt's economic regulations, and the president withdrew his threat.

The modern Supreme Court meets from the first Monday in October until the end of June. (In the past, members of the Court also rode around the countryside hearing appeals of trial-court decisions during the summer months. They were not relieved of this duty until 1891, when additional

Justices Serving on the Rehnquist Court

William Rehnquist, chief justice, 1986–

William J. Brennan Jr., 1956–1990
Byron R. White, 1962–1993
Thurgood Marshall, 1967–1991
Harry A. Blackmun, 1970–1994
Lewis F. Powell Jr., 1972–1987
John Paul Stevens, 1975–
Sandra Day O'Connor, 1981–
Antonin Scalia, 1986–
Anthony M. Kennedy, 1988–
David H. Souter, 1990–
Clarence Thomas, 1991–
Ruth Bader Ginsburg, 1993–
Stephen G. Breyer, 1994–

For almost 150 years of its existence, the Supreme Court made do with cramped quarters that it shared with other institutions of government. For example, when the federal government moved to the new capital city, Washington, D.C., in 1800, the Supreme Court took up offices in the basement of the Capitol building, where it remained for sixty years. In 1860, the Court moved upstairs to the old Senate Chamber (recently vacated by the Senate, which now had its own wing in the Capitol). The Court continued in that space for another seventy-five years. Toward the end of that time, Chief Justice William Howard Taft (a former president, and the only person to serve as both chief justice and president) convinced Congress to appropriate money for a permanent home for the Court. The building (above) opened its doors for the Court session that began in October 1935.

Inside, the justices conduct their most important business behind closed doors, in the Conference Room. Cases, of course, are heard in open court, and justices talk frequently with their clerks, relying on them to research the law and contribute opinions that serve as the basis for Court decisions. Yet no one but the nine justices is allowed in meetings in the Conference Room.

federal courts were established to take over those duties.) When the Court is in session, the justices listen to lawyers' arguments in several cases during a period of two weeks. For the next two weeks, they study the cases they have just heard and write opinions. Then the justices repeat the two-week cycle of hearing cases and deciding them. A quorum of six justices is needed, and cases are decided by majority vote. If there is a tie, the decision of the lower court is upheld unless the case is reargued.

The Court decides which cases it will review, except for a few that it must hear. If four justices find a case important or interesting, the Court will hear it. The Court's refusal to hear a case may not necessarily mean that it accepts a lower court's judgment. The justices may have concluded that the issues involved are too political for them to decide. Alternatively, the justices themselves may disagree so strongly about the issues that the Court is not ready to review the case.

The Supreme Court's judgments are called *opinions*. They represent the views that a majority of the justices are willing to accept. *Majority opinions* are written by one justice and passed to the others for comments. There is room for negotiation and compromise. Yet some justices may choose to write *concurring opinions*. These agree with the majority's conclusion but differ over the reasoning. Other justices may find the majority's view unacceptable. They may choose to write *dissenting opinions*. These explain why those writers think the Court's decision is incorrect. Both concurring and dissenting opinions can become future majority opinions.

Occasionally, amendments to the Constitution have reversed Court decisions. For example, the Court's ruling in *Chisholm v. Georgia* (1793) offended the states. Two citizens of South Carolina had sued Georgia for payment of Revolutionary War debts. Lawyers for Georgia refused to appear in court. They claimed Georgia was a sovereign and independent state. The Supreme Court ruled in favor of the South Carolinians and reminded Georgia that the people, not the states, were sovereign. In response, the states passed the Eleventh Amendment. It in effect gives a state the power to refuse to be sued by citizens of another state, by removing such lawsuits from federal jurisdiction.

Supreme Court judgments have helped to preserve the Constitution that the Framers created. They have also adapted it to changing times and different circumstances. In this way, the Supreme Court has brought an eighteenth-century document, written in the days of horses and coaches, into the space age.

Ambassadors; Checks and Balances; Chief Justice; Congress; Consuls; Equity; Executive Branch; Federal Courts; Framers; Impeachment; Judicial Activism; Judicial Branch; Judicial Restraint; Judicial Review; Jurisdiction; Law; President; Quorum; Treaties; U.S. Constitution, Article I; U.S. Constitution, Article III; U.S. Constitution, Eleventh Amendment

Tariffs

Taxes on products shipped from abroad to be sold in a country.

Tariffs can be used to protect a country's manufacturing and agriculture, because they make imported goods more expensive. They can also serve to raise revenue. At the Constitutional Convention, southern delegates opposed export taxes because that would discourage foreign countries from buying cotton, rice, indigo, and other crops vital to the southern economy. Northern delegates supported tariffs because they would protect the infant industries of the North. As the result of a compromise, the Constitution gives Congress control over foreign commerce and allows it to set tariffs on goods entering the nation but not to collect taxes on exports leaving the nation for sale abroad.

Commerce Clause; Congress; Constitutional Convention; Delegates; Export Taxes; Imports; Revenue

Taxation, Power of

A government's authority and ability to require citizens to pay for the nation's defense and general welfare.

The American colonists were not permitted to elect representatives to the British Parliament, and they complained when they were taxed without their consent. With this in mind, the Framers wrote Article I, section 7, of the Constitution, requiring that all proposals to raise revenue originate in the House of Representatives. They wanted the house of Congress most directly responsible to the people—the House of Representatives—to control the purse strings of government. In Article I, section 8, the Framers gave Congress the power to "lay and collect taxes." Congress not only raises money but also decides how it will be spent. However, the system of checks and balances found in the Constitution gives the president and the courts the power to block decisions of Congress.

Checks and Balances; Congress; Framers; House of Representatives; President; Revenue; Senate; U.S. Constitution, Article I

Term Limits

Legal restrictions on the number of times public officials may be reelected to the same office.

Supporters of term limits argue that they make elections more democratic by removing officeholders' advantages over challengers. They also claim that new officeholders will be more likely than long-established politicians to listen to voters' wishes. Opponents of term limits claim that it is more democratic to allow voters to decide whether to reelect an officeholder. They say regularly scheduled elections are, in effect, term limits.

Term limits have been a part of American politics since the earliest days. Under the Articles of Confederation, seven of the new states wrote term limits into their constitutions. The Articles of Confederation themselves included term limits on delegates to the Confederation Congress. Article IV specified that no delegate could serve more than three years in any six-year period. Critics argued that this clause drove capable people out of government after only a short time.

Term limits were debated at the Constitutional Convention. They were included in the Virginia Plan and in the New Jersey Plan, but they were left out of the final draft of the Constitution. During the debate over ratification, Antifederalists such as George Mason and Melancton Smith faulted the Constitution for not including term limits. In the Federalist Papers, articles supporting ratification, Alexander Hamilton and James Madison argued that frequent elections—they were set to be held every two years—would keep lawmakers from ignoring the wishes of the people.

The Framers expected that many new lawmakers would join Congress every two years, and in fact 40 percent of the First Congress did not return as part of the Second Congress. In the 1800s, many elections resulted in a 50 percent turnover rate. However, by the early 1990s, nearly 90 percent of the members of Congress had served more than one term.

Twenty-three states reacted to this by limiting the number of times their representatives in Congress could be reelected. In *U.S. Term Limits v. Thornton* (1995), the Supreme Court, exercising its power of judicial review, overturned these restrictions by ruling that they were unconstitutional. That same year a constitutional amendment on term limits failed to pass Congress. It was not the first time such a measure had been rejected.

Nevertheless, term limits remain an issue that some people hope to see introduced into the Constitution. Since 1951, the Twenty-second Amendment has kept the president from serving more than two terms.

Supporters of term limits want this restriction extended to members of Congress.

Amendment Process; Amendments, Unratified; Antifederalists; Articles of Confederation; Congress; Constitutional Convention; Delegates; Federalist Papers; Framers; House of Representatives; Judicial Review; New Jersey Plan; President; Ratification; States; Supreme Court; Virginia Plan

Territories

Lands belonging to the United States that are not states.

According to Article IV of the Constitution, Congress has the power to make laws regarding American territories. New states may be formed from territories and admitted to the Union. The Northwest Ordinance of 1787 served as a guideline for Congress. It allowed a territorial government to be set up once 5,000 male voters had settled the land. They could form their own legislature and send one nonvoting delegate to Congress. When the population grew to 60,000 people, they could draw up a state constitution and ask Congress to be admitted to the Union. If accepted, they would be treated as equals with the older states. In 1959, Alaska and Hawaii became the most recent territories admitted as states.

Congress; States; U.S. Constitution, Article IV

Three-Fifths Compromise

Counting every five slaves as three free people for purposes of direct taxes and representation in the House of Representatives.

This was one of the North-South compromises made by the Framers at the Constitutional Convention. It prevented the South from dominating the House of Representatives at the expense of the North. The Confederation Congress had already used the same ratio of slaves to free people in a 1783 bill to raise revenue. Found in Article I, section 2, of the Constitution, it was eliminated by section 2 of the Fourteenth Amendment, which required that everyone ("excluding Indians not taxed") be counted equally.

Apportionment; Capitation Tax; Census; Confederation Congress; Constitutional Convention; Framers; House of Representatives; Native Americans; New Jersey Plan; Revenue; Slavery; U.S. Constitution, Article I; U.S. Constitution, Fourteenth Amendment; Virginia Plan

Treason

Waging war against the United States or siding with the enemies of the United States and giving them aid and comfort.

"Despite [the Framers'] clear understanding of the role slavery would play in the new republic, use of the words 'slaves' and 'slavery' was carefully avoided in the original document. Political representation . . . was to be based on the population of 'free Persons' in each State, plus three-fifths of all 'other Persons.' Moral principles against slavery, for those who had them, were compromised. . . .

"[W]e must be careful, when focusing on the events . . . in Philadelphia two centuries ago, that we not overlook the momentous events which followed, and thereby lose our proper sense of perspective. . . ."

Justice Thurgood Marshall, "The Bicentennial Speech," May 1987

Born in the West Indies, Alexander Hamilton served as an aide to General George Washington during the War for Independence. After the war he served in the Confederation Congress.

In 1786, at the Annapolis Convention, Hamilton proposed that a constitutional convention be called. At that convention, Hamilton proposed to centralize governmental power. He wanted an executive in each state, appointed by the national government, to have power to reject state laws. Under Hamilton's plan, the president would be elected for life. The delegates set Hamilton's plan aside.

Hamilton played a much more important role in winning ratification of the Constitution. He wrote a large number of the Federalist Papers, the articles that so influenced public opinion in favor of the new government.

In 1789, Hamilton became secretary of the treasury. He recommended measures to stabilize the nation's finances and to promote American industry. He also became the leader of a political party, the Federalists.

He left the national government in 1795. Becoming involved in New York State politics, he often clashed with New York lawyer—and Vice President of the United States—Aaron Burr, who killed him in a duel in 1804.

This definition of treason is found in Article III, section 3, of the Constitution. The definition is important because it describes certain specific activities, not ideas, statements, or opinions. It prevents citizens from being accused of treason for merely criticizing the government. As a result, people have been able to form opposition parties and challenge the political party in power without fear of arrest.

In order to convict people of treason, at least two witnesses must have observed the same specific disloyal activities. They must also be prepared to swear to what they saw in court, or a suspect may choose to confess and accept punishment.

Citizenship; Parties, Political; U.S. Constitution, Article III

Treasury, U.S. Department of the

The executive department in charge of coining money and collecting revenues to pay the government's expenses.

It is mentioned in Article I, section 6, of the Constitution. Among its other modern duties are selling government bonds to raise money, managing national banks, supervising the Secret Service, and making sure that the government receives excise taxes from the sale of alcohol, firearms, and tobacco. Congress created the Treasury Department in 1789.

Congress; Excise Taxes; Executive Departments; Money and Coinage; Revenue; U.S. Constitution, Article I

Treaties

Agreements among independent nations to create, change, or end international relationships.

Examples include alliances, defense pacts, and trade agreements. Article II, section 2, of the Constitution gives the president the power to make treaties. However, to take effect, these must be approved by two-thirds of the members of the Senate. One of the most famous treaties rejected by the Senate was the 1919 Treaty of Versailles. It was intended to end World War I and to make the United States a member of the League of Nations, the forerunner of the United Nations.

According to Article VI, treaties are part of the supreme law of the land, and every state must accept them. Nevertheless, in *Missouri v. Holland* (1920), the state of Missouri challenged a U.S. treaty with Canada protecting birds that migrated between the two nations. The state felt that the treaty interfered with its reserved powers under the Tenth Amendment to the Constitution. The Supreme Court rejected Missouri's claim, because of the supremacy clause.

President; Reserved Powers; States; Supremacy Clause; Supreme Court; U.S. Constitution, Article II; U.S. Constitution, Article VI; U.S. Constitution, Tenth Amendment

U

Unicameral Legislature

A lawmaking body that has a single chamber, or house.

Today, Nebraska is the only state with a unicameral legislature. The United States once was governed by a single house of lawmakers. The Continental Congresses and the Confederation Congress were one-chamber legislatures, with each state having the same number of votes as the others.

At the Constitutional Convention, the authors of the New Jersey Plan wanted to keep the Confederation's unicameral legislature, because it treated the small states as equals with the large states. They rejected the Virginia Plan, because it had favored states with large populations. However, the Convention adopted the Connecticut Compromise. It gave small states equality of representation with the large states in a Senate. It also recognized the power of the large states by creating a House of Representatives, elected by the people. This two-chamber, or bicameral, system is found in Article I of the Constitution.

Bicameral Legislature; Confederation Congress; Congress; Connecticut Compromise; Continental Congresses; House of Representatives; New Jersey Plan; Senate; U.S. Constitution, Article I; Virginia Plan

U.S. Constitution

The basic law that creates the government of the United States and defines and limits its powers.

The thirty-four entries following this one take up different elements of the U.S. Constitution—the seven Articles and twenty-seven amendments—in sequential order. This entry discusses the Constitution generally.

It is the oldest written plan of government still in use. In 1787, fifty-five delegates to the Constitutional Convention prepared the original 4,300-word document, and thirty-nine of them signed it. The Constitution was ratified by the required nine states in June 1788. It replaced the Articles of Confederation, the first plan of government for the United States. The Framers of the Constitution created a republic, but not a democracy, because they did not entirely trust the judgment of ordinary people. In

Visitors to the National Archives in Washington, D.C., examine the Declaration of Independence and part of the Constitution. The documents have been displayed there since 1952, in a helium-filled case that preserves their brittle paper. At night, the entire case descends to a chamber built to withstand a nuclear explosion. All five pages of the original Constitution are brought out only on September 17, the anniversary of its signing and, since 1919, a day of celebration.

The Constitution was not always treated so reverently. For more than 130 years, it was kept in cabinets or folded up in a tin box. It was stored for nine years at an orphanage. Its first permanent display, at the Library of Congress from 1924 to 1941, was in a glass box dubbed the "Shrine of the Constitution." During World War II, it was stored in Fort Knox, with the nation's gold reserves—a clear sign of the value people placed in the physical document by that time.

order to win the support of southern states, they made slavery part of the basic law of the United States—with no changes permitted until 1808. (Some of the Framers seem to have thought that the Constitution was a compromise that would end slavery after 1808.)

The Constitution promotes federalism by setting up a national government and preserving the state governments. It enumerates the express powers of the national government. The states exercise both reserved powers and concurrent powers. The Constitution also follows the principle of separation of powers, by dividing the national government into three distinct branches: a legislature, an executive, and a judiciary. Relations among them are determined by checks and balances. Because these branches share responsibilities and may block one another's decisions, no one branch can dominate the others.

To give the Constitution flexibility, the Framers set up procedures for amendments. Twenty-seven formal amendments have been added to the original document. They have made the Constitution more democratic, changed government procedures, and eliminated provisions about slavery. The Framers also left some matters to be filled in later by Congress. In addition, they wrote some deliberately vague statements into the text that would have to be interpreted by the federal courts.

Amendment Process;
Articles of Confederation;
Checks and Balances;
Concurrent Powers;
Congress; Constitution;
Constitutional Convention;
Executive Branch;
Express Powers; Federal
Courts; Federalism;
Framers; Judicial Branch;
Legislative Branch;
Preamble; Ratification;
Representative Democracy;
Reserved Powers;
Separation of Powers;
Slavery

The article that establishes the legislative branch of the national government and outlines its powers.

Section 1 puts all legislative power in the Congress. That body has two chambers, the House of Representatives and the Senate. It is the only branch of the national government with the power to make laws. (This has been modified, in the sense that federal agencies, such as the Environmental Protection Agency and the Federal Trade Commission, issue rulings that are much like laws.)

Section 2 deals with elections, terms, and qualifications for members of the House of Representatives. Members are elected every two years. Each state decides who is qualified to vote (now subject to the Fifteenth, Nineteenth, Twenty-fourth, and Twenty-sixth amendments). To be qualified for office, a representative must be at least twenty-five years old, a citizen of the United States for seven years, and a resident of the state where the election is held.

For purposes of apportionment, each state is divided into districts of 30,000 people. (Because Congress fixed the number of seats in the House at 435 in 1910, each member of the House now represents about 630,000 people.) The number of representatives given to each state depends on the size of its population, with every five slaves counting as three free persons. (This was a result of the Connecticut Compromise and compromises on slavery and taxation. The Thirteenth and Fourteenth amendments eliminated the part about slaves.) A census, taken every ten years, sets the number of representatives allowed to each state. Each state must have at least one representative. When a seat is vacant, the governor of a state calls a special election to replace a representative. The House has the power to choose its Speaker and other officers. It is also given the power to bring charges of misconduct against any of them that may result in impeachment.

Section 3 takes up elections, terms, and qualifications for the Senate. Each state is entitled to two senators, to be chosen by the state's legislature. (The Seventeenth Amendment provides that they be elected by the people. If a vacancy occurs, the governor of the state calls a special election to choose a replacement, or the state legislature may allow the governor to appoint someone temporarily.) Senators serve for six years, but their terms overlap so that one-third of the Senate is elected every two years. To be qualified for office, candidates must be at least thirty years old, a citizen of the United States for nine years, and a resident of the state where the election is held.

The vice president serves as president of the Senate but can vote only to break a tie. The Senate may choose other presiding officers, including the president pro tempore. It may also hire and remove such officials as a chaplain and secretary. They are not members of the legislature.

The Senate has the sole power to act as a trial court in impeachment cases. The chief justice presides when a president is tried. (The vice president presides over trials involving ambassadors, heads of executive departments, federal judges, and other officials.) The vote of two-thirds of the senators present is necessary for conviction. (President Andrew Johnson was the first president to be tried, and he escaped conviction by one vote. Seven federal judges have been found guilty and removed from office.)

Section 4 covers the method of holding elections and the requirements for meetings. State legislatures may decide the times, places, and manner of holding elections, but Congress may make changes. (Congress has decided that unless a state constitution sets a different date, all congressional elections are to be held in even-numbered years on the Tuesday after the first Monday in November.) The Constitution requires Congress to meet at least once a year and sets the first Monday in December for the start of the session. (The Twentieth Amendment changed the starting date to January 3.)

Section 5 focuses on rules and procedures. Each chamber decides whether its members meet the qualifications for service. A majority of the members make up a quorum, allowing them to do their work. The houses can set up their own rules and procedures, and may censure (scold) or expel their members for misbehaving. To expel a member requires a two-thirds vote. Each house must publish a journal of its activities, except for matters of national security that have to be kept secret. (In addition to the *House Journal* and *Senate Journal*, which are published at the end of each session, the *Congressional Record* gives a daily account of what the lawmakers do and say.) Both houses must stay in session for the same amount of time and in the same place. Neither may adjourn for more than three days or move to another place without the consent of the other.

Section 6 defines the rights of lawmakers. Members of the House and the Senate are paid, by the federal government, an amount set by law. (The Twenty-seventh Amendment prevents salary increases from taking effect until after the next congressional elections.) While meeting in session, and while traveling to or from a session, lawmakers cannot be arrested, except for treason, felony, or a breach of the peace. They have unrestricted freedom of speech and cannot be arrested or tried for what they say in Congress. They may not accept any other job in the federal government while serving in Congress. (This guarantees the separation of powers.)

Section 7 describes the making of laws. All money-related bills must be introduced in the House of Representatives. (The Framers thought the House would pay more attention to the people's wishes than the Senate, because House members serve shorter terms than senators.) Bills that have passed the House and Senate must be signed by the president to become law. If the president objects to a bill, it can be returned to the chamber that first proposed it. The president's objections are written into that chamber's journal of proceedings. The bill can still become law if two-thirds of the members of each house vote to pass it again. How each lawmaker voted must be recorded in the journals. If a president fails to sign a bill ten days after receiving it, not counting Sundays, it automatically becomes law. If, however, Congress adjourns during those ten days, it will not become law if left unsigned. The president's approval is required for every order, resolution, and vote that is passed by both houses, except for the decision to adjourn. If the president disapproves, these can be passed again by a two-thirds vote in each chamber.

Section 8 describes the powers of Congress. Seventeen express powers of Congress and one implied power are listed. (1) To raise and collect taxes, duties, and imposts on foreign goods sold in the United States, and excises on goods made in the United States; to pay debts; and to provide for defense and the general well-being of the nation. Duties, imposts, and excises must be the same throughout the nation. (Under the Confederation, states charged different amounts.) (2) To borrow money against the credit of the United States. (3) To regulate commerce with foreign nations, among the states, and with Indian tribes. (4) To create uniform laws for the naturalization of foreigners who want to become citizens, as well as for bankruptcies. (Under the Confederation, states had their own bankruptcy laws.) (5) To coin money, set its value and that of foreign money, and create a standard for weights and measures. (These also varied from state to state during the Confederation.) (6) To punish counterfeiting of U.S. securities (bonds) and money. (7) To set up post offices and postal roads. (Congress passed a law in 1970 making the Post Office Department an independent agency, the United States Postal

President Franklin D. Roosevelt is shown here addressing a joint session of Congress on December 8, 1941. One day earlier, Japanese warplanes had attacked the U.S. Naval Station at Pearl Harbor, Hawaii. Japan followed the attack by declaring war on the United States, and Roosevelt was appearing before legislators to request an official declaration of war, a power the Constitution gives to Congress. The vote in Congress was almost unanimous; only Congresswoman Jeannette Rankin of Montana, a pacifist, voted against the declaration of war. A few days later, after Germany, an ally of Japan, had declared war on the United States, Congress voted a second declaration. The roles were cast for U.S. participation in World War II.

Presidents and visiting foreign dignitaries appear before joint sessions of Congress only rarely. They do so in the House of Representatives, since that chamber is much larger than the Senate and can seat the full Congress. Normally, a president will appear before Congress only to deliver the state of the union message.

Service, rather than an executive department of the government.) (8) To promote progress in science and the arts and to protect authors and inventors by granting them copyrights and patents for their work. (9) To establish federal courts to decide appropriate cases (as determined under Article III), which may be appealed to the Supreme Court. (10) To protect citizens and ships in international waters. (11) To declare war and grant letters of marque and reprisal. (12) To raise and support armies. Appropriations for the Army must be voted on every two years. (This was meant to keep the Army under civilian control.) (13) To create and support a navy. (14) To make rules for the organization and discipline of the land and naval military forces. (The Framers never imagined that the nation would have an air force.) (15) To call out the state militias to enforce the laws of the land, put down rebellions, and defend against foreign invasions. (16) To make arrangements for organizing, arming, and disciplining the militias and for taking charge of them when they are called up for national duty. The states have the right to appoint officers and train the militias, according to rules set by Congress. (The militias are now called the National Guard.) (17) To make laws for the District of Columbia and all other properties owned and operated by the national government, including forts and dockyards. (18) To make all laws considered necessary and proper for carrying out the powers given to Congress by the Constitution. (This "necessary and proper" clause, also known as

the elastic clause, stretches legislative power so that it can be applied to situations and items the Framers never imagined, such as the space program. It gives Congress implied powers.)

Section 9 describes powers denied to Congress, in a list of eight clauses. (1) The lawmakers cannot ban the international slave trade until 1808, but they may tax the importation of slaves. (In 1808, Congress did ban it.) (2) They may not suspend the writ of habeas corpus, except when there is a rebellion or a danger to public safety. (3) They may not punish individuals by passing bills of attainder or ex post facto laws. (The power to punish is a duty of the courts, not Congress.) (4) They may not order a capitation or any other direct tax, unless it is based on the number of people living in each state as calculated by the census. (5) They may not place export taxes on items from any state that are shipped for sale abroad. (This was a part of a compromise on commerce to satisfy the South. The southern economy depended on overseas sales of agricultural products.) (6) They may not pass laws favoring any state over others in commerce, or requiring ships headed for one state to pay duties in another. (7) They may not spend government money without first passing an appropriations bill. (This is a form of checks and balances, because it lets Congress control the funds a president can spend. The Constitution also requires that the public be informed of all government monies raised and spent.) (8) They may not grant titles of nobility or accept any benefits from foreign governments. This is designed to prevent the creation of an American aristocracy and to prevent bribery by other nations.

Section 10 mentions powers denied to the states, in three clauses, to ensure federal control over foreign affairs, war, and trade. (1) The states may not enter into any treaties, alliances, or confederations; grant letters of marque and reprisal; coin money; give credit to borrowers; make anything but gold or silver the legal requirement for paying debts; pass bills of attainder or ex post facto laws; pass laws canceling responsibilities or duties required by contracts; or grant titles of nobility. (2) They may not pass imposts or duties on foreign or locally made goods, except for inspection fees, without the consent of Congress. If monies are collected for these taxes, they must be turned over to the national government, minus expenses. (3) They may not tax ships' tonnage, keep troops or warships in peacetime, enter into any agreement with other states or a foreign nation, or fight a war (unless actually invaded or in immediate danger of an invasion), without the consent of Congress. (Congress has approved interstate agreements such as the Port of New York and New Jersey Authority; the two states share control over area airports, rivers, and harbors.)

Adjournment; Ambassadors; Apportionment; Appropriations; Bankruptcy; Bill; Bill of Attainder; Breach of the Peace; Bribery; Capitation Tax; Census; Checks and Balances; Citizenship; Commerce Clause; Confederation Congress; Congress; Connecticut Compromise; Copyright; Counterfeiting; Debts; Defense; District of Columbia; Duties and Imposts; Elastic Clause; Excise Taxes; Export Taxes; Ex Post Facto Laws; Express Powers; Federal Courts; Felonies; Habeas Corpus, Writ of; House of Representatives; Impeachment; Journals; Letters of Marque and Reprisal; Militia; Patents; Poll Taxes; President; President Pro Tempore of the Senate; Quorum; Resolutions; Senate; Separation of Powers; Slavery; Speaker of the House of Representatives; Supreme Court; Treason; Treaties; U.S. Constitution, Thirteenth Amendment; U.S. Constitution, Fourteenth Amendment; U.S. Constitution, Fifteenth Amendment; U.S. Constitution, Seventeenth Amendment; U.S. Constitution, Twentieth Amendment; U.S. Constitution, Twenty-fourth Amendment; U.S. Constitution, Twenty-sixth Amendment; U.S. Constitution, Twenty-seventh Amendment; Vice President

U.S. Constitution, Article II

The article that establishes the executive branch of the national government and outlines its powers.

Section 1 describes the election, qualifications for office, and payment of the president and the election of the vice president. The president has executive power. The president and the vice president hold office for four years. (The Twenty-second Amendment essentially limits them to two four-year terms.) The original method of electing them required the states to choose members of an electoral college, called presidential electors. Each state had as many electors as it had senators and representatives. Electors met in their own states and cast two ballots for president. One of their votes had to be given to someone living outside the state. (This was meant to encourage the selection of the best people, well known nationwide.) In each state, the electors made up a list of all the candidates receiving their votes. They checked the list, signed it, and sent it to the president of the Senate. That person counted the votes from all the states in front of Congress. The person with a majority of the electors' votes became president, and the first runner-up became vice president.

In the event of a tie for president, the House of Representatives chose the president from among the five candidates who received the highest number of votes in the electoral college, with each state having one vote in the House. (This gave the small states equality with the large states in the choice of a president.) Members from two-thirds of the states had to be present, and a majority of their votes was required for election. If there was a tie for vice president, the Senate chose a vice president from among them. (This whole procedure has been replaced by the Twelfth Amendment.) Article II gives Congress the power to decide when electors should be chosen and the day they must vote.

To be qualified for office, a president must be a natural-born citizen of the United States, at least thirty-five years old, and a resident of the United States for fourteen years. The vice president carries out the duties and powers of the president if the president is removed from office, dies, or is disabled. (The Twenty-fifth Amendment clears up uncertainties about presidential succession by stating that the vice president becomes the president, not a temporary caretaker, when the office of president is vacant. In addition, it describes procedures to be used when a president becomes seriously disabled or when the office of vice president is vacant.) In addition, Congress may pass a law to provide for a situation when both offices of the president and vice president are vacant.

The president receives a salary that may not be increased or decreased during a term of office. The president may not receive any other payments from the government or from the states. Before taking office, the president will swear (the only oath specifically described in the Constitution), "I do solemnly swear (or affirm) that I will faithfully execute the Office of President of the United States, and will to the best of my Ability, preserve, protect, and defend the Constitution of the United States."

Section 2 describes the powers of the president. The president is commander in chief of the Army and Navy, and of the states' militias when they are called up to serve the nation. (The military thus is kept under civilian control.) The president may ask the heads of executive departments for their opinions in writing. (This led to the creation of the cabinet.) The president may grant reprieves and pardons for crimes against the United States, except cases involving impeachment. With the advice and consent of the Senate, the president may make treaties, appoint ambassadors, consuls, justices of the Supreme Court, and other public officials to be established by law. Congress may allow the president to make some appointments alone. When the Senate is not in session, the president may fill vacancies, but the terms of those officials will expire at the end of the next Senate session.

Section 3 takes up the duties of the president. The president shall give Congress information on the state of the nation and recommend laws for it to pass. The president may call special sessions of Congress. If the law-makers disagree about adjournment, the president may set a date for their sessions to end. The president shall receive ambassadors and other public officials and grant commissions to military officers. Finally, the president shall take care that the laws are carried out.

Section 4 concerns removal from office. The president, vice president, and all civilian public officials can be removed from office if they are impeached (or charged) and then convicted of treason, bribery, or other high crimes and misdemeanors, a centuries-old phrase usually taken to mean major abuses of power or violations of public trust in connection with official duties.

Adjournment; Advice and Consent; Ambassadors; Bribery; Cabinet; Checks and Balances; Commander in Chief; Congress; Consuls; Crimes and Misdemeanors; Electoral College; Executive Branch; Executive Departments; House of Representatives; Impeachment; Militia; Oaths of Office; Pardons and Reprieves; President; Presidential Succession; Senate; Supreme Court; Treason; Treaties; U.S. Constitution, Twelfth Amendment; U.S. Constitution, Twenty-second Amendment; U.S. Constitution, Twenty-fifth Amendment; Vice President

U.S. Constitution, Article III

The article that establishes the judicial branch of the national government and outlines its powers.

Section 1 sets up the federal courts. The power to hear and decide certain types of cases is given to a Supreme Court and unspecified lower courts that Congress may create. (Congress has established ninety-one federal district courts to try cases and eleven courts of appeal to review cases from the district courts. It has also set up other special courts, such as the Customs Court.) Judges usually hold office for life, unless they are found guilty of misconduct. (This guarantees that the judiciary will be an independent branch of government.) They are to be paid regularly, and their salaries may not be lowered while they continue to hold office.

Section 2 describes the kinds of cases to be heard in federal courts. Judges may try cases involving the common law, equity, statutes, treaties, or the law of the seas, and cases affecting ambassadors, consuls, and other public officials. It may also decide controversies between two or more states, when the United States is involved, between citizens of different states, between citizens of the same state claiming land granted by different states, between a state and its citizens, and between a state and foreign states or citizens of foreign states. (The Eleventh Amendment took away the federal courts' power to try cases between a state and citizens of another state.) The Supreme Court acts as a trial court in cases concerning ambassadors, consuls, and other government officials and lawsuits involving states. In all other cases, it serves as the nation's highest court of appeals. All crimes, except those with the penalty of impeachment, must be tried by jury. Trials have to be held in the state where the crime was committed or, if not within a state, at a place Congress may decide by law. (The Fifth, Sixth, and Seventh amendments have spelled out in greater detail the rights of people accused of crimes.)

Section 3 concerns treason. The crime of treason is defined as waging war against the United States or siding with the nation's enemies, giving them aid and comfort. People can be convicted of treason only if at least two witnesses testify against them in open court. These witnesses must swear to having seen the suspects commit the same treasonable action. (This is the only crime defined in the Constitution. Because treason is so open to interpretation, the Framers wanted to prevent its being used for political purposes.) Congress has the power to set a punishment for treason, but the penalty may not include corruption of the blood or forfeiture.

Congress; Corruption of the Blood and Forfeiture; Federal Courts; Impeachment; Jury Trial, Right to; Supreme Court; Treason; U.S. Constitution, Fifth Amendment; U.S. Constitution, Sixth Amendment; U.S. Constitution, Seventh Amendment; U.S. Constitution, Eleventh Amendment

U.S. Constitution, Article IV

The article that outlines relations among the states.

Section 1 says each state must give full faith and credit to the official acts of other states. In other words, they must respect each other's laws, court decisions, and records concerning such matters as marriages, divorces, births, deaths, and wills.

Section 2 concerns treatment of citizens. Each state must give citizens from other states the same privileges and immunities it gives to its own citizens. This section does not prevent states from requiring citizens of other states to live within the state for a fixed period of time in order to qualify for driver's licenses, welfare, or voting privileges. Fugitives who have committed treason, felonies, or other crimes must be sent back to the state where the crime was committed if that state's governor demands their return. (On rare occasions, if it is thought that a fugitive will not receive justice, he or she is not sent back.) Fugitive slaves must be returned to their owners. (This was canceled by the Thirteenth Amendment.)

Section 3 deals with admitting new states. Congress may admit states to the Union. No new state can be formed within an existing state or by combining two existing states or parts of states without the approval of Congress and the consent of the state legislatures involved. (Nothing is said about the right of a state to leave the Union.) Congress has the power to control and protect federal territories and lands. (This allows the government to create national parks, for example, and to govern territories.)

Section 4 describes the national government's obligations to states. The states are guaranteed a republican form of government and protection against invasion or domestic violence.

Congress; Domestic Violence; Felonies; Full Faith and Credit; Privileges and Immunities;

Republican Form of Government; Treason; U.S. Constitution, Thirteenth Amendment

U.S. Constitution, Article V

The article that describes the process of amending the Constitution.

To propose an amendment requires a two-thirds vote in both houses of Congress (currently, 290 members of the House of Representatives and 67 senators). Alternatively, two-thirds of the state legislatures (currently, 34 states) may request a special convention to offer amendments. A proposed amendment is ratified when three-fourths of the state legislatures or special conventions held in three-fourths of the states (currently, 38 states) vote their approval.

Amendment Process; Congress; Convention; House of Representatives; Ratification; Senate;

U.S. Constitution, individual amendments

U.S. Constitution, Article VI

The article that establishes the supremacy of the national government over the state governments.

The government agrees to pay all national debts owed under the Articles of Confederation. The Constitution, national laws, and treaties are declared the supreme law of the land. Members of Congress and the state legislatures, national and state public officials, and judges must take an oath to support the Constitution. No religious test, however, shall ever be required in order to hold office.

Articles of Confederation; Debts; Oaths of Office; Religious Tests; Supremacy Clause; Treaties

U.S. Constitution, Article VII

The article that outlines the process for ratifying the Constitution.

The approval of nine of the original thirteen states is sufficient to put the Constitution into effect. (Eleven states ratified the Constitution by 1788. North Carolina did not join the Union until 1789. Rhode Island, which had not sent any delegates to the Constitutional Convention, waited until 1790.)

Constitutional Convention; Ratification

U.S. Constitution, First Amendment (1791)

First Amendment
Congress shall make no law respecting an establishment of religion, or prohibiting the free exercise thereof; or abridging the freedom of speech, or of the press, or the right of the people peaceably to assemble, and to petition the Government for a redress of grievances.

In August 1963, some 250,000 civil-rights protesters gathered in Washington, D.C., between the Washington Monument (visible here) and the Lincoln Memorial. From the memorial, Martin Luther King Jr. delivered his "I Have a Dream" speech.

The amendment guaranteeing these basic liberties: freedom of religion, freedom of speech, freedom of the press, freedom of assembly, and freedom to petition the government to right wrongs.

As colonists, Americans had often been denied these important rights. They made sure that state constitutions protected their basic liberties. In 1787, Antifederalists demanded amendments to guarantee these American freedoms and others in return for their approval of the new Constitution. Modern Americans continue to value their First Amendment freedoms, but they are also concerned about what they consider basic social and economic rights, such as equal pay for equal work. These are not found in the Constitution.

Antifederalists; Assembly, Freedom of; Bill of Rights; Petition the Government for a Redress of Grievances, Right to; Press, Freedom of the; Religion, Freedom of; Speech, Freedom of

Second Amendment
A well regulated Militia, being necessary to the security of a free State,
the right of the people to keep and
bear Arms, shall not be infringed.

U.S. Constitution, Second Amendment (1791)

The amendment establishing the right to bear arms, on the grounds that a well-regulated militia is essential to a state's security.

Colonists had insisted on owning and keeping personal weapons. They considered weapons necessary for hunting food and for defending themselves. Private ownership of arms also allowed them to serve as volunteers in a militia. The militia fought the standing army of professional British soldiers to win independence. After the Revolution, Americans continued to be suspicious of standing armies. They demanded the right to keep their own arms, which they considered necessary to defend themselves from the military power of a tyrannical government.

In modern times, ownership of guns has become controversial. Gun-control groups have formed to oppose private ownership of handguns, known as "Saturday Night Specials," used for crimes. They want stricter laws requiring that guns be registered with the police. They also object to rapid-fire, automatic weapons, which they regard as unnecessary for hunting or self-defense but helpful to criminals. In general, they note that the right to bear arms is linked in this amendment to the phrase "a well regulated Militia," suggesting that some restrictions of purely private ownership are permissible. Other groups, including hunters and people who shoot in competitions as well as many citizens concerned about their ability to defend themselves against criminals, do not want any limitation of what they see as their unrestricted Second Amendment rights.

Arms, Right to Bear; Bill of Rights; Militia

Third Amendment
No Soldier shall, in time of peace be
quartered in any house, without the
consent of the Owner, nor in time of
war, but in a manner to be prescribed
by law.

U.S. Constitution, Third Amendment (1791)

The amendment banning the practice of quartering troops.

Colonists resented the British for forcing them to house soldiers in their homes during peacetime. Their privacy was often disturbed by off-duty, rowdy, drunken Redcoats. The British, however, felt that colonists should contribute to the cost of defending their lands by feeding and housing the troops. The Third Amendment allows soldiers to be quartered in private homes only with the homeowners' consent. In wartime, laws must regulate the housing of troops.

Bill of Rights; Privacy; Quartering of Troops

U.S. Constitution, Fourth Amendment (1791)

The amendment limiting government searches and seizures.

Fourth Amendment
The right of the people to be secure in their persons, houses, papers, and effects, against unreasonable searches and seizures, shall not be violated, and no Warrants shall issue, but upon probable cause, supported by Oath or affirmation, and particularly describing the place to be searched, and the persons or things to be seized.

Colonists had objected to British abuse of general search warrants, called writs of assistance. These allowed officials to ransack colonial homes and businesses at will on the pretext of tracking down smugglers. This amendment protects the privacy of people's homes, possessions, papers, and bodies. Government officials must have permission to enter a home and examine its contents or occupants. They must first convince a judge that a search is necessary. Then the court may issue a warrant, or written permission. It describes in detail where the search will take place and what may be taken away as evidence. In most cases, illegally obtained evidence cannot be used in court. Advances in modern technology, such as telephones and computers, have created new problems in balancing privacy with the need to gather evidence.

Bill of Rights; Privacy; Searches and Seizures

U.S. Constitution, Fifth Amendment (1791)

Fifth Amendment
No person shall be held to answer for a capital, or otherwise infamous crime, unless on a presentment or indictment of a Grand Jury, except in cases arising in the land or naval forces, or in the Militia, when in actual service in time of War or public danger; nor shall any person be subject for the same offence to be twice put in jeopardy of life or limb, nor shall be compelled in any criminal case to be a witness against himself, nor be deprived of life, liberty, or property, without due process of law; nor shall private property be taken for public use, without just compensation.

The amendment outlining the rights of people accused of committing major crimes.

These safeguards were part of the English legal tradition, familiar to American colonists. Unfortunately, the British government did not always grant the colonists their rights as British subjects. The amendment requires that a grand jury must charge individuals with a crime before they can be brought to trial. This ensures that there is sufficient reason to hold suspects under arrest and try them. Further, suspects cannot be subjected to double jeopardy by being tried twice for the same crime. They are protected from self-incrimination, because they cannot be forced to make a confession. Their lives, liberty, or property may not be taken away unless they receive due process, meaning a fair trial. These requirements do not apply to members of the armed services in wartime. In addition, the Fifth Amendment prevents the government from simply taking away private property for public purposes under eminent domain. It requires that property owners be paid a fair price for their land.

Some modern Americans resent all the rights given to people accused of serious crimes. They believe this amendment makes it difficult to convict them. Civil-liberties groups, however, remind Americans that everyone is innocent until proved guilty. They try to make sure that the Fifth Amendment guarantees are enforced.

Bill of Rights; Double Jeopardy; Due Process of Law; Eminent Domain; Grand Jury; Property Rights; Self-Incrimination

Sixth Amendment

In all criminal prosecutions, the accused shall enjoy the right to a speedy and public trial, by an impartial jury of the State and district wherein the crime shall have been committed, which district shall have been previously ascertained by law, and to be informed of the nature and cause of the accusation; to be confronted with the witnesses against him; to have compulsory process for obtaining witnesses in his favor, and to have the Assistance of Counsel for his defense.

U.S. Constitution, Sixth Amendment (1791)

The amendment listing the rights of people brought to trial in criminal cases.

Most of these rights have existed since the 1100s in England, but American colonists were not always treated as British citizens. Often they were tried far from their homes, in Admiralty courts, applying the law of the seas. According to the Sixth Amendment, persons accused of serious crimes have the right to a speedy and public trial. They have to be tried by an impartial jury in a court located near the area where the crime took place. They must be told of the charges brought against them. They also have the right to question witnesses who testify against them. The government must help them compel favorable witnesses to come to court and testify for them. Finally, they have the right to the help of an attorney. Like their colonial ancestors, modern Americans have taken the right to a fair trial very seriously, and the Supreme Court in recent decades has interpreted these rights more broadly; for example, the Court has ruled that if the accused cannot pay for a lawyer, the government must supply one.

Accused, Rights of the; Bill of Rights; Jury Trial, Right to

Seventh Amendment

In Suits at common law, where the value in controversy shall exceed twenty dollars, the right of trial by jury shall be preserved, and no fact tried by a jury, shall be otherwise reexamined in any Court of the United States, than according to the rules of the common law.

U.S. Constitution, Seventh Amendment (1791)

The amendment establishing the right to a jury trial in civil cases where the amount involved exceeds $20.

In lawsuits, colonists preferred to be tried by juries of townspeople rather than judges appointed by British officials. They felt they would receive a fairer hearing. Today, federal courts try only the cases that involve large amounts of money.

Bill of Rights; Common Law; Jury Trial, Right to

Eighth Amendment

Excessive bail shall not be required, nor excessive fines imposed, nor cruel and unusual punishments inflicted.

U.S. Constitution, Eighth Amendment (1791)

The amendment prohibiting very high bail, heavy fines, and cruel and unusual punishments.

As early as the 1200s, the English began to pass laws to prevent courts from imposing unreasonable fees. These laws allowed people to leave jail before their trials or were substituted as punishment for crimes. Cruel and unusual punishments were banned in 1689, but executing, branding, whipping, and disabling people were still permitted. Americans accepted these English penalties. Over time, however, many of these punishments were abandoned as inhumane.

Modern Americans have debated whether the death penalty is a cruel and unusual punishment. In *Furman v. Georgia* (1972), the Supreme Court used the Eighth Amendment for the first time to reject the death penalty. Later, the Court set requirements that must be met in order to sentence a criminal to be executed. Even so, the debate continues whether the death penalty is an appropriate punishment for murder.

Bail; Bill of Rights; Cruel and Unusual Punishment; Death Penalty

U.S. Constitution, Ninth Amendment [1791]

Ninth Amendment

The enumeration in the Constitution, of certain rights, shall not be construed to deny or disparage others retained by the people.

The amendment stating that the rights of the American people are not limited to just the ones specifically mentioned in the Constitution.

The amendment restates a basic belief of the Framers. The national government can exercise only express powers, those listed in the Constitution. Where the Constitution is silent, the national government cannot prevent people from exercising their reserved rights, which are not specifically listed in detail in either the Constitution or the Bill of Rights. Many of the Framers feared that such a list would probably be incomplete, and that any omission might help make the national government too powerful. In modern times, for example, the Supreme Court has sometimes interpreted privacy to be one of these rights.

Bill of Rights; Denied Powers; Express Powers; Privacy; Rights Retained by the People

U.S. Constitution, Tenth Amendment [1791]

Tenth Amendment

The powers not delegated to the United States by the Constitution, nor prohibited by it to the States, are reserved to the States respectively, or to the people.

The amendment reserving unspecified powers and rights to the states and to the people.

The amendment let the states and the people keep all powers other than those granted to the national government in the Constitution, or prohibited to the states by the Constitution. During debates in the Constitutional Convention, in the states during ratification, and in the First Congress, some officials were concerned that the new national government would become too powerful, weaken the states, and oppress the people. The amendment was intended to reassure them that the national government was limited in what it could do and where it could do it.

Nevertheless, the power of the national government gradually expanded, at the expense of the states. For example, during the twentieth century, Congress invaded traditional state functions to set standards for wages and hours of work, clean air, the employment and schooling of minorities, and help for the poor. In the 1980s and 1990s, states began to challenge the national government again and reclaim what they saw as their reserved powers.

Bill of Rights; Constitutional Convention; Elastic Clause; Federal Government; Police Powers; Ratification; Reserved Powers; States; States' Rights

U.S. Constitution, Eleventh Amendment (1798)

Eleventh Amendment
The Judicial power of the United States shall not be construed to extend to any suit in law or equity, commenced or prosecuted against one of the United States by Citizens of another State, or by Citizens or Subjects of any Foreign State.

The amendment limiting lawsuits against states in federal courts.

Lawsuits against one state brought by citizens of another state or by citizens of a foreign nation have to be decided in state courts. The amendment overturns part of Article III, section 2, of the Constitution. Originally, the Supreme Court was given the power to act as a trial court in these lawsuits, to guarantee impartiality. In *Chisholm v. Georgia* (1793), the Supreme Court ruled in favor of two citizens of South Carolina who sued the state of Georgia. They wanted to be paid for supplies sold to the state during the War for Independence. Georgia sent no lawyers to court, because the state felt that in trying the case, the national government was challenging Georgia's sovereign powers. After the Court's decision, five other states were sued by the British and Loyalists (Americans who had sided with the British during the War for Independence) seeking payment for their lands, seized during the Revolution. Favorable decisions would have ruined the states' economies, which were based on land sales. The amendment solved their problems.

By an oversight, this amendment was not declared ratified until 1798, but the required number of states actually approved it by February 1795.

Amendment Process; Civil Law; Federal Courts; Jurisdiction; Ratification; States; Supreme Court; U.S. Constitution, Article III

U.S. Constitution, Twelfth Amendment (1804)

Twelfth Amendment
The Electors shall meet in their respective states, and vote by ballot for President and Vice-President, one of whom, at least, shall not be an inhabitant of the same state with themselves; they shall name in their ballots the person voted for as President, and in distinct ballots the person voted for as Vice-President, and they shall make distinct lists of all persons voted for as President, and of all persons voted for as Vice-President, and of the number of votes for each, which lists they shall

The amendment providing for separate election of the president and the vice president.

The amendment introduces different ballots for the president and vice president. Each has to receive a majority of all electoral votes (currently, at least 270 out of 538) to be elected. If a presidential candidate fails to receive a majority, the House of Representatives decides the election from among the top three vote getters. Members from two-thirds of the states must be present. Each state has one vote, and the candidate who receives a majority wins. The Senate uses the same procedure to elect the vice president, if necessary, with senators choosing between the two top sign and certify, and transmit sealed to the seat of the government of the United States, directed to the President of the Senate; —The President of the Senate shall, in the presence of the Senate and House of Representatives, open all the certificates and the votes shall then be counted; —The person having the greatest number of votes for President, shall be the President, if such number be a majority of the whole number of Electors appointed; and if no person have such majority, then from the persons having the highest numbers not exceeding three on the list of those voted for as President, the House of Representatives shall choose immediately, by ballot, the President. But in choosing the President, the votes shall be taken by states, the representation from each state having one vote; a quorum for this purpose shall consist of a member or members from two-thirds of the states, and a majority of all the states shall be necessary to a choice. And if the House of Representatives shall not choose a President whenever the right of choice shall devolve upon them, before the fourth day of March next following, then the Vice-President shall act as President, as in the case of the death or other constitutional disability of the President. —The person having the greatest number of votes as Vice-President, shall be the Vice-President, if such number be a majority of the whole number of Electors appointed, and if no person have a majority, then from the two highest numbers on the list, the Senate shall choose the Vice-President; a quorum for the purpose shall consist of two-thirds of the whole number of Senators, and a majority of the whole number shall be necessary to a choice. But no person constitutionally ineligible to the office of President shall be eligible to that of Vice-President of the United States.

contenders. If the House cannot choose a president before the new term begins, the vice president temporarily acts as president.

The amendment changes Article II, section 1, of the Constitution. Originally, the runner-up in a presidential election was made vice president. Once political parties developed, this method of electing a president created problems. The election of 1796 resulted in a president from one party, John Adams, a Federalist, and a vice president from another, Thomas Jefferson, a Democratic-Republican. The election of 1800 produced a tie between the Democratic-Republican Party's candidates for president and vice president, Thomas Jefferson and Aaron Burr. As the Constitution required, the House of Representatives had to break the tie. Because of political maneuvering, the members voted thirty-six times before making Jefferson president. Everyone agreed changes were needed.

Americans continue to elect their president and vice president as the Twelfth Amendment requires. There have been many close elections since 1800 that might have resulted in an electoral-vote tie, and whenever a strong third-party candidate has run for president, the possibility exists that no candidate will win a majority of the electoral vote. To date, however, only one presidential election and one for vice president have been decided by Congress under the terms of the Twelfth Amendment. The 1824 election went to the House of Representatives when Andrew Jackson received the most electoral votes, but not a majority. The Twelfth Amendment does not require the House to select the person who came in first, and in fact it gave the presidency to John Quincy Adams, who had come in second, behind Jackson, out of four candidates. (Jackson defeated Adams decisively in the 1828 election and was reelected in 1832.) In 1836, it took the Senate to choose Richard M. Johnson as President Martin Van Buren's vice president, because Johnson, who was Van Buren's running mate in the election, failed to win a majority of the electoral votes for vice president. (Neither presidential candidate in 1876 won a clear majority, but that was because the outcome of the voting in several states was disputed. In this case, Congress ended up creating a special electoral commission of representatives, senators, and Supreme Court justices, which awarded all of the disputed electoral votes to the Republican, Rutherford B. Hayes, giving him a one-vote majority in the electoral college.) Under certain circumstances, the Twenty-fifth Amendment has given Congress additional responsibilities in choosing a vice president.

Electoral College; Popular Vote; President; U.S. Constitution, Twenty-fifth Amendment

Section 1. Neither slavery nor involuntary servitude, except as a punishment for crime whereof the party shall have been duly convicted, shall exist within the United States, or any place subject to their jurisdiction.

Section 2. Congress shall have power to enforce this article by appropriate legislation.

Fourteenth Amendment

Section 1. All persons born or naturalized in the United States and subject to the jurisdiction thereof, are citizens of the United States and of the State wherein they reside. No State shall make or enforce any law which shall abridge the privileges or immunities of citizens of the United States; nor shall any State deprive any person of life, liberty, or property, without due process of law; nor deny to any person within its jurisdiction the equal protection of the laws.

Section 2. Representatives shall be apportioned among the several States according to their respective numbers, counting the whole number of persons in each State, excluding Indians not taxed. But when the right to vote at any election for the choice of electors for President and Vice President of the United States, Representatives in Congress, the Executive and Judicial Officers of a State, or the members of the Legislature thereof, is denied to any of the male inhabitants of such State, being twenty-one years of age, and citizens of the United States, or in any way abridged, except for participation in rebellion, or other crime, the basis of representation therein shall be reduced in the proportion which the number of such male citizens shall bear to the whole number of male citizens twenty-one years of age in such State.

U.S. Constitution, Thirteenth Amendment (1865)

The amendment officially ending slavery, the condition of legal ownership of some people by others, in which the people declared to be slaves can be forced to work against their will and can be bought and sold at any time.

The amendment frees all slaves forever. Slavery was recognized in the Constitution in Article I, section 2, and by the Supreme Court in *Scott v. Sandford* (1857). In the *Scott* case, the Court decided that slaves were legally property and could not file suit in court for their freedom, even if justified. An amendment was needed to change the Constitution and overturn a Court decision. President Abraham Lincoln's 1863 Emancipation Proclamation was not sufficient. It was only a temporary measure and affected only the Confederate states during the Civil War.

Capitation Tax; Extradition; Involuntary Servitude; Slavery; U.S. Constitution, Article I; U.S. Constitution, Fourteenth Amendment; U.S. Constitution, Fifteenth Amendment

U.S. Constitution, Fourteenth Amendment (1868)

The amendment defining national citizenship and describing the rights of citizenship.

American citizens are people who are born in the United States or come from abroad and swear their allegiance to the United States. They are also citizens of the state where they live. States are forbidden to pass or enforce any law that denies American citizens equal privileges and immunities. They must treat citizens from other states and their own citizens in the same way. States may not take away people's lives, liberty, or property without due process of law. They must grant everyone within their borders equal protection of the laws.

The Fourteenth Amendment was intended to remedy the effects of Black Codes, passed in the South, after the Civil War. Under the codes, former slaves could not own guns, vote, serve on juries, or give testimony in court. They could be arrested for staying out past curfews, being absent from work, or loitering. In the 1873 *Slaughter-House Cases*, the Supreme Court ruled that states could not deny people their rights as citizens of the national government. They could, however, determine and limit their rights as state citizens. In other decisions, most notably *Plessy v. Ferguson* (1896), the Court upheld southern laws separating people by race.

In the 1950s, however, the Court reinterpreted the Fourteenth Amendment and moved to end such segregation. *Brown v. the Board of Education of Topeka* (1954), for example, sparked a social movement that

Section 3. No person shall be a Senator or Representative in Congress, or elector of President and Vice President, or hold any office, civil or military, under the United States, or under any State, who, having previously taken an oath, as a member of Congress, or as an officer of the United States, or as a member of any State legislature, or as an executive or judicial officer of any State, to support the Constitution of the United States, shall have engaged in insurrection or rebellion against the same, or given aid or comfort to the enemies thereof. But Congress may by a vote of two-thirds of each House, remove such disability.

Section 4. The validity of the public debt of the United States, authorized by law, including debts incurred for payment of pensions and bounties for services in suppressing insurrection or rebellion, shall not be questioned. But neither the United States nor any State shall assume or pay any debt or obligation incurred in aid of insurrection or rebellion against the United States, or any claim for the loss or emancipation of any slave; but all such debts, obligations and claims shall be held illegal and void.

Section 5. The Congress shall have power to enforce, by appropriate legislation, the provisions of this article.

Fifteenth Amendment

Section 1. The right of citizens of the United States to vote shall not be denied or abridged by the United States or by any State on account of race, color, or previous condition of servitude.

Section 2. The Congress shall have power to enforce this article by appropriate legislation.

eventually resulted in desegregated schools. Gradually, laws treating people differently according to their race, place of birth, or gender began to disappear. In fact, in a wide variety of cases during the twentieth century, the Supreme Court has interpreted the "equal protection" clause of this amendment to apply the Bill of Rights to state laws as well as federal laws. Thus the Court has "incorporated" part of the Bill of Rights into the Fourteenth Amendment.

The amendment also replaces part of Article I, section 2, of the Constitution. This section counted every five slaves as three free people for purposes of representation in Congress and taxation. Instead, former slaves were to be treated as full citizens. A state's representation in Congress would be reduced if freed male slaves age twenty-one or older were denied the right to vote in federal or state elections. This part of the amendment was never enforced. As long as the U.S. Army occupied the South after the Civil War, until 1877 in some cases, soldiers made sure that blacks could take part in elections.

The amendment also disqualifies from public office any Confederate official who had originally sworn to uphold the Constitution. Congress was permitted to remove the penalty. Finally, the amendment states that the United States would pay Union pensions, bonuses, and debts, but it would not pay for Confederate war debts or for freeing slaves. This settlement was accepted by both the North and South.

The amendment was meant to guarantee the rights of a group—black men—long mistreated and excluded from civil life in the United States. However, it also marks the first time that women, both white and black—another group long kept from participating in politics—were specifically denied the right to vote by the wording of the Constitution.

Bill of Rights; Census; Citizenship; Equal Protection of the Laws; Incorporation of the Bill of Rights; Jury Trial, Right to; Segregation and Desegregation; Slavery; Supreme Court; U.S. Constitution, Article I; U.S. Constitution, Thirteenth Amendment; U.S. Constitution, Fifteenth Amendment; Women's Rights

U.S. Constitution, Fifteenth Amendment (1870)

The amendment extending the right to vote to all men, regardless of race.

The amendment prevents the national government or the states from using race, color, or former enslavement to prevent males over age twenty-one from voting. It was intended to make black males full citizens and, incidentally, to help keep the Republican Party in power through

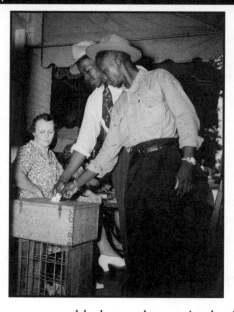

Two African Americans are shown here casting ballots in the Mississippi Democratic Party's primary election in July 1946. Two years earlier, in *Smith v. Allwright* (1944), the Supreme Court had ruled that state parties could not exclude blacks from membership. In many southern states, where the Democratic Party was by far in the majority, the winner of a primary election was assured of winning the general election against a Republican opponent in the fall. (In many places, the Republican Party did not even nominate candidates.) Thus, when state parties excluded blacks, they effectively denied them a voice in the general election. Despite the ruling, a number of states continued to find ways to prevent blacks and poor whites from voting. Sometimes they levied a poll tax, or they might require them to read and "interpret" a passage of the Constitution to the satisfaction of a local election official.

their votes. Never before had the national government exercised power over elections. This was a matter traditionally reserved to the states. Soon after the amendment was passed, however, it was ignored. Southern Democrats returned to power in Congress and took up other matters. When the U.S. Army withdrew from occupation duties in the South in 1877, blacks were kept from voting by state laws, poll taxes, difficult reading tests, and threats of harm. Most northern states did not encourage blacks to take part in elections either. Laws passed almost a hundred years later, in the 1960s, finally guaranteed blacks their voting rights.

Civil Rights; Elections; Poll Taxes; Segregation and Desegregation; Slavery; U.S. Constitution, Thirteenth Amendment; U.S. Constitution, Fourteenth Amendment; Voting Rights

Sixteenth Amendment
The Congress shall have power to lay and collect taxes on incomes, from whatever source derived, without apportionment among the several States, and without regard to any census or enumeration.

U.S. Constitution, Sixteenth Amendment (1913)

The amendment allowing the government to collect an income tax.

This amendment gives Congress the power to tax incomes without regard to population. It changed part of Article I, section 9, of the Constitution, which required that taxes paid by individuals be calculated according to the population in each state. It also overturned a Supreme Court decision.

Traditionally, the government had raised the money it needed from direct taxes, tariffs, and excise taxes. Income taxes were used in 1862 to finance the costs of the Civil War. In 1872, wartime income-tax laws were allowed to expire until 1894, when the Treasury was short of money again. In 1894, people were taxed 2 percent of earnings over $4,000; businesses paid 2 percent of their incomes. In *Pollock v. Farmers' Loan and Trust Co.* (1895), the Supreme Court ruled that an income tax violated the Constitution, because it was based on earnings, not population. With the passage of the amendment, income taxes gradually became a major source of government revenue.

Capitation Tax; Excise Taxes; Income Taxes; Tariffs; Taxation, Power of; U.S. Constitution, Article I

Seventeenth Amendment

The Senate of the United States shall be composed of two Senators from each State, elected by the people thereof, for six years; and each Senator shall have one vote. The electors in each State shall have the qualifications requisite for electors of the most numerous branch of the State legislatures.

When vacancies happen in the representation of any State in the Senate, the executive authority of such State shall issue writs of election to fill such vacancies: Provided, That the legislature of any State may empower the executive thereof to make temporary appointments until the people fill the vacancies by election as the legislature may direct.

This amendment shall not be so construed as to affect the election or term of any Senator chosen before it becomes valid as part of the Constitution.

Eighteenth Amendment

Section 1. After one year from the ratification of this article the manufacture, sale, or transportation of intoxicating liquors within, the importation thereof into, or the exportation thereof from the United States and all territory subject to the jurisdiction thereof for beverage purposes is hereby prohibited.

Section 2. The Congress and the several States shall have concurrent power to enforce this article by appropriate legislation.

Section 3. This article shall be inoperative unless it shall have been ratified as an amendment to the Constitution by the legislatures of the several States, as provided in the Constitution, within seven years from the date of the submission hereof to the States by the Congress.

U.S. Constitution, Seventeenth Amendment (1913)

The amendment providing for the direct election of senators.

Senators are to be elected by the same people who are qualified to vote for the most numerous branch of the state legislature. Each state still has two senators, each serving a six-year term. Vacancies are filled by new elections. State legislatures may permit the governor to make a temporary appointment until an election is held.

The amendment changed Article I, section 3, of the Constitution, which gave state legislatures the power to choose senators. After the Civil War, large corporations bribed state lawmakers to get them to elect senators favorable to business interests. The amendment was designed to remedy corruption and make senatorial elections more democratic. Today, the costs of campaigning are so high that candidates again need personal wealth or rich supporters to run for the Senate.

Elections; Legislative Branch; Popular Vote; Senate; States; U.S. Constitution, Article I

U.S. Constitution, Eighteenth Amendment (1919)

The amendment prohibiting the sale of alcoholic drinks.

One year after ratification, the manufacture, sale, and transportation of alcoholic beverages became illegal. Congress and the states shared the power of enforcing the amendment. This was the first and only time that a change was made in the Constitution to regulate people's private conduct. This was also the first time that an amendment included a seven-year time limit for approval.

The Anti-Saloon League and the Women's Christian Temperance Union had long crusaded for a nationwide ban on alcohol. Maine had adopted a prohibition law in 1851. By 1917, when the United States entered World War I, twenty-six more states had followed Maine's example. During wartime, the grain and sugar used to produce liquor were needed to feed soldiers and civilians.

Prohibition gained support because it was basically an antiurban, antiforeigner, antiworker, anti-Catholic movement at a time when anti-immigrant sentiment ran high. Members of the movement believed that immigrant workers in eastern industrial cities got drunk and neglected their responsibilities. Prohibitionists wanted to restore what they saw as traditional American values. However, Prohibition quickly became both unpopular and unsuccessful.

Amendment Process; Imports; Prohibition; U.S Constitution, Twenty-first Amendment

Nineteenth Amendment

The right of citizens of the United States to vote shall not be denied or abridged by the United States or by any State on account of sex.

Congress shall have power to enforce this article by appropriate legislation.

Twentieth Amendment

Section 1. The terms of the President and Vice President shall end at noon on the 20th day of January, and the terms of Senators and Representatives at noon on the 3d day of January, of the years in which such terms would have ended if this article had not been ratified; and the terms of their successors shall then begin.

Section 2. The Congress shall assemble at least once in every year, and such meeting shall begin at noon on the 3d day of January, unless they shall by law appoint a different day.

Section 3. If, at the time fixed for the beginning of the term of the President, the President elect shall have died, the Vice President elect shall become President. If a President shall not have been chosen before the time fixed for the beginning of his term, or if the President elect shall have failed to qualify, then the Vice President elect shall act as President until a President shall have qualified; and the Congress may by law provide for the case wherein neither a President elect nor a Vice President elect shall have qualified, declaring who shall then act as President, or the manner in which one who is to act shall be selected, and such person shall act accordingly until a President or Vice President shall have qualified.

Section 4. The Congress may by law provide for the case of the death of any

Twentieth Amendment is continued on the next page

U.S. Constitution, Nineteenth Amendment (1920)

The amendment allowing women to vote.

The amendment gives females the right to vote in both state and national elections and lets Congress pass whatever laws are needed to put it into effect. It also overturned a Supreme Court decision. Women had long demanded legal and political rights. In 1869, Wyoming and Utah became the first U.S. territories to give women political equality. Following their lead, the first states to do so were all in the West—Wyoming (as a state in 1890), Colorado (1893), and Utah (as a state) and Idaho (both in 1896). By then, however, in *Minor v. Happersett* (1875), the Supreme Court had ruled that women were not denied their rights as citizens simply because they could not vote. By 1897, twenty-seven states permitted women to vote in some elections, but the remaining states were under no obligation to do so. For decades, women continued to demonstrate and protest for an amendment to secure voting rights nationwide. They made such valuable contributions on the home front during World War I (1917–1918) that they could no longer be denied the amendment they wanted.

Elections; Equal Rights Amendment; States; Supreme Court; Territories; U.S. Constitution, Fifteenth Amendment; Voting Rights; Women's Rights

U.S. Constitution, Twentieth Amendment (1933)

The amendment shortening the time between Election Day and the beginning of the new Congress and presidential administration.

The amendment sets January 3 as the day each new Congress will meet and January 20 as the day an incoming president and vice president will be sworn in. It replaces part of Article I, section 4, of the Constitution. Originally, a Congress elected in November of an even-numbered year did not necessarily meet until thirteen months later. Presidents elected in November had to wait until March to take office. Meanwhile, defeated members of Congress and an outgoing president went on serving for months, passing laws and appointing people to office. They were compared to lame ducks whose wings had been clipped. This is why the Twentieth Amendment is known as the "Lame Duck Amendment."

The amendment also provides for presidential succession. If an incoming president dies before he can take office, the vice president becomes president. If a president does not qualify for office in time, the vice president acts as president until the president can take over. (This can happen if a president fails to get a majority of the votes in the electoral college,

In this photograph, President Gerald R. Ford addresses a new session of Congress in January 1977. Ford, who had lost the 1976 presidential election, was a lame duck, with just two weeks remaining in office.

Twentieth Amendment continued

of the persons from whom the House of Representatives may choose a President whenever the right of choice shall have devolved upon them, and for the case of the death of any of the persons from whom the Senate may choose a Vice President whenever the right of choice shall have devolved upon them.

Section 5. Sections 1 and 2 shall take effect on the 15th day of October following the ratification of this article.

Section 6. This article shall be inoperative unless it shall have been ratified as an amendment to the Constitution by the legislatures of three-fourths of the several States within seven years from the date of its submission.

Twenty-first Amendment

Section 1. The eighteenth article of amendment to the Constitution of the United States is hereby repealed.

Section 2. The transportation or importation into any State, Territory, or Possession of the United States for delivery or use therein of intoxicating liquors, in violation of the laws thereof, is hereby prohibited.

Section 3. This article shall be inoperative unless it shall have been ratified as an amendment to the Constitution by conventions in the several States, as provided in the Constitution, within seven years from the date of the submission hereof to the States by the Congress.

and the House of Representatives has difficulty choosing a winner.) If neither the new president nor the vice president qualifies, Congress may pass a law to solve the problem. Finally, if the House has to choose a president or the Senate must vote in a vice president, and the candidate then dies, Congress must find a replacement.

Congress; Elections; Electoral College; House of Representatives; Lame Ducks; President;

Presidential Succession; Senate; U.S. Constitution, Article I; Vice President

U.S. Constitution, Twenty-first Amendment (1933)

The amendment repealing Prohibition.

This amendment repealed, or canceled, the Eighteenth Amendment. Once again, people could legally manufacture, sell, and transport alcoholic beverages. However, states could still enforce their own prohibition laws. (Kansas, Mississippi, and Oklahoma chose to continue the ban.)

Congress realized that Prohibition was a failure. During the 1920s, the Eighteenth Amendment had turned many otherwise honest, hardworking Americans into criminals. They were willing to make their own liquor or to deal with mobsters and smugglers to get it. Notorious gangsters, such as Chicago's Al Capone, controlled the illegal-liquor business, killing off their competitors. They also ran private nightclubs where people could buy alcoholic drinks, often served in teacups.

By the 1930s, Congress had another reason to repeal Prohibition. The American economy had suffered a severe collapse, known as the Great Depression. Businesses closed, and many Americans lost their jobs. If the lawmakers allowed the liquor industry to start up again, more people could be put to work. They sent the Twenty-first Amendment to the states and required them to hold special conventions to approve repeal. They chose this method of ratification because Prohibition supporters were still in control of some state legislatures. It was the only time conventions were held to ratify an amendment.

Amendment Process; Convention; Prohibition; U.S. Constitution, Eighteenth Amendment

Twenty-second Amendment

Section 1. No person shall be elected to the office of the President more than twice, and no person who has held the office of President, or acted as President, for more than two years of a term to which some other person was elected President shall be elected to the office of President more than once. But this Article shall not apply to any person holding the office of President when this Article was proposed by the Congress, and shall not prevent any person who may be holding the office of President, or acting as President, during the term within which this Article becomes operative from holding the office of President or acting as President during the remainder of such term.

Section 2. This article shall be inoperative unless it shall have been ratified as an amendment to the Constitution by the legislatures of three-fourths of the several States within seven years from the date of its submission to the States by the Congress.

U.S. Constitution, Twenty-second Amendment (1951)

The amendment setting term limits for presidents.

The amendment restricts a president to two terms in office. It also specifies that a vice president who succeeds to the presidency and serves as president for more than two years of a predecessor's term (that is, more than one-half of a term) may serve only one full term in addition to the incomplete term. An exception was made for the president at the time, Harry S. Truman, who had served out nearly all of the late President Franklin D. Roosevelt's fourth term before being elected to a full term in 1948. Roosevelt had died in office in April 1945, less than three months after beginning his fourth term.

The Constitution does not state how many terms a president may serve. Alexander Hamilton, one of the Framers of the Constitution, had wanted the president to serve for life. Most other Framers feared that a president who served too long could have too much power, like a monarch. In fact, American presidents followed George Washington's example as the first president and did not seek reelection after two terms in office. This became an established American tradition (but not the law) until Roosevelt, a Democrat, decided to run for a third term in 1940, with the Great Depression not completely over and World War II already under way in Europe and Asia. In 1947, when members of the Republican Party won a majority of seats in Congress, they decided to make the tradition a part of the Constitution. Despite objections from Democrats, they succeeded.

Congress; Elections; Framers; Parties, Political; President; Term Limits; Vice President

Twenty-third Amendment

Section 1. The District constituting the seat of Government of the United States shall appoint in such manner as the Congress may direct:

A number of electors of President and Vice President equal to the whole number of Senators and Representatives in Congress to which the District would be entitled if it were a State, but in no event more than the least populous State; they shall be in addition to those appointed by the States, but they shall be considered, for the purposes of the election of President and Vice President, to be electors appointed by

U.S. Constitution, Twenty-third Amendment (1961)

The amendment letting residents of the District of Columbia vote in presidential elections if otherwise qualified to vote.

Residents of the District of Columbia may choose as many members of the electoral college as the least populated state in the nation, meaning three. (This way the district does not have more power than a state in choosing the president. If an election must be decided by the House of Representatives, however, the district cannot take part, because it has no voting representatives in Congress.)

Previously, only citizens living in states could vote. The Framers of the Constitution had not expected most people to live in the District of Columbia full-time. Government officials would come to Washington, D.C., for a few months to conduct their business and then return to their a State; and they shall meet in the District and perform such duties as provided by the twelfth article of amendment.

Section 2. The Congress shall have power to enforce this article by appropriate legislation.

home states. However, during the twentieth century, the permanent population grew. The number of federal programs and projects greatly increased, and government workers began to live in the district year-round. So did the people who supplied them with food, products, and services. By the 1960s, the population of the district was 750,000. While they lived in the nation's capital, they could not vote. The Twenty-third amendment remedied this injustice.

Congress; District of Columbia; Elections; Electoral College; Federal Government; House of Representatives; President; Voting Rights

Twenty-fourth Amendment

Section 1. The right of citizens of the United States to vote in any primary or other election for President or Vice President, for electors for President or Vice President, or for Senator or Representative in Congress, shall not be denied or abridged by the United States or any State by reason of failure to pay any poll tax or other tax.

Section 2. The Congress shall have power to enforce this article by appropriate legislation.

U.S. Constitution, Twenty-fourth Amendment (1964)

The amendment banning poll taxes.

The national government and the states may not deny citizens the right to vote in national elections because they failed to pay poll taxes or any other taxes. Congress can pass laws to enforce this amendment. In the early days of the American republic, paying poll taxes demonstrated that citizens were financially independent and that they were solid members of their communities. Their votes were less likely to be bought by office seekers. Their judgments were less likely to be affected by their emotions. In the South, after the Civil War, these taxes were used to prevent poor whites and blacks from voting. By 1962, when Congress passed the amendment, only five states still had poll taxes. Ratification took place during the civil-rights movement of the 1960s, which made blacks full American citizens.

Capitation Tax; Citizenship; Civil Rights; Congress; Elections; Poll Taxes; Ratification; Segregation and Desegregation; States

Twenty-fifth Amendment

Section 1. In case of the removal of the President from office or of his death or resignation, the Vice President shall become President.

Section 2. Whenever there is a vacancy in the office of the Vice President, the President shall nominate a Vice President who shall take office upon confirmation by a majority vote of both Houses of Congress.

Section 3. Whenever the President transmits to the President pro tempore of the Senate and the Speaker of the

U.S. Constitution, Twenty-fifth Amendment (1967)

The amendment making arrangements to replace a disabled president temporarily and to fill vacancies in the office of president and vice president.

If a president dies or resigns from office, the vice president becomes president. If the office of vice president is vacant, the president selects a new vice president, to be approved a majority vote in Congress. The vice president serves as acting president when the president sends Congress a letter stating inability to fulfill presidential duties. When the president is ready to take charge again, Congress must be notified. The vice president can also become acting president if the president is disabled and fails to inform Congress. In that case, the vice president and a majority of the cabinet, or some other group that Congress chooses, have to send

House of Representatives his written declaration that he is unable to discharge the powers and duties of his office, and until he transmits to them a written declaration to the contrary, such powers and duties shall be discharged by the Vice President as Acting President.

Section 4. Whenever the Vice President and a majority of either the principal officers of the executive departments or of such other body as Congress may by law provide, transmit to the President pro tempore of the Senate and the Speaker of the House of Representatives their written declaration that the President is unable to discharge the powers and duties of his office, the Vice President shall immediately assume the powers and duties of the office as Acting President.

Thereafter, when the President transmits to the President pro tempore of the Senate and the Speaker of the House of Representatives his written declaration that no inability exists, he shall resume the powers and duties of his office unless the Vice President and a majority of either the principal officers of the executive department or of such other body as Congress may by law provide, transmit within four days to the President pro tempore of the Senate and the Speaker of the House of Representatives their written declaration that the President is unable to discharge the powers and duties of his office. Thereupon Congress shall decide the issue, assembling within forty-eight hours for that purpose if not in session. If the Congress, within twenty-one days after receipt of the latter written declaration, or, if Congress is not in session, within twenty-one days after Congress is required to assemble, determines by two-thirds vote of both Houses that the President is unable to discharge the powers and duties of his office, the Vice President shall continue to discharge the

Congress a letter stating that the president is not able to carry out official responsibilities. To resume official duties, the president must inform Congress that the disability has ended. If necessary, the vice president and a majority of the cabinet, or some other group that Congress may select, have four days to challenge the president's judgment. Then Congress decides the issue.

This amendment removes uncertainties in Article II, section 1, of the Constitution about the vice president's right to become president upon the death of a president. When President William Henry Harrison died in 1841, his successor, John Tyler, started the tradition that a vice president was sworn in as president. The Constitution was not clear about this. It could be argued that the vice president was to serve only until a new president could be elected. Nevertheless, other vice presidents who became president were not treated as temporary substitutes. This tradition finally became a part of the Constitution.

The amendment also eliminates an omission in the Constitution concerning vice-presidential vacancies. Between 1812 and 1963, seven vice presidents died in office, one resigned, and eight succeeded to the presidency (because of the death of the president) without having a new vice president selected. In 1963, when Vice President Lyndon B. Johnson became president after President John F. Kennedy was assassinated, he was worried because he had had a heart attack and his possible successor, the Speaker of the House, was old. Johnson pressed Congress for an amendment on vice-presidential replacements. The new procedure was first applied in 1973. Vice President Spiro Agnew resigned following criminal charges against him, and Gerald R. Ford replaced him. Then, in 1974, when President Richard M. Nixon resigned in the face of apparently certain impeachment and conviction in the Watergate scandal, Ford became president and named Nelson A. Rockefeller as his vice president. Neither Ford nor Rockefeller was elected by the American people.

Finally, the amendment solves the problem of presidential disability. Article II, section 1, of the Constitution does not state whether a president can return to office after leaving because of a disability. So a number of presidents carried out their duties despite serious illnesses. In 1919, President Woodrow Wilson suffered a disabling stroke. His doctors concealed the serious nature of his illness from officials and from the public. His wife, Edith, secretly ran the government in his name, and the vice president took over the president's social duties.

same as Acting President; otherwise, the President shall resume the powers and duties of his office.

In the 1950s, President Dwight D. Eisenhower remembered Wilson's example when he had a heart attack and other illnesses. He exchanged letters with his vice president outlining the emergency procedures they would take to keep the government running. In the 1960s, under President Johnson's prodding, Congress and the states finally approved a method for handling presidential disability. The disability provisions of the Twenty-fifth Amendment were used for the first time in the 1980s when President Ronald Reagan had cancer surgery and Vice President George Bush temporarily assumed the duties of president.

Congress; President; Presidential Disability; Presidential Succession; Speaker of the House of Representatives; U.S. Constitution, Article II; Vice President

U.S. Constitution, Twenty-sixth Amendment (1971)

Twenty-sixth Amendment

Section 1. The right of citizens of the United States, who are eighteen years of age or older, to vote shall not be denied or abridged by the United States or by any State on account of age.

Section 2. The Congress shall have power to enforce this article by appropriate legislation.

The amendment giving voting rights to young adults.

The amendment lets people who are at least eighteen years old take part in national and state elections. Congress can pass laws to enforce this amendment. During the 1960s, young people were active members of the civil-rights movement to grant equality to blacks. In the late 1960s and early 1970s, they demonstrated against being drafted to fight in the Vietnam War. They also argued that if they were old enough to die in a war, they were old enough to vote for the people who could send them off to war. With many reform-minded politicians having been elected in 1968, Congress reduced the voting age from twenty-one to eighteen by passing the Voting Rights Act of 1970, affecting about 11 million people. In *Oregon v. Mitchell* (1970), however, the Supreme Court decided that

Nineteen-year-old Karen Rogers is pictured here voting in the 1972 Illinois primary election. The nationwide congressional and presidential elections that year were the first after ratification of the Twenty-sixth Amendment extended voting rights to eighteen-, nineteen-, and twenty-year-olds. Rogers is about to pull the lever that will close the voting-booth curtain, thus giving her the opportunity to cast her ballot away from public scrutiny.

Congress had no power to change state and local election laws. Some states had already let older teenagers vote, but they set differing age requirements. A constitutional amendment was needed to give uniform voting rights to younger Americans nationwide. The states approved it only about three months after Congress proposed it. This was the fastest ratification any amendment ever received.

Amendment Process; Congress; Elections; Ratification; States; Supreme Court; Voting Rights

Twenty-seventh Amendment
No law, varying the compensation for the services of the Senators and Representatives, shall take effect, until an election of Representatives shall have intervened.

U.S. Constitution, Twenty-seventh Amendment (1992)

The amendment limiting pay raises for members of Congress.

Salary increases for senators and representatives go into effect only after the next congressional election has taken place. This amendment was first proposed by James Madison in 1789, but by 1791 only six states had approved it. No more ratifications took place until Ohio accepted it in 1873. The amendment surfaced again in the late 1970s and 1980s, when Wyoming, Maine, and Colorado ratified it after objecting to a wave of recent congressional pay increases. Members of Congress raised their salaries by unrecorded votes so the people back home would not know how their representatives and senators voted. Anger at Congress mounted, and other states rushed to approve the amendment. Their ratifications were valid because no time limit had been set. It had taken two hundred years, but Madison's amendment was finally added to the Constitution.

Amendment Process; Amendments, Unratified; Compensation; Congress; Elections; Ratification

V

Veto

The power to reject or turn down proposed legislation.

Article I, section 7, of the Constitution gives the president the right to decide whether to sign a bill passed by Congress into law. A veto occurs when the president refuses to sign a bill and sends it back to the lawmakers with his objections. If the legislative branch is still meeting, two-thirds of the members of each house may pass the bill again. It then becomes law. This is called *overriding a veto*. If Congress sends a bill to the president and adjourns within ten days (not counting Sundays), and the president does not sign it, it does not become law. This is known as a *pocket veto*, because the president has figuratively put the bill in a pocket and "forgotten" it. (A president might do this to avoid vetoing a bill, perhaps because doing so would attract bad media attention or anger important legislators.) If, however, Congress sends the president a bill and the president does not sign it or return it within ten days while Congress remains in session, the bill becomes law. (A president might let this happen to avoid signing a bill opposed by the administration but so popular in Congress that a veto would be overridden.) The following presidents vetoed the most bills: Franklin D. Roosevelt, 635 vetoes in just over twelve years; Grover Cleveland, 584 in eight years; Harry S. Truman, 250 in almost eight years; and Dwight D. Eisenhower, 181 in eight years.

Like many other parts of the Constitution, the presidential veto was the result of a compromise. During the Constitutional Convention, the Framers debated who should exercise this power. Most Framers were determined to place limits on the legislature. Despite the listing of express powers, they truly feared that a House of Representatives elected by ordinary citizens might act against the interests of the better-informed and wealthy classes. So they were determined to thwart the will of the people, if necessary. They hoped the presidential veto would accomplish this.

Under the Virginia Plan, the president and a council of judges could accept or reject laws passed by Congress. James Madison, George Mason, James Wilson, and Gouverneur Morris supported the proposal. Elbridge Gerry, Nathaniel Gorham, Alexander Martin, Caleb Strong, and John Rutledge opposed it. They argued that it violated the separation of powers.

Wilson later suggested that the president alone be given the right to reject acts of Congress. Alexander Hamilton and Rufus King supported Wilson, but the idea was widely criticized. For example, Pierce Butler and Benjamin Franklin felt that the plan was too monarchical. Mason feared that the president would refuse to consent to much-needed laws until Congress approved his appointees to office. Like the British, American politicians might have to resort to bribery and corruption to get things done. Gunning Bedford Jr. opposed all plans for a veto. He believed that each branch of government should simply do its job; the president should not be able to challenge laws passed by the House of Representatives, because the people knew best what they wanted. Finally, Morris proposed that a presidential veto be overridden by a two-thirds vote of each house of Congress. Daniel Carroll, James Wilson, and Hugh Williamson helped convince the other delegates to accept this arrangement.

This cartoon ridicules President Andrew Jackson, who is portrayed as trampling the Constitution and assuming the powers of a monarch. Critics of Jackson took this view in part because of his 1832 veto of a bill to recharter the Second Bank of the United States. Jackson regarded the bank as unconstitutional. He also had a unique view of the balance of power among the three branches of government, seeing each branch as its own judge of the Constitution and the laws. In his veto message to Congress on the bank bill, he wrote, "The Congress, the Executive, and the Court must each for itself be guided by its own opinion of the Constitution. Each public officer who takes an oath to support the Constitution swears that he will support it as he understands it, and not as it is understood by others."

Two hundred years later, Americans debated presidential-veto procedures once again. In 1996, Congress passed the Line Item Veto Act, to take effect in 1997. According to Article I, section 7, a veto applied to an entire bill. The new law allowed the president to strike out specific spending items and tax breaks from a bill while letting the rest of the bill become law. To satisfy the people who elected them, members of Congress often added expensive local projects to the laws they were writing. The president was supposed to be able to use the line-item veto to eliminate such wasteful spending. However, Congress could then pass the canceled sections again as separate bills. If the president vetoed them again, Congress could override that veto by a two-thirds majority vote.

President Bill Clinton used the line-item veto to delete eighty-two individual items from eleven separate laws, including a tax break for New York City hospitals. Lawyers for New York City brought a lawsuit, challenging the new law. After a lower court ruled against him, the president appealed to the Supreme Court. In *Clinton v. City of New York* (1998), the Court struck down the line-item veto. It ruled that the new law violated the specific procedures for passing bills outlined in Article I, section 7. These procedures could be changed only by an amendment. Many state governors already have line-item vetoes. They were written into state constitutions.

Adjournment; Appointment to Office; Bill; Checks and Balances; Congress; Constitutional Convention; Delegates; Executive Branch; Express Powers; Framers; House of Representatives; Law; Legislative Branch; President; Separation of Powers; Supreme Court; U.S. Constitution, Article I; Virginia Plan

Vice President

The government official whose constitutional duty, mentioned in Article I, section 3, of the Constitution, is to preside over the Senate and cast the deciding vote when ties occur.

According to Article II, section 1, the vice president is to assume "the powers and duties" of the office of president if the president dies in office or is unable to carry out his duties. The Twenty-fifth Amendment clarifies this by saying that in the event of the removal, death, or resignation of the president, the vice president "shall become president." That is, the vice president does not merely carry out the duties of the office of president but becomes president.

The Framers had not originally planned to have a vice president. When Alexander Hamilton addressed the Constitutional Convention in June

1787, he proposed that a vice president be chosen to preside over the Senate. This suggestion was ignored. Finally, the Committee on Postponed Matters used the idea of a vice president to solve a problem about electing the president. They created an electoral college and required each elector to cast two ballots for president, with each vote going to a candidate from a different state. To make the second vote important, the runner-up in the election would become vice president.

During debates on this proposal, Nathaniel Gorham complained that the vice president might be a "very obscure" person with few votes. Hugh Williamson objected that the position was unnecessary. George Mason argued that the vice presidency would be dangerous because it would combine powers of both the executive branch and the legislative branch (because of the vice president's role as president of the Senate). Nevertheless, the office was created.

Amendments to the Constitution have changed the way vice presidents are chosen and have given them more duties. The Twelfth Amendment separated the election of the president and vice president. Since it was passed in 1804, electors in the electoral college have cast one ballot for president and a separate one for vice president. This way, there is no confusion over which candidate they prefer for which position.

Under the Twentieth Amendment, the date the president and vice president take their oaths of office was moved from March 4 to January 20. If the president-elect, the person elected president in November, dies before taking office, the vice president–elect becomes president in January.

The Twenty-fifth Amendment gave the vice president a new responsibility. Along with the heads of the executive departments, the vice president is to inform Congress whenever a president is unfit to carry out the duties of the office of president. While the president is disabled, the vice president is to serve as acting president. The vice president and the cabinet also have a role to play in the event they disagree with the president about the nature or length of the disability.

The Constitution did not provide for replacing the vice president in case the office was vacated by death, resignation, or impeachment. Many times in American history the office of vice president has been vacant. In some cases, the vice president was elevated to the office of president. In other cases, a vice president died or resigned. In addition to providing for the succession or temporary replacement of the president, the Twenty-fifth Amendment gave the president power to name a new vice president if the office of vice president is vacant. A majority in Congress has to approve the choice. In the 1970s, through this method, Gerald R. Ford and Nelson A. Rockefeller became the nation's only unelected vice presidents.

Only ten vice presidents out of the forty-five who have held the office served a second term. Eight vice presidents—John Tyler, Millard Fillmore, Andrew Johnson, Chester A. Arthur, Theodore Roosevelt, Calvin Coolidge, Harry S. Truman, and Lyndon B. Johnson—became president because the president died. Four of them were later elected to their own terms as president. One vice president—Gerald R. Ford—became president when a president resigned. Throughout the 1800s and 1900s, only one woman, Representative Geraldine Ferarro of New York, was nominated for vice president by a major political party.

Apart from their few constitutional duties, vice presidents often did not have much to do until the late twentieth century. There were some exceptions, but most vice presidents did not play a role in the decisions of presidents and their cabinets. Finally, in the late 1970s, they were sent on more diplomatic missions abroad, began taking part in cabinet meetings and serving on the National Security Council, and chaired important committees. In the 1970s, President Jimmy Carter and Vice President Walter F. Mondale developed an especially close working relationship, as did President Bill Clinton and Vice President Al Gore in the 1990s.

Cabinet; Congress; Constitutional Convention; Electoral College; Executive Branch; Executive Departments; Framers; House of Representatives; Impeachment; Legislative Branch; Oaths of Office; Parties, Political; President; Presidential Succession; Senate; Separation of Powers; States; U.S. Constitution, Article I; U.S. Constitution, Article II; U.S. Constitution, Twelfth Amendment; U.S. Constitution, Twentieth Amendment; U.S. Constitution, Twenty-fifth Amendment

Virginia Plan

A draft proposal to correct the defects of the Articles of Confederation.

The fifteen planks of the Virginia Plan were drawn up by James Madison and presented to the Constitutional Convention by Edmund Randolph. They provided the delegates with a number of recommendations to discuss and debate when the convention first met. On the whole, the plan represented the interests of the large states. This led the small states to develop their own ideas in the New Jersey Plan. The Connecticut Compromise worked out an arrangement satisfactory to both.

The Virginia Plan called for a two-chamber legislature chosen on the basis of wealth and state population. Members of the lower house were to be elected by the people and to be paid for their service. They could not be reelected for a period of years. During their term in Congress, they could not hold any other public office. The upper house was to be elected by the lower house. Its members were to be subject to the same restrictions as the lower house. Each house could pass laws for the whole nation. The national legislature could also veto acts of state legislatures if these violated the agreement that created the Union. If states failed to fulfill their duties to the Union, the legislature could use force against them.

The Virginia Plan also created an executive and a judicial branch. The executive was to be chosen by the legislature and was ineligible for a second term. The legislature would put national laws into effect. The executive and judges from the national courts would serve as a "council of revision." They could examine every act of national and state legislatures and veto laws. The legislatures could override the veto. A judicial branch would be set up, with judges serving for life. (The pay of judges and the executive could not be changed during their service.) The national legislature would set up trial courts and a supreme court to hear appeals.

The Virginia Plan also included proposals concerning the states. New states were to be admitted by the national legislature. The national government would guarantee each state a republican form of government. It would also guarantee each state's existing boundaries.

The remainder of the plan proposed that the Confederation Congress would stay in power until the new agreement took effect. It also provided a procedure for ratification. The Confederation Congress had to approve the agreement and then submit it to assemblies of representatives recommended by state legislatures and chosen for that purpose by the people. The plan also provided that the new national legislature would not have to consent to amendments. In addition, it required all officials of the national government to take an oath to support the agreement.

Articles of Confederation; Bicameral Legislature; Confederation Congress; Congress; Connecticut Compromise; Constitutional Convention; Delegates; Executive Branch; Law; Legislative Branch; New Jersey Plan; Ratification; Republican Form of Government; Supreme Court; Veto

Virginia Statute for Religious Freedom

A law giving Virginians the right to worship as they chose and barring the state from setting up an official religion or religious tests for officeholders.

Passed in 1786, it was originally drafted by Thomas Jefferson in 1777. He was influenced by the writings of the English political philosopher

George Mason could not bear politicians or committee work. So in 1775, when George Washington was made commander in chief of the Continental Army, Mason only reluctantly replaced his friend in the Virginia constitutional convention. He then made a lasting impact on American history by writing most of the Virginia Constitution of 1776. It contained his Declaration of Rights, which became a model for the Declaration of Independence, for states' bills of rights, and for the nation's Bill of Rights.

Sixty-two years old when he came to the Constitutional Convention, Mason wanted a stronger national government, but he did not want it to be a democracy. He feared that majorities would oppress minorities. Yet he defended the people's right to choose at least one house of Congress. He was very disappointed with the delegates' compromises on slavery. Mason wanted to end the slave trade—even though he had more than 300 slaves.

Toward the end of the Convention, Mason asked the delegates to include a bill of rights, but he was turned down. He wholeheartedly supported Edmund Randolph's proposal to allow state ratifying conventions to add amendments to the Constitution. When that measure was defeated as well, Mason refused to sign the document and became a leading Antifederalist.

John Locke. In matters of religion, Jefferson argued, the state had no right to make regulations. The people's right to freedom of conscience could never be surrendered to a government. James Madison was responsible for getting the Virginia legislature to pass the statute. It was a model for the First Amendment's guarantee of freedom of religion.

Religion, Freedom of; Religious Tests; Second Treatise on Government; *U.S. Constitution, First Amendment*

Voting Rights

The freedom to elect officeholders.

At the Constitutional Convention, the delegates had to decide who was qualified to vote for members of the House of Representatives. (The people would elect the Senate and the president indirectly through the states.) The Committee of Detail recommended that the people eligible to vote for the most numerous branch in state legislatures should vote for representatives to Congress. When the committee's report was debated, James Madison, Gouverneur Morris, and John Dickinson wanted to limit the vote to property owners. Morris feared that people without property would simply sell their votes to the rich. Madison feared that those people would outnumber property owners and combine against them. He believed that ownership of land was the best protection of liberty.

George Mason, Oliver Ellsworth, Nathaniel Gorham, John Rutledge, Pierce Butler, and Benjamin Franklin were among those who supported the committee's report. Mason argued that every man with an interest in society should be able to take part in elections. These people included merchants, parents of children, and monied men as well as property owners. Ellsworth added that everyone who paid a tax should be allowed to vote for the officials who would collect and spend his money. Franklin reminded the delegates that Britain had limited the right to vote and then oppressed nonvoters. This made them less patriotic. Ellsworth also offered a practical argument. Since many of the states already allowed people without property to vote, these citizens would be reluctant to ratify a constitution that excluded them from elections. The report of the Committee of Detail was accepted, and Article I, section 2, of the Constitution left voting qualifications to the states.

When the Constitution was ratified, voting was restricted to males. In many states there were some property qualifications until the 1830s. Amendments to the Constitution gradually extended the right to vote to black males, in the Fifteenth Amendment; women, in the Nineteenth Amendment; people living in Washington, D.C., in the Twenty-third Amendment; and eighteen- to twenty-year-olds, in the Twenty-sixth Amendment. Two other amendments affected voting rights. The Seventeenth Amendment gave American voters the right to elect their senators, and the Twenty-fourth Amendment eliminated a qualification for voting, the payment of poll taxes. Congress passed civil-rights acts to remove other obstacles to voting, such as the requirement that citizens prove that they could read. In addition, where state officials were still reluctant to register black voters, federal-government officials placed the names of these citizens on lists of those qualified to vote.

Civil Rights; Congress; Constitutional Convention; Delegates; Elections; House of Representatives; Poll Taxes; President; Ratification; Senate; U.S. Constitution, Article I; U.S. Constitution, Fifteenth Amendment; U.S. Constitution, Seventeenth Amendment; U.S. Constitution, Nineteenth Amendment; U.S. Constitution, Twenty-third Amendment; U.S. Constitution, Twenty-fourth Amendment; U.S. Constitution, Twenty-sixth Amendment

War Powers

The ability to decide whether the United States will fight an enemy and how the troops will be trained and maintained.

Under the Articles of Confederation, a state could go to war only with the consent of the other states meeting in the Confederation Congress. At the Constitutional Convention, the Framers chose to give the power to wage war to the national government. There was hardly any debate about the decision. The delegates remembered how difficult it was to get the states to contribute troops and supplies to the Continental Army during the War for Independence. They were also convinced that a stronger national government was needed to deal with Great Britain and Spain. Britain still occupied forts and trading posts in the Northwest. This violated the peace treaty of 1783, which had ended the War for Independence. In 1784, Spain closed the Mississippi River to American shipping. The Confederation was too weak to do much about these problems.

Following the principles of separation of powers and checks and balances, the Framers divided the power to wage war between the president and Congress. Under Article I, section 10, of the Constitution, states are denied the power to wage war unless they have to fight off a threatened invasion before Congress is able to act. They can, however, train militias and appoint officers, under rules set by Congress. Article II, section 2,

This photograph shows American soldiers during the Allied invasion of Normandy, France, in June 1944. The amphibious landing was one of the decisive events of World War II. It gained a foothold in German-occupied France and directly contributed to the defeat of Germany. Yet it was very costly in lives lost, both on the beaches of Normandy and in the fighting that raged for weeks afterward.

World War II was the last time in the twentieth century that Congress voted a declaration of war. In the early 1950s (during the Korean War), and again in the 1960s and early 1970s (during the Vietnam War), presidents committed U.S. troops abroad without express authority from Congress. As long as U.S. soliders were fighting in the field, few in Congress felt free to oppose these actions.

To reassert its authority, Congress passed the War Powers Act in 1973, overriding a presidential veto to do so. The act allows a president to commit U.S. troops abroad for no more than sixty days without the specific authorization of Congress.

makes the president the commander in chief of the nation's armed forces, and of the state militias when they are called up in time of war. However, according to Article I, section 8, only Congress can declare war. In addition, Congress is responsible for raising and supporting armies and navies and for making military rules and regulations. This division of responsibility worked well for over 150 years.

By the mid-twentieth century, however, modern technology shifted more responsibility for making military decisions to the president. The last time Congress issued a formal declaration of war was on December 8, 1941, the day after the Japanese launched a surprise attack against the American naval base at Pearl Harbor, Hawaii. As a result of the declaration, the United States entered World War II. The development of atomic bombs in 1945 and rocket delivery systems in the 1950s raised important questions about the future of the war powers. If, as military planners claimed, there might be no more than ten minutes' warning before a nuclear-missile attack, Congress would not have time to declare war. The president might have to act quickly to order a retaliatory strike without getting permission from the lawmakers.

Even in nonnuclear conflicts, presidents have taken military action before consulting the legislative branch. In the second half of the twentieth century, they have sent armed forces to fight overseas without official declarations of war from Congress. In 1950, President Harry S. Truman ordered American troops to South Korea to repel an attack by North Korea as part of what became a United Nations military operation. Congress cooperated with him by voting funds for the Korean War. The conflict ended in a cease-fire in 1953.

American military personnel were already in South Vietnam when Congress passed the Gulf of Tonkin Resolution in early August 1964. This resolution, and not a formal declaration of war, let President Lyndon B. Johnson use a quickly growing number of American forces to help South Vietnam resist attacks by North Vietnam. In 1969 and 1970, Congress was not initially told about military operations in nearby Laos or the secret air war over neighboring Cambodia. When the lawmakers did learn that President Richard M. Nixon had widened the war by letting American ground forces invade Cambodia, they canceled the resolution. American forces were not withdrawn from Vietnam until after the signing in 1973 of the Paris Peace Accords.

Presidents Ronald Reagan and George Bush also sent American forces to fight, in Grenada and the Persian Gulf respectively, without formal declarations of war. Presidents Bush and Bill Clinton ordered troops to keep the peace in Somalia and the former Yugoslavia, respectively. (Presidents have assigned American forces to peacekeeping duties and service at foreign bases since World War II, to honor treaty agreements and United Nations requests.) No one questioned their right to make these troop commitments, despite debates over the wisdom of the actions.

Although modern presidents have stretched their war powers, they cannot entirely ignore Congress. After all, the lawmakers can hold hearings to criticize a president's military decisions. For example, in 1987, President Reagan and his advisers were questioned about the government's secret arms sales to Iran and the use of that money to fund Nicaraguan rebels in violation of American law. More importantly, Congress can refuse to pay for military actions if the lawmakers disapprove of a president's decisions or if they are not kept informed of military developments; practically speaking, however, it is usually difficult for Congress to vote against funding to support soldiers who have already been sent into harm's way. Still, despite the growth of presidential war powers, the constitutional division of responsibility between the president and Congress is still in place.

Articles of Confederation; Checks and Balances; Commander in Chief; Confederation Congress; Constitutional Convention; Defense; Delegates; Executive Branch; Foreign Affairs; Framers; Legislative Branch; Militia; President; Resolutions; Separation of Powers; U.S. Constitution, Article I; U.S. Constitution, Article II

Weights and Measures

Standards set for trade and scientific purposes.

The woman was photographed in front of the White House, the president's residence, in Washington, D.C., in the early 1900s. At the time, women were barred from voting in many states (and in almost every country in the world). Many people were calling for an amendment to the Constitution to grant women the right to vote nationwide. This woman protested the issue in a way calculated to win public attention. Although the president is not involved in the amendment process, the presidency and the White House are very much at the center of public life. Even in the early 1900s, the media focused on the president more than on any other public official. By posing in front of the White House—and posing a rhetorical question of the president—she assured herself an audience.

The Articles of Confederation gave the Confederation Congress power to set standards for weights and measures. Article I, section 8, of the Constitution continued this arrangement. If each state were left to its own devices, trade could be seriously affected. For example, if a pound contained sixteen ounces in one state and twelve in another, it would be difficult to conduct business. Similarly, if measurements differed from state to state, it would be hard to duplicate scientific experiments and make sure each produced the same or similar results.

Articles of Confederation; Confederation Congress; U.S. Constitution, Article I

Women's Rights

The requirement that females receive equal treatment under the law.

Women were not specifically mentioned in the Constitution. Although women had made sacrifices and proved their worth during the War for Independence, they were not granted the rights of American citizenship. They were treated as children under the law, to be protected by their

fathers, older brothers, or husbands. They were not allowed to own property or to control their own money, except in the few states where widows were allowed to do so. (All of this was common around the world at that time.) In 1839, the Mississippi Married Women's Property Act gave them some legal rights over what they owned. Nine years later, New York State adopted a similar measure. By 1900, every state had followed suit. By 1921, twenty states let women serve on juries.

Women gained the right to vote very gradually. Women voted in New Jersey elections until 1807, when the law was changed to exclude them. In 1838, widows with children in school were allowed to vote in Kentucky school board elections. The first women's rights convention was held in Seneca Falls, New York, in 1848 to protest the way women were treated. In 1890, Wyoming became the first state to guarantee voting rights for women in its constitution. Gradually other states made similar arrangements. However, it was not until 1920, when the Nineteenth Amendment to the Constitution was ratified, that women finally gained the right to vote nationwide.

Women also fought for the right to be educated. In 1778, the Quakers started a school to educate rural mothers so they could teach their children. In 1821, in Troy, New York, Emma Willard opened the first school for women to receive public funding. The first public high school for women was started three years later in Worcester, Massachusetts. In 1837, Oberlin College admitted women and Mount Holyoke, a women's college, was founded. Other colleges became coeducational between 1853 (Antioch College) and 1987 (Goucher College). Women also claimed the right to receive graduate education and to enter the legal and medical professions. In 1885, Bryn Mawr became the first college to offer graduate programs for women.

Women often faced difficulties in the workplace. At first, they supported state laws to protect them from hazardous jobs and unreasonable wages and hours. These laws were overturned by the Supreme Court, because they interfered with business property rights. In the modern era, however, women rejected such special and, in effect, exclusionary treatment. They won the right to equal pay for equal work in 1963, though enforcement has been inconsistent. The Civil Rights Act of 1964 made it illegal to discriminate based on sex. Women worked hard for passage of the Equal Rights Amendment of 1972, but it failed to be ratified in the time period set by Congress. They soon won other victories, however. Title IX of the Education Amendments of 1972, for example, banned discrimination against women in college admissions, funding for athletic programs, hiring, and firing at educational institutions receiving federal funds. In 1976, they gained admission to the nation's military academies.

Under the right to privacy, women gained greater control of their own bodies. For the most part, laws no longer prevented them from using contraceptives or ending unwanted pregnancies. The Family and Medical Leave Act of 1993 allowed women up to twelve weeks of unpaid leave away from their jobs to care for newborn or adopted children. Still, such problems as affordable child care, workplace promotions, and violence against women remained to be solved.

Apportionment; Census; Civil Rights; Due Process of Law; Equal Rights Amendment; House of Representatives; Law; Privacy; Property Rights; Ratification; Supreme Court; U.S. Constitution, Article I; U.S. Constitution, Nineteenth Amendment

We the People of the United States, in Order to form a more perfect Union, establish Justice, insure domestic Tranquility, provide for the common defense, promote the general Welfare, and secure the Blessings of Liberty to ourselves and our Posterity, do ordain and establish this Constitution for the United States of America.

ARTICLE I

Section 1. All legislative Powers herein granted shall be vested in a Congress of the United States, which shall consist of a Senate and House of Representatives.

Section 2. The House of Representatives shall be composed of Members chosen every second Year by the People of the several States, and the Electors in each State shall have the Qualifications requisite for Electors of the most numerous Branch of the State Legislature.

No Person shall be a Representative who shall not have attained to the Age of twenty five Years, and been seven Years a Citizen of the United States, and who shall not, when elected, be an Inhabitant of that State in which he shall be chosen.

Representatives and direct Taxes shall be apportioned among the several States which may be included within this Union, according to their respective Numbers, which shall be determined by adding to the whole Number of free Persons, including those bound to Service for a Term of Years, and excluding Indians not taxed, three fifths of all other Persons. The actual Enumeration shall be made within three Years after the first Meeting of the Congress of the United States, and within every subsequent Term of ten Years, in such Manner as they shall by Law direct. The Number of Representatives shall not exceed one for every thirty Thousand, but each State shall have at Least one Representative; and until such enumeration shall be made, the State of New Hampshire shall be entitled to chuse three, Massachusetts eight, Rhode-Island and Providence Plantations one, Connecticut five, New-York six, New Jersey four, Pennsylvania eight, Delaware one, Maryland six, Virginia ten, North Carolina five, South Carolina five, and Georgia three.

When vacancies happen in the Representation from any State, the Executive Authority thereof shall issue Writs of Election to fill such Vacancies.

Power to impeach

The House of Representatives shall chuse their Speaker and other Officers; and shall have the sole Power of Impeachment.

The Senate

Choosing senators (Procedures were changed by the 17th Amendment)

Section 3. The Senate of the United States shall be composed of two Senators from each State, chosen by the Legislature thereof, for six Years; and each Senator shall have one Vote.

Immediately after they shall be assembled in Consequence of the first Election, they shall be divided as equally as may be into three Classes. The Seats of the Senators of the first Class shall be vacated at the Expiration of the second Year, of the second Class at the Expiration of the fourth Year, and of the third Class at the Expiration of the sixth Year, so that one third may be chosen every second Year; and if Vacancies happen by Resignation, or otherwise, during the Recess of the Legislature of any State, the Executive thereof may make temporary Appointments until the next Meeting of the Legislature, which shall then fill such Vacancies.

Qualifications for becoming a senator

No Person shall be a Senator who shall not have attained to the Age of thirty Years, and been nine Years a Citizen of the United States, and who shall not, when elected, be an Inhabitant of that State for which he shall be chosen.

The Vice President of the United States shall be President of the Senate, but shall have no Vote, unless they be equally divided.

The Senate shall chuse their other Officers, and also a President pro tempore, in the Absence of the Vice President, or when he shall exercise the Office of President of the United States.

Power to try and judge those impeached by the House of Representatives

The Senate shall have the sole Power to try all Impeachments. When sitting for that Purpose, they shall be on Oath or Affirmation. When the President of the United States is tried, the Chief Justice shall preside: And no Person shall be convicted without the Concurrence of two thirds of the Members present.

Judgment in Cases of Impeachment shall not extend further than to removal from Office, and disqualification to hold and enjoy any Office of honor, Trust or Profit under the United States: but the Party convicted shall nevertheless be liable and subject to Indictment, Trial, Judgment and Punishment, according to Law.

Congress

Section 4. The Times, Places and Manner of holding Elections for Senators and Representatives, shall be prescribed in each State by the Legislature thereof; but the Congress may at any time by Law make or alter such Regulations, except as to the Places of chusing Senators.

When Congress shall meet

The Congress shall assemble at least once in every Year, and such Meeting shall be on the first Monday in December, unless they shall by Law appoint a different Day.

How Congress shall conduct business

Section 5. Each House shall be the Judge of the Elections, Returns and Qualifications of its own Members, and a Majority of each shall constitute a Quorum to do Business; but a smaller Number may adjourn from day to day, and may be authorized to compel the Attendance of absent Members, in such Manner, and under such Penalties as each House may provide.

Each House may determine the Rules of its Proceedings, punish its Members for disorderly Behaviour, and, with the Concurrence of two thirds, expel a Member.

Each House shall keep a Journal of its Proceedings, and from time to time publish the same, excepting such Parts as may in their Judgment require Secrecy; and the Yeas and Nays of the Members of either House on any question shall, at the Desire of one fifth of those Present, be entered on the Journal.

Neither House, during the Session of Congress, shall, without the Consent of the other, adjourn for more than three days, nor to any other Place than that in which the two Houses shall be sitting.

Salaries and special protections (Qualified by the 27th Amendment)

Section 6. The Senators and Representatives shall receive a Compensation for their Services, to be ascertained by Law, and paid out of the Treasury of the United States. They shall in all Cases, except Treason, Felony and Breach of the Peace, be privileged from Arrest during their Attendance at the Session of their respective Houses, and in going to and returning from the same; and for any Speech or Debate in either House, they shall not be questioned in any other Place.

Restrictions on holding other federal offices

No Senator or Representative shall, during the Time for which he was elected, be appointed to any civil Office under the Authority of the United States, which shall have been created, or the Emoluments whereof shall have been encreased during such time; and no Person holding any Office under the United States, shall be a Member of either House during his Continuance in Office.

Bills to raise money by taxation must come from the House and be approved by the Senate

Section 7. All Bills for raising Revenue shall originate in the House of Representatives; but the Senate may propose or concur with Amendments as on other Bills.

Bills passed by the House and Senate go to the president for approval. If the president vetoes (rejects) a bill, it still may become law if approved by a two-thirds majority of both houses of Congress.

Every Bill which shall have passed the House of Representatives and the Senate, shall, before it become a Law, be presented to the President of the United States: If he approve he shall sign it, but if not he shall return it, with his Objections to that House in which it shall have originated, who shall enter the Objections at large on their Journal, and proceed to reconsider it. If after such Reconsideration two thirds of that House shall agree to pass the Bill, it shall be sent, together with the Objections, to the other House, by which it shall likewise be reconsidered, and if approved by two thirds of that House, it shall become a Law. But in all such Cases the Votes of both Houses shall be determined by Yeas and Nays, and the Names of the Persons voting for and against the Bill shall be entered on the Journal of each House respectively. If any Bill shall not be returned by the President within ten Days (Sundays excepted) after it shall have been presented to him, the Same shall be a Law, in like Manner as if he had signed it, unless the Congress by their Adjournment prevent its Return, in which Case it shall not be a Law.

Every Order, Resolution, or Vote to which the Concurrence of the Senate and House of Representatives may be necessary (except on a question of Adjournment) shall be presented to the President of the United States; and before the Same shall take Effect, shall be approved by him, or being disapproved by him, shall be repassed by two thirds of the Senate and House of Representatives, according to the Rules and Limitations prescribed in the Case of a Bill.

Congress has the power to:

— set and collect taxes

— borrow money

— regulate commerce

— set rules for naturalization and bankruptcy

— print and coin money

— punish counterfeiters

— create post offices
— issue patents and copyrights

— set up lower federal courts
— punish pirates

— declare war

— create an army and a navy

Section 8. The Congress shall have Power To lay and collect Taxes, Duties, Imposts and Excises, to pay the Debts and provide for the common Defence and general Welfare of the United States; but all Duties, Imposts and Excises shall be uniform throughout the United States;

To borrow Money on the credit of the United States;

To regulate Commerce with foreign Nations, and among the several States, and with the Indian Tribes;

To establish an uniform Rule of Naturalization, and uniform Laws on the subject of Bankruptcies throughout the United States;

To coin Money, regulate the Value thereof, and of foreign Coin, and fix the Standard of Weights and Measures;

To provide for the Punishment of counterfeiting the Securities and current Coin of the United States;

To establish Post Offices and post Roads;

To promote the Progress of Science and useful Arts, by securing for limited Times to Authors and Inventors the exclusive Right to their respective Writings and Discoveries;

To constitute Tribunals inferior to the supreme Court;

To define and punish Piracies and Felonies committed on the high Seas, and Offences against the Law of Nations;

To declare War, grant Letters of Marque and Reprisal, and make Rules concerning Captures on Land and Water;

To raise and support Armies, but no Appropriation of Money to that Use shall be for a longer Term than two Years;

To provide and maintain a Navy;

To make Rules for the Government and Regulation of the land and naval Forces;

— call up the militia

To provide for calling forth the Militia to execute the Laws of the Union, suppress Insurrections and repel Invasions;

To provide for organizing, arming, and disciplining, the Militia, and for governing such Part of them as may be employed in the Service of the United States, reserving to the States respectively, the Appointment of the Officers, and the Authority of training the Militia according to the discipline prescribed by Congress;

— govern the District of Columbia

To exercise exclusive Legislation in all Cases whatsoever, over such District (not exceeding ten Miles square) as may, by Cession of particular States, and the Acceptance of Congress, become the Seat of the Government of the United States, and to exercise like Authority over all Places purchased by the Consent of the Legislature of the State in which the Same shall be, for the Erection of Forts, Magazines, Arsenals, dock-Yards, and other needful Buildings; —And

— make laws necessary to enforce these powers

To make all Laws which shall be necessary and proper for carrying into Execution the foregoing Powers, and all other Powers vested by this Constitution in the Government of the United States, or in any Department or Officer thereof.

Congress does not have the power to:

— prevent the importation of slaves before the year 1808

Section 9. The Migration or Importation of such Persons as any of the States now existing shall think proper to admit, shall not be prohibited by the Congress prior to the Year one thousand eight hundred and eight, but a Tax or duty may be imposed on such Importation, not exceeding ten dollars for each Person.

— unjustly imprison someone without a court ruling

The Privilege of the Writ of Habeas Corpus shall not be suspended, unless when in Cases of Rebellion or Invasion the public Safety may require it.

— declare someone guilty without holding a fair trial, or try someone for an act that was not considered a crime at the time it was committed

No Bill of Attainder or ex post facto Law shall be passed.

No Capitation, or other direct, Tax shall be laid, unless in Proportion to the Census or Enumeration herein before directed to be taken.

— tax goods exported by states

No Tax or Duty shall be laid on Articles exported from any State.

— grant special favors to individual states

No Preference shall be given by any Regulation of Commerce or Revenue to the Ports of one State over those of another; nor shall Vessels bound to, or from, one State, be obliged to enter, clear, or pay Duties in another.

— withdraw money from the Treasury

No Money shall be drawn from the Treasury, but in Consequence of Appropriations made by Law; and a regular Statement and Account of the Receipts and Expenditures of all public Money shall be published from time to time.

— give titles of nobility or accept personal gifts from foreign visitors

No Title of Nobility shall be granted by the United States: And no Person holding any Office of Profit or Trust under them, shall, without the Consent of the Congress, accept of any present, Emolument, Office, or Title, of any kind whatever, from any King, Prince, or foreign State.

Section 10. No State shall enter into any Treaty, Alliance, or Confederation; grant Letters of Marque and Reprisal; coin Money; emit Bills of Credit; make any Thing but gold and silver Coin a Tender in Payment of Debts; pass any Bill of Attainder, ex post facto Law, or Law impairing the Obligation of Contracts, or grant any Title of Nobility.

No State shall, without the Consent of the Congress, lay any Imposts or Duties on Imports or Exports, except what may be absolutely necessary for executing its inspection Laws; and the net Produce of all Duties and Imposts, laid by any State on Imports or Exports, shall be for the Use of the Treasury of the United States; and all such Laws shall be subject to the Revision and Controul of the Congress.

No State shall, without the Consent of Congress, lay any Duty of Tonnage, keep Troops, or Ships of War in time of Peace, enter into any Agreement or Compact with another State, or with a foreign Power, or engage in War, unless actually invaded, or in such imminent Danger as will not admit of delay.

The states do not have the power to:
- make treaties or alliances with foreign countries
- issue money
- collect taxes on imports or exports
- keep troops or warships in peacetime
- go to war with another state or country

THE EXECUTIVE BRANCH (Presidency)

ARTICLE II

Section 1. The executive Power shall be vested in a President of the United States of America. He shall hold his Office during the Term of four Years, and, together with the Vice President, chosen for the same Term, be elected, as follows:

Choosing the president and vice president (Procedures were changed by the 12th Amendment)

Each State shall appoint, in such Manner as the Legislature thereof may direct, a Number of Electors, equal to the whole Number of Senators and Representatives to which the State may be entitled in the Congress: but no Senator or Representative, or Person holding an Office of Trust or Profit under the United States, shall be appointed an Elector.

The Electors shall meet in their respective States, and vote by Ballot for two Persons, of whom one at least shall not be an Inhabitant of the same State with themselves. And they shall make a List of all the Persons voted for, and of the Number of Votes for each; which List they shall sign and certify, and transmit sealed to the Seat of the Government of the United States, directed to the President of the Senate. The President of the Senate shall, in the Presence of the Senate and House of Representatives, open all the Certificates, and the Votes shall then be counted. The Person having the greatest Number of Votes shall be the President, if such Number be a Majority of the whole Number of Electors appointed; and if there be more than one who have such Majority, and have an equal Number of Votes, then the House of Representatives shall immediately chuse by Ballot one of them for President; and if no Person have a Majority, then from the five highest on the List the said House shall in like Manner chuse the President. But in chusing the President, the Votes shall be taken by States, the Representation from each State having one Vote; a quorum for this Purpose shall consist of a Member or Members from two thirds of the States, and a Majority of all the States shall be necessary to a Choice. In every Case, after the Choice of the President, the Person having the greatest Number of Votes of the Electors shall be the Vice President. But if there should remain two or more who have equal Votes, the Senate shall chuse from them by Ballot the Vice President.

The Congress may determine the Time of chusing the Electors, and the Day on which they shall give their Votes; which Day shall be the same throughout the United States.

Qualifications for becoming president

No Person except a natural born Citizen, or a Citizen of the United States, at the time of the Adoption of this Constitution, shall be eligible to the Office of President; neither shall any Person be eligible to that Office who shall not have attained to the Age of thirty five Years, and been fourteen Years a Resident within the United States.

Provisions for the vice president to become president should the president die or be removed from office (Clarified by the 25th Amendment)

In Case of the Removal of the President from Office, or of his Death, Resignation, or Inability to discharge the Powers and Duties of the said Office, the Same shall devolve on the Vice President, and the Congress may by Law provide for the Case of Removal, Death, Resignation or Inability, both of the President and Vice President, declaring what Officer shall then act as President, and such Officer shall act accordingly, until the Disability be removed, or a President shall be elected.

President's salary

The President shall, at stated Times, receive for his Services, a Compensation, which shall neither be encreased nor diminished during the Period for which he shall have been elected, and he shall not receive within that Period any other Emolument from the United States, or any of them.

President's oath of office

Before he enter on the Execution of his Office, he shall take the following Oath or Affirmation: —"I do solemnly swear (or affirm) that I will faithfully execute the Office of President of the United States, and will to the best of my Ability, preserve, protect and defend the Constitution of the United States."

The president has the power to:
– command the nation's armed forces

Section 2. The President shall be Commander in Chief of the Army and Navy of the United States, and of the Militia of the several States, when called into the actual Service of the United States; he may require the Opinion, in writing, of the principal Officer in each of the executive Departments, upon any Subject relating to the Duties of their respective

- grant pardons

- make treaties and appointments
  (with the Senate's approval)

Offices, and he shall have Power to grant Reprieves and Pardons for Offences against the United States, except in Cases of Impeachment.

He shall have Power, by and with the Advice and Consent of the Senate, to make Treaties, provided two thirds of the Senators present concur; and he shall nominate, and by and with the Advice and Consent of the Senate, shall appoint Ambassadors, other public Ministers and Consuls, Judges of the supreme Court, and all other Officers of the United States, whose Appointments are not herein otherwise provided for, and which shall be established by Law: but the Congress may by Law vest the Appointment of such inferior Officers, as they think proper, in the President alone, in the Courts of Law, or in the Heads of Departments.

The President shall have Power to fill up all Vacancies that may happen during the Recess of the Senate, by granting Commissions which shall expire at the End of their next Session.

The president's responsibilities are to:

- communicate with Congress

- convene or adjourn Congress in case of a disagreement

- receive ambassadors

- execute laws

- commission officers

Section 3. He shall from time to time give to the Congress Information of the State of the Union, and recommend to their Consideration such Measures as he shall judge necessary and expedient; he may, on extraordinary Occasions, convene both Houses, or either of them, and in Case of Disagreement between them, with Respect to the Time of Adjournment, he may adjourn them to such Time as he shall think proper; he shall receive Ambassadors and other public Ministers; he shall take Care that the Laws be faithfully executed, and shall Commission all the Officers of the United States.

Conditions under which a president and other federal officers may be removed from office

Section 4. The President, Vice President and all civil Officers of the United States, shall be removed from Office on Impeachment for, and Conviction of, Treason, Bribery, or other high Crimes and Misdemeanors.

THE JUDICIAL BRANCH (Courts)

Judicial power is given to the Supreme Court and lower courts

Federal judges hold office for life and can be removed only if impeached and convicted

ARTICLE III

Section 1. The judicial Power of the United States, shall be vested in one supreme Court, and in such inferior Courts as the Congress may from time to time ordain and establish. The Judges, both of the supreme and inferior Courts, shall hold their Offices during good Behaviour, and shall, at stated Times, receive for their Services, a Compensation, which shall not be diminished during their Continuance in Office.

Jurisdiction of the federal courts (Limited by the 11th Amendment)

Section 2. The judicial Power shall extend to all Cases, in Law and Equity, arising under this Constitution, the Laws of the United States, and Treaties made, or which shall be made, under their Authority; —to all Cases affecting Ambassadors, other public Ministers and Consuls; —to all Cases of admiralty and maritime Jurisdiction; —to Controversies to which the United

States shall be a Party; —to Controversies between two or more States; —between a State and Citizens of another State; —between Citizens of different States; —between Citizens of the same State claiming Lands under Grants of different States, and between a State, or the Citizens thereof, and foreign States, Citizens or Subjects.

In all Cases affecting Ambassadors, other public Ministers and Consuls, and those in which a State shall be Party, the supreme Court shall have original Jurisdiction. In all the other Cases before mentioned, the supreme Court shall have appellate Jurisdiction, both as to Law and Fact, with such Exceptions, and under such Regulations as the Congress shall make.

Anyone accused of committing a federal crime has the right to a trial by jury

The Trial of all Crimes, except in Cases of Impeachment, shall be by Jury; and such Trial shall be held in the State where the said Crimes shall have been committed; but when not committed within any State, the Trial shall be at such Place or Places as the Congress may by Law have directed.

Definition and punishment of treason

Section 3. Treason against the United States, shall consist only in levying War against them, or in adhering to their Enemies, giving them Aid and Comfort. No Person shall be convicted of Treason unless on the Testimony of two Witnesses to the same overt Act, or on Confession in open Court.

The Congress shall have Power to declare the Punishment of Treason, but no Attainder of Treason shall work Corruption of Blood, or Forfeiture except during the Life of the Person attainted.

RELATIONS BETWEEN THE STATES AND THE FEDERAL GOVERNMENT

ARTICLE IV

States shall uphold each others' laws, records, and court decisions

Section 1. Full Faith and Credit shall be given in each State to the public Acts, Records, and judicial Proceedings of every other State. And the Congress may by general Laws prescribe the Manner in which such Acts, Records and Proceedings shall be proved, and the Effect thereof.

Section 2. The Citizens of each State shall be entitled to all Privileges and Immunities of Citizens in the several States.

Fugitives from the law in one state may be extradited, or returned, to that state. (This also applied to slaves until slavery was abolished by the 13th Amendment)

A Person charged in any State with Treason, Felony, or other Crime, who shall flee from Justice, and be found in another State, shall on Demand of the executive Authority of the State from which he fled, be delivered up, to be removed to the State having Jurisdiction of the Crime.

No Person held to Service or Labour in one State, under the Laws thereof, escaping into another, shall, in Consequence of any Law or Regulation therein, be discharged from such Service or Labour, but shall be delivered up on Claim of the Party to whom such Service or Labour may be due.

Conditions of admitting new states to the Union

Section 3. New States may be admitted by the Congress into this Union; but no new State shall be formed or erected within the Jurisdiction of any other State; nor any State be formed by the Junction of two or more States, or Parts of States, without the Consent of the Legislatures of the States concerned as well as of the Congress.

The Congress shall have Power to dispose of and make all needful Rules and Regulations respecting the Territory or other Property belonging to the United States; and nothing in this Constitution shall be so construed as to Prejudice any Claims of the United States, or of any particular State.

Each state is guaranteed a republican form of government and federal protection

Section 4. The United States shall guarantee to every State in this Union a Republican Form of Government, and shall protect each of them against Invasion; and on Application of the Legislature, or of the Executive (when the Legislature cannot be convened) against domestic Violence.

PROVISIONS FOR CHANGING THE CONSTITUTION

A proposal to amend the Constitution must be approved by two-thirds of the Congress or two-thirds of the states

An amendment becomes law when three-fourths of the state legislatures approve of it

ARTICLE V

The Congress, whenever two thirds of both Houses shall deem it necessary, shall propose Amendments to this Constitution, or, on the Application of the Legislatures of two thirds of the several States, shall call a Convention for proposing Amendments, which, in either Case, shall be valid to all Intents and Purposes, as Part of this Constitution, when ratified by the Legislatures of three fourths of the several States, or by Conventions in three fourths thereof, as the one or the other Mode of Ratification may be proposed by the Congress; Provided that no Amendment which may be made prior to the Year One thousand eight hundred and eight shall in any Manner affect the first and fourth Clauses in the Ninth Section of the first Article; and that no State, without its Consent, shall be deprived of its equal Suffrage in the Senate.

THE CONSTITUTION IS THE HIGHEST LAW OF THE LAND

Federal and state officers and judges are bound to uphold the Constitution

ARTICLE VI

All Debts contracted and Engagements entered into, before the Adoption of this Constitution, shall be as valid against the United States under this Constitution, as under the Confederation.

This Constitution, and the Laws of the United States which shall be made in Pursuance thereof; and all Treaties made, or which shall be made, under the Authority of the United States, shall be the supreme Law of the Land; and the Judges in every State shall be bound thereby, any Thing in the Constitution or Laws of any State to the Contrary notwithstanding.

The Senators and Representatives before mentioned, and the Members of the several State Legislatures, and all executive and judicial Officers, both of the United States and of the several States, shall be bound by Oath or

Affirmation, to support this Constitution; but no religious Test shall ever be required as a Qualification to any Office or public Trust under the United States.

PROVISIONS FOR RATIFYING THE CONSTITUTION

ARTICLE VII

The Ratification of the Conventions of nine States, shall be sufficient for the Establishment of this Constitution between the States so ratifying the Same.

Done in Convention by the Unanimous Consent of the States present the Seventeenth Day of September in the Year of our Lord one thousand seven hundred and Eighty seven and of the Independence of the United States of America the Twelfth. In witness whereof We have hereunto subscribed our Names.

Go. WASHINGTON—Presidt and deputy from Virginia

NEW HAMPSHIRE
John Langdon
Nicholas Gilman

MASSACHUSETTS
Nathaniel Gorham
Rufus King

CONNECTICUT
Wm. Saml. Johnson
Roger Sherman

NEW YORK
Alexander Hamilton

NEW JERSEY
Wil: Livingston
David Brearley
Wm. Paterson
Jona: Dayton

PENNSYLVANIA
B. Franklin
Thomas Mifflin
Robt. Morris
Geo. Clymer
Thos. FitzSimons
Jared Ingersoll
James Wilson
Gouv. Morris

DELAWARE
Geo: Read
Gunning Bedford Jun.
John Dickinson
Richard Bassett
Jaco: Broom

MARYLAND
James McHenry
Dan: of St Thos Jenifer
Danl. Carroll

VIRGINIA
John Blair
James Madison Jr.

NORTH CAROLINA
Wm. Blount
Rich'd. Dobbs Spaight
Hugh Williamson

SOUTH CAROLINA
J. Rutledge
Charles Cotesworth
Pinckney
Charles Pinckney
Pierce Butler

GEORGIA
William Few
Abr. Baldwin

Attest: William Jackson, Secretary.

Articles in Addition to, and Amendment of, the Constitution of the United States of America, Proposed by Congress, and Ratified by the Legislatures of the Several States, Pursuant to the Fifth Article of the Original Constitution.

FIRST AMENDMENT

Fundamental Rights

Guarantees freedom of religion, speech, the press, and peaceable assembly

ARTICLE I

Congress shall make no law respecting an establishment of religion, or prohibiting the free exercise thereof; or abridging the freedom of speech, or of the press, or the right of the people peaceably to assemble, and to petition the Government for a redress of grievances.

SECOND AMENDMENT

Right to Security

Guarantees the right to bear arms

ARTICLE II

A well regulated Militia, being necessary to the security of a free State, the right of the people to keep and bear Arms, shall not be infringed.

THIRD AMENDMENT

Quartering Soldiers

Guarantees that citizens will not be required to shelter soldiers in their homes

ARTICLE III

No Soldier shall, in time of peace be quartered in any house, without the consent of the Owner, nor in time of war, but in a manner to be prescribed by law.

FOURTH AMENDMENT

Searches and Seizures

Prohibits unreasonable searches and seizures of persons or property (to protect privacy)

ARTICLE IV

The right of the people to be secure in their persons, houses, papers, and effects, against unreasonable searches and seizures, shall not be violated, and no Warrants shall issue, but upon probable cause, supported by Oath or affirmation, and particularly describing the place to be searched, and the persons or things to be seized.

FIFTH AMENDMENT

Rights of Defendants

Guarantees accused persons a fair and legal trial and that no one may be tried twice for the same crime; forced to testify against oneself; or have private property taken away for public use without fair compensation

ARTICLE V

No person shall be held to answer for a capital, or otherwise infamous crime, unless on a presentment or indictment of a Grand Jury, except in cases arising in the land or naval forces, or in the Militia, when in actual service in time of War or public danger; nor shall any person be subject for the same offence to be twice put in jeopardy of life or limb, nor shall be compelled in any criminal case to be a witness against himself, nor be deprived of life, liberty, or property, without due process of law; nor shall private property be taken for public use, without just compensation.

SIXTH AMENDMENT

Jury in Criminal Cases

Guarantees accused persons the right to a speedy trial by jury in criminal cases and legal counsel

ARTICLE VI

In all criminal prosecutions, the accused shall enjoy the right to a speedy and public trial, by an impartial jury of the State and district wherein the crime shall have been committed, which district shall have been previously ascertained by law, and to be informed of the nature and cause of the accusation; to be confronted with the witnesses against him; to have compulsory process for obtaining witnesses in his favor, and to have the Assistance of Counsel for his defence.

SEVENTH AMENDMENT

Jury in Civil Cases

Guarantees accused persons the right to a trial by jury in civil cases where the damages exceed $20

ARTICLE VII

In Suits at common law, where the value in controversy shall exceed twenty dollars, the right of trial by jury shall be preserved, and no fact tried by a jury, shall be otherwise re-examined in any Court of the United States, than according to the rules of the common law.

EIGHTH AMENDMENT

Excessive Punishment

Prohibits unreasonable bail or fines and cruel and unusual punishment

ARTICLE VIII

Excessive bail shall not be required, nor excessive fines imposed, nor cruel and unusual punishments inflicted.

NINTH AMENDMENT

Other Rights of Citizens

Affirms that citizens are entitled to other rights not listed in the Constitution

ARTICLE IX

The enumeration in the Constitution, of certain rights, shall not be construed to deny or disparage others retained by the people.

TENTH AMENDMENT

Other Rights of States

Affirms that powers not given to the federal government by the Constitution belong to the states or the people

ARTICLE X

The powers not delegated to the United States by the Constitution, nor prohibited by it to the States, are reserved to the States respectively, or to the people.

ELEVENTH AMENDMENT

Lawsuits Against States

Affirms that citizens of one state cannot sue the government of another state in a federal court

ARTICLE XI

The Judicial power of the United States shall not be construed to extend to any suit in law or equity, commenced or prosecuted against one of the United States by Citizens of another State, or by Citizens or Subjects of any Foreign State.

TWELFTH AMENDMENT

Presidential Election Procedures

Provides for the separate election of
presidents and vice presidents and
clarifies the electoral college procedure

ARTICLE XII

The Electors shall meet in their respective states, and vote by ballot for President and Vice President, one of whom, at least, shall not be an inhabitant of the same state with themselves; they shall name in their ballots the person voted for as President, and in distinct ballots the person voted for as Vice-President, and they shall make distinct lists of all persons voted for as President, and of all persons voted for as Vice-President, and of the number of votes for each, which lists they shall sign and certify, and transmit sealed to the seat of the government of the United States, directed to the President of the Senate; —The President of the Senate shall, in the presence of the Senate and House of Representatives, open all the certificates and the votes shall then be counted; —The person having the greatest number of votes for President, shall be the President, if such number be a majority of the whole number of Electors appointed; and if no person have such majority, then from the persons having the highest numbers not exceeding three on the list of those voted for as President, the House of Representatives shall choose immediately, by ballot, the President. But in choosing the President, the votes shall be taken by states, the representation from each state having one vote; a quorum for this purpose shall consist of a member or members from two-thirds of the states, and a majority of all the states shall be necessary to a choice. And if the House of Representatives shall not choose a President whenever the right of choice shall devolve upon them, before the fourth day of March next following, then the Vice-President shall act as President, as in the case of the death or other constitutional disability of the President. The person having the greatest number of votes as Vice-President, shall be the Vice-President, if such number be a majority of the whole number of Electors appointed, and if no person have a majority, then from the two highest numbers on the list, the Senate shall choose the Vice-Presiden; a quorum for the purpose shall consist of two-thirds of the whole number of Senators, and a majority of the whole number shall be necessary to a choice. But no person constitutionally ineligible to the office of President shall be eligible to that of Vice-President of the United States.

THIRTEENTH AMENDMENT

Abolition of Slavery

Prohibits slavery and other forms of
forced labor

ARTICLE XIII

Section 1. Neither slavery nor involuntary servitude, except as a punishment for crime whereof the party shall have been duly convicted, shall exist within the United States, or any place subject to their jurisdiction.

Section 2. Congress shall have power to enforce this article by appropriate legislation.

FOURTEENTH AMENDMENT

Rights of Citizens

Defines citizenship and prohibits states from denying anyone "due process of law" and "equal protection," specifically to protect the civil rights of the newly-freed slaves

ARTICLE XIV

Section 1. All persons born or naturalized in the United States and subject to the jurisdiction thereof, are citizens of the United States and of the State wherein they reside. No State shall make or enforce any law which shall abridge the privileges or immunities of citizens of the United States; nor shall any State deprive any person of life, liberty, or property, without due process of law; nor deny to any person within its jurisdiction the equal protection of the laws.

Section 2. Representatives shall be apportioned among the several States according to their respective numbers, counting the whole number of persons in each State, excluding Indians not taxed. But when the right to vote at any election for the choice of electors for President and Vice President of the United States, Representatives in Congress, the Executive and Judicial officers of a State, or the members of the Legislature thereof, is denied to any of the male inhabitants of such State, being twenty-one years of age, and citizens of the United States, or in any way abridged, except for participation in rebellion, or other crime, the basis of representation therein shall be reduced in the proportion which the number of such male citizens shall bear to the whole number of male citizens twenty-one years of age in such State.

Section 3. No person shall be a Senator or Representative in Congress, or elector of President and Vice President, or hold any office, civil or military, under the United States, or under any State, who, having previously taken an oath, as a member of Congress, or as an officer of the United States, or as a member of any State legislature, or as an executive or judicial officer of any State, to support the Constitution of the United States, shall have engaged in insurrection or rebellion against the same, or given aid or comfort to the enemies thereof. But Congress may by a vote of two-thirds of each House, remove such disability.

Section 4. The validity of the public debt of the United States, authorized by law, including debts incurred for payment of pensions and bounties for services in suppressing insurrection or rebellion, shall not be questioned. But neither the United States nor any State shall assume or pay any debt or obligation incurred in aid of insurrection or rebellion against the United States, or any claim for the loss or emancipation of any slave; but all such debts, obligations and claims shall be held illegal and void.

Section 5. The Congress shall have power to enforce, by appropriate legislation, the provisions of this article.

FIFTEENTH AMENDMENT

Voting Rights

Affirms that citizens may not be denied the right to vote because of their race or color

SIXTEENTH AMENDMENT

Income Taxes

Gives Congress the power to collect federal income taxes

SEVENTEENTH AMENDMENT

Senatorial Election Procedures

Provides for the election of senators by the direct vote of the people of each state, rather than by the state legislatures

EIGHTEENTH AMENDMENT

Prohibition

Prohibits the manufacture or sale of alcoholic beverages (Repealed by the 21st Amendment)

ARTICLE XV

Section 1. The right of citizens of the United States to vote shall not be denied or abridged by the United States or by any State on account of race, color, or previous condition of servitude.

Section 2. The Congress shall have power to enforce this article by appropriate legislation.

ARTICLE XVI

The Congress shall have power to lay and collect taxes on incomes, from whatever source derived, without apportionment among the several States, and without regard to any census or enumeration.

ARTICLE XVII

The Senate of the United States shall be composed of two Senators from each State, elected by the people thereof, for six years; and each Senator shall have one vote. The electors in each State shall have the qualifications requisite for electors of the most numerous branch of the State legislatures.

When vacancies happen in the representation of any State in the Senate, the executive authority of such State shall issue writs of election to fill such vacancies: Provided, That the legislature of any State may empower the executive thereof to make temporary appointments until the people fill the vacancies by election as the legislature may direct.

This amendment shall not be so construed as to affect the election or term of any Senator chosen before it becomes valid as part of the Constitution.

ARTICLE XVIII

Section 1. After one year from the ratification of this article the manufacture, sale, or transportation of intoxicating liquors within, the importation thereof into, or the exportation thereof from the United States and all territory subject to the jurisdiction thereof for beverage purposes is hereby prohibited.

Section 2. The Congress and the several States shall have concurrent power to enforce this article by appropriate legislation.

Section 3. This article shall be inoperative unless it shall have been ratified as an amendment to the Constitution by the legislatures of the several States, as provided in the Constitution, within seven years from the date of the submission hereof to the States by the Congress.

ARTICLE XIX

The right of citizens of the United States to vote shall not be denied or abridged by the United States or by any State on account of sex.

Congress shall have power to enforce this article by appropriate legislation.

ARTICLE XX

Section 1. The terms of the President and Vice President shall end at noon on the 20th day of January, and the terms of Senators and Representatives at noon on the 3d day of January, of the years in which such terms would have ended if this article had not been ratified; and the terms of their successors shall then begin.

Section 2. The Congress shall assemble at least once in every year, and such meeting shall begin at noon on the 3d day of January, unless they shall by law appoint a different day.

Section 3. If, at the time fixed for the beginning of the term of the President, the President elect shall have died, the Vice President elect shall become President. If a President shall not have been chosen before the time fixed for the beginning of his term, or if the President elect shall have failed to qualify, then the Vice President elect shall act as President until a President shall have qualified; and the Congress may by law provide for the case wherein neither a President elect nor a Vice President elect shall have qualified, declaring who shall then act as President, or the manner in which one who is to act shall be selected, and such person shall act accordingly until a President or Vice President shall have qualified.

Section 4. The Congress may by law provide for the case of the death of any of the persons from whom the House of Representatives may choose a President whenever the right of choice shall have devolved upon them, and for the case of the death of any of the persons from whom the Senate may choose a Vice President whenever the right of choice shall have devolved upon them.

Section 5. Sections 1 and 2 shall take effect on the 15th day of October following the ratification of this article.

Section 6. This article shall be inoperative unless it shall have been ratified as an amendment to the Constitution by the legislatures of three-fourths of the several States within seven years from the date of its submission.

TWENTY-FIRST AMENDMENT

Repeal of Prohibition

Repeals (cancels) the 18th Amendment

ARTICLE XXI

Section 1. The eighteenth article of amendment to the Constitution of the United States is hereby repealed.

Section 2. The transportation or importation into any State, Territory, or possession of the United States for delivery or use therein of intoxicating liquors, in violation of the laws thereof, is hereby prohibited.

Section 3. This article shall be inoperative unless it shall have been ratified as an amendment to the Constitution by conventions in the several States, as provided in the Constitution, within seven years from the date of the submission hereof to the States by the Congress.

TWENTY-SECOND AMENDMENT

Presidential Terms of Offices

Limits a president to two terms of office

ARTICLE XXII

Section 1. No person shall be elected to the office of the President more than twice, and no person who has held the office of President, or acted as President, for more than two years of a term to which some other person was elected President shall be elected to the office of President more than once. But this Article shall not apply to any person holding the office of President when this Article was proposed by the Congress, and shall not prevent any person who may be holding the office of President, or acting as President, during the term within which this Article becomes operative from holding the office of President or acting as President during the remainder of such term.

Section 2. This article shall be inoperative unless it shall have been ratified as an amendment to the Constitution by the legislatures of three-fourths of the several States within seven years from the date of its submission to the States by the Congress.

TWENTY-THIRD AMENDMENT

District of Columbia Voting Rights

Gives citizens living in the District of Columbia (Washington, D.C.) the right to vote for president and vice president

ARTICLE XXIII

Section 1. The District constituting the seat of Government of the United States shall appoint in such manner as the Congress may direct:

A number of electors of President and Vice President equal to the whole number of Senators and Representatives in Congress to which the District would be entitled if it were a State, but in no event more than the least populous State; they shall be in addition to those appointed by the States, but they shall be considered, for the purposes of the election of President and Vice President, to be electors appointed by a State; and they shall meet in the District and perform such duties as provided by the twelfth article of amendment.

Section 2. The Congress shall have power to enforce this article by appropriate legislation.

ARTICLE XXIV

Section 1. The right of citizens of the United States to vote in any primary or other election for President or Vice President, for electors for President or Vice President, or for Senator or Representative in Congress, shall not be denied or abridged by the United States or any State by reason of failure to pay any poll tax or other tax.

Section 2. The Congress shall have power to enforce this article by appropriate legislation.

ARTICLE XXV

Section 1. In case of the removal of the President from office or of his death or resignation, the Vice President shall become President.

Section 2. Whenever there is a vacancy in the office of the Vice President, the President shall nominate a Vice President who shall take office upon confirmation by a majority vote of both Houses of Congress.

Section 3. Whenever the President transmits to the President pro tempore of the Senate and the Speaker of the House of Representatives his written declaration that he is unable to discharge the powers and duties of his office, and until he transmits to them a written declaration to the contrary, such powers and duties shall be discharged by the Vice President as Acting President.

Section 4. Whenever the Vice President and a majority of either the principal officers of the executive departments or of such other body as Congress may by law provide, transmit to the President pro tempore of the Senate and the Speaker of the House of Representatives their written declaration that the President is unable to discharge the powers and duties of his office, the Vice President shall immediately assume the powers and duties of the office as Acting President.

Thereafter, when the President transmits to the President pro tempore of the Senate and the Speaker of the House of Representatives his written declaration that no inability exists, he shall resume the powers and duties of his office unless the Vice President and a majority of either the principal officers of the executive department or of such other body as Congress may by law provide, transmit within four days to the President pro tempore of the Senate and the Speaker of the House of Representatives their written declaration that the President is unable to discharge the powers and duties of his office. Thereupon Congress shall decide the issue, assembling within forty-eight hours for that purpose if not in session. If the Congress, within twenty-one days after receipt of the latter written declaration, or, if Congress is not in session, within twenty-one days after Congress is required to assemble, determines by two-thirds vote of both Houses that the President is unable to discharge the powers and duties of his office, the Vice President shall continue to discharge the same as Acting President; otherwise, the President shall resume the powers and duties of his office.

TWENTY-SIXTH AMENDMENT

Voting Age

Gives citizens 18 years old or older the right to vote

ARTICLE XXVI

Section 1. The right of citizens of the United States, who are eighteen years of age or older, to vote shall not be denied or abridged by the United States or by any State on account of age.

Section 2. The Congress shall have power to enforce this article by appropriate legislation.

TWENTY-SEVENTH AMENDMENT

Congressional Pay

Bans midterm congressional pay raises

ARTICLE XXVII

No law, varying the compensation for the services of the Senators and Representatives, shall take effect until an election of Representatives shall have intervened.

Books

Abraham, Henry. *Justices and Presidents: A Political History of Appointments to the Supreme Court.* 3rd ed. New York: Oxford University Press, 1991.

Alderman, Ellen, and Caroline Kennedy. *In Our Defense: The Bill of Rights in Action.* paperback ed. New York: Avon Books, 1992.

———. *The Right to Privacy.* paperback ed. New York: Vintage Books, 1997.

Anderson, Thornton. *Creating the Constitution: The Convention of 1787 and The First Congress.* University Park: The Pennsylvania State University Press, 1993.

Bailyn, Bernard. *The Ideological Origins of the American Revolution.* Cambridge: Harvard University Press, 1992.

Banning, Lance. *The Sacred Fire of Liberty: James Madison and the Founding of the Federal Republic.* Ithaca: Cornell University Press, 1995.

Beard, Charles A. *An Economic Interpretation of the Constitution of the United States.* paperback ed. New Brunswick: Rutgers University Press, 1998.

Beer, Samuel. *To Make a Nation: The Rediscovery of American Federalism.* Cambridge: Harvard University Press, 1993.

Bernikow, Louise. *The American Women's Almanac: An Inspiring and Irreverent Women's History.* New York: Berkley Books, 1997.

Bernstein, Richard B., and Jerome Agel. *Amending America: If We Love the Constitution So Much, Why Do We Keep Trying to Change It?* New York: Times Books, 1993.

Bowen, Catherine Drinker. *Miracle at Philadelphia: The Story of the Constitutional Convention May to September 1787.* Boston: Little, Brown and Company, 1986.

Castro, William R. *The Supreme Court in the Early Republic: The Chief Justiceships of John Jay and Oliver Ellsworth.* Columbia: University of South Carolina Press, 1995.

Chase, Harold W., and Craig R. Ducat, eds. *Edward S. Corwin's The Constitution and What It Means Today.* paperback ed. Princeton: Princeton University Press, 1978.

Chidsey, Donald Barr. *The Birth of the Constitution: An Informal History.* New York: Crown Publishers, 1964.

Collier, Christopher, and James Lincoln Collier. *Decision in Philadelphia: The Constitutional Convention of 1787.* New York: Random House, 1986.

Conley, Patrick T., and John P. Kaminski. *The Bill of Rights and the States: The Colonial and Revolutionary Origins of American Liberties.* Madison, Wisc.: Madison House, 1992.

———. *The Constitution and the States: The Role of the Original Thirteen States in the Framing and Ratification of the Constitution.* Madison, Wisc.: Madison House, 1988.

Cronin, Thomas E. *Inventing the American Presidency.* Lawrence: The University Press of Kansas, 1989.

Currie, David P. *The Constitution of the United States: A Primer for the People.* Chicago: University of Chicago Press, 1988.

Elkins, Stanley, and Eric McKitrick. *The Age of Federalism: The Early American Republic, 1788–1800.* New York: Oxford University Press, 1993.

Elliott, Stephen P., gen. ed. *Reference Guide to the United States Supreme Court.* New York: Facts On File, 1986.

Epstein, David F. *The Political Theory of The Federalist.* Chicago: University of Chicago Press, 1984.

Farrand, Max. *The Framing of the Constitution of the United States.* paperback ed. New Haven: Yale University Press, 1991.

———, ed. *The Records of the Federal Convention of 1787.* 3 vols. New Haven: Yale University Press, 1986.

Feerick, John D. *The Twenty-fifth Amendment: Its Complete History and Applications.* New York: Fordham University Press, 1992.

Fiorina, M.P. *Congress: Keystone of the Washington Establishment.* 2nd ed. New Haven: Yale University Press, 1989.

Fish, Peter Graham. *The Office of Chief Justice.* Charlottesville: University Press of Virginia, 1984.

Fisher, Louis. *Judicial Power and the Constitution.* New York: Macmillan, 1990.

Gillespie, Michael A., and Michael Lienesch, eds. *Ratifying the Constitution.* Lawrence: The University Press of Kansas, 1989.

Grimes, Alan P. *Democracy and the Amendments to the Constitution.* Lanham, Maryland: University Press of America, 1987.

Gunther, Gerald. *Constitutional Law.* 13th ed. Westbury, New York: The Foundation Press, 1997.

Hall, Kermit L. *The Supreme Court and Judicial Review in American History.* Washington, D.C.: The American Historical Association, 1985.

———, ed. *Oxford Companion to the Supreme Court.* New York: Oxford University Press, 1992.

Hickok, Eugene W., Jr. *The Bill of Rights: Original Meaning and Current Understanding.* Charlottesville: University Press of Virginia, 1991.

Hutson, James H., ed. *Supplement to Max Farrand's The Records of the Federal Convention of 1787.* New Haven: Yale University Press, 1987.

Kammen, Michael. *A Machine That Would Go of Itself: The Constitution in American Culture.* paperback ed. New York: St. Martin's Press, 1993.

Keefe, W.J., and M.S. Ogul. *The American Legislative Process.* 9th ed. Old Tappen, N.J.: Prentice-Hall, 1996.

Kesler, Charles R., ed. *Saving the Revolution: The Federalist Papers and the American Founding.* New York: The Free Press, 1987.

Kukla, Jon, ed. *The Bill of Rights: A Lively Heritage.* Richmond: Virginia State Library and Archives, 1987.

Kurland, Philip B., and Ralph Lerner, eds. *The Founders' Constitution.* Chicago: University of Chicago Press, 1987.

Kutler, Stanley I, ed. *The Supreme Court and the Constitution: Readings in American Constitutional History.* 3rd ed. New York: W.W. Norton, 1984.

Lacey, Michael J., and Knud Haakonssen, eds. *A Culture of Rights: The Bill of Rights in Philosophy, Politics, and Law, 1791 and 1991.* Cambridge: Cambridge University Press, 1992.

Levy, Leonard W., ed. *The Encyclopedia of the American Presidency*. New York: Macmillan, 1998.

Lienesch, Michael. *New Order of the Ages: Time, the Constitution, and the Making of Modern American Political Thought.* Princeton: Princeton University Press, 1988.

Lutz, Donald S. *Popular Consent and Popular Control: Whig Political Theory in the Early State Constitutions.* Baton Rouge: Louisiana State University Press, 1980.

Madison, James. *Notes of Debates in the Federal Convention of 1787.* New York: W.W. Norton & Company, 1987.

Main, Jackson Turner. *The Anti-Federalists: Critics of the Constitution, 1781–1788.* Chapel Hill: University of North Carolina Press, 1961.

Mayer, David N. *The Constitutional Thought of Thomas Jefferson.* paperback ed. Charlottesville: University Press of Virginia, 1995.

McCloskey, Robert G. *The American Supreme Court.* 2nd ed., rev. by Sanford Levinson. Chicago: The University of Chicago Press, 1993.

McCoy, Drew R. *The Last of the Fathers: James Madison and the Republican Legacy.* paperback ed. Cambridge: Cambridge University Press, 1991.

McDonald, Forrest. *Alexander Hamilton: A Biography.* paperback. New York: W.W. Norton, 1982.

———. *Novus Ordo Seclorum: The Intellectual Origins of the Constitution.* Lawrence: University Press of Kansas, 1985.

Miller, John C. *The Federalist Era, 1789–1801.* paperback ed. Prospect Heights, Ill.: Waveland Press, 1998.

Miller, William. *The Business of May Next: James Madison and the Founding.* paperback. Charlottesville: University Press of Virginia, 1994.

Morgan, Edmund S. *Inventing the People: The Rise of Popular Sovereignty in England and America.* paperback ed. New York: W.W. Norton, 1989

Morris, Richard B. *The Forging of the Union, 1781–1789.* New York: Harper & Row, 1987.

Murphy, Walter, and C. Herman Pritchett, eds. *Courts, Judges, and Politics.* 4th ed., paperback. Blacklick, Ohio: McGraw Hill College Division, 1986.

Nedelsky, Jennifer. *Private Property and the Limits of American Constitutionalism.* paperback ed. Chicago: University of Chicago Press, 1994.

O'Brien, David M. *Storm Center: The Supreme Court in American Politics.* paperback ed. New York: W.W. Norton, 1995.

Onuf, Peter S. *The Origins of the Federal Republic: Jurisdictional Controversies in the United States, 1775–1787.* Philadelphia: University of Pennsylvania. 1983.

Padover, Saul K. *The Living U.S. Constitution: Historical Background to Landmark Supreme Court Decisions, with Introductions, Indexed Guide, and Pen Portraits of the Signers.* 3rd ed., rev. by Jacob W. Landynski. New York: Plume, 1995.

Perry, Michael. *The Constitution in the Courts: Law or Politics?* paperback ed. New York: Oxford University Press, 1996.

Peters, William. *A More Perfect Union.* New York: Crown Publishers, 1987.

Phelps, Glenn A. *George Washington and American Constitutionalism.* Lawrence: The University Press of Kansas, 1993.

Rakove, Jack N. *Original Meanings: Politics and Ideas in the Making of the Constitution.* New York: Alfred A. Knopf, 1996.

Reid, John Phillip. *Constitutional History of the American Revolution.* Madison: University of Wisconsin Press, 1995.

Ripley, R.B. *Congress: Process and Policy.* 3rd ed. New York: W.W. Norton, 1983.

Rossiter, Clinton. *1787: The Grand Convention.* New York: Macmillan, 1966.

Rutland, Robert A. *The Birth of the Bill of Rights, 1776–1791.* Chapel Hill: University of North Carolina Press, 1955.

Schlesinger, Arthur M. Jr. *The Imperial Presidency.* reprint. Bridgewater, N.J.: Replica Books, 1998.

Schwartz, Bernard. *A History of the Supreme Court.* New York: Oxford University Press, 1993.

———. *The Great Rights of Mankind: A History of the American Bill of Rights.* Madison, Wisc.: Madison House, 1992.

———, ed. *The Bill of Rights: A Documentary History.* New York: Chelsea House, 1971.

Sharp, James Roger. *American Politics in the Early Republic: The New Nation in Crisis.* New Haven: Yale University Press, 1993

Swisher, Carl B. *American Constitutional Development.* reprint. Westport, Conn.: Greenwood Press, 1978.

Tuck, Richard. *Natural Rights Theories: Their Origins and Development.* paperback ed. Cambridge: Cambridge University Press, 1982.

Veit, Helen E., Kenneth R. Bowling, and Charlene Bangs Bickford, eds. *Creating the Bill of Rights: The Documentary Record from the First Federal Congress.* Baltimore: Johns Hopkins University Press, 1991.

Zuckert, Michael P. *Natural Rights and the New Republicanism.* Princeton: Princeton University Press, 1994.

Web Sites

The Federal Judiciary Homepage, Administrative Office of the U.S. Courts, www.uscourts.gov

Government Printing Office, www.access.gpo.gov

National Archives and Records Administration, www.nara.gov

Official Federal Government Web Sites, Library of Congress, lcweb.loc.gov/global/executive/fed.html

Supreme Court Collection, Legal Information Institute, Cornell University School of Law, supct.law.cornell.edu/supct

Thomas: Legislative Information on the Internet, Library of Congress, thomas.loc.gov/

U.S. House of Representatives, www.house.gov

United States Legislative Branch, Library of Congress, lcweb.loc.gov/global/legislative/congress.html

U.S. Senate, www.senate.gov

Page numbers that appear in boldface type indicate major entries on a topic. Turning to those pages first will give the best overview of a subject. Page numbers appearing after a subentry (such as "attorney," following "accused, rights of the") point to specific aspects of an entry or topic.

C

cabinet, **17,** 41, 54, 96, 151, 170, 175, 176
Calhoun, John C., 116, 135, 175
California, 49, 65, 106, 133
Cambodia, 181
Canada, 11, 30, 79, 142
Cannon, Joseph G., 129
capital, U.S. *See* District of Columbia
capital punishment. *See* death penalty
capitation tax, **18,** 40, 69, 87, 126, 149, 164
capitol building, U.S., 42, 138
Capone, Al, 167
Carlisle, John G., 129
Carroll, Daniel, 31, 61, 115, 173
Carter, Jimmy, 97, 176
Catholics, 113
Cato (pseudonym), 5
Causby v. United States (1946), 107
censorship, 102
census, 7, **18,** 46, 64, 95, 145, 149
Centinel (pseudonym), 5
Centinel, The (newspaper), 109
Central Hudson Gas & Electric Corporation v. Public Service Commission of New York (1980), 131-132
Central Intelligence Agency (CIA), 17, 53, 61
Champion v. Ames (1903), 23
Chandler v. Florida (1981), 103
Chaplinsky v. New Hampshire (1942), 131
Chase, Salmon P., 19, 89
Chase, Samuel, 67
checks and balances, 1, 14, **18-19,** 27, 53, 55, 59, 65, 67, 74, 76, 78, 82, 83, 97, 114, 117, 118, 124, 132, 139, 144, 149, 173, 179
Cherokee, 86. *See also* Native Americans
Cheves, Langdon, 128
Chicago, Burlington and Quincy Railroad Co. v. Chicago (1897), 70
chief justice, **19,** 24, 59, 66, 137
child labor, 3, 4, 23, 73, 77, 116
Chinese Americans, 20
Chinese Exclusion Act (1882), 20
Chisholm v. Georgia (1793), 138, 160
Christmas, 111
Church of England, 110, 113
citizenship, 3, **19-20,** 26, 27, 69-71, 86, 88, 97, 105, 124, 128, 145-146, 147, 151, 154, 160, 162, 166, 182
civil law, **20,** 70, 79, 158
civil liberties, 9, **20,** 83, 157. *See also* religion, freedom of; speech, freedom of
civil rights, 15, **20-21,** 59, 69-71, 77, 83, 121-122, 135-136, 168-169, 171; due process, 70, 73, 162-164; equal protection of the laws, 50-51, 70-71, 162-164; freedom of assembly, 11-12, 155; freedom of association, 12, 155; habeas corpus, 63-64; police powers and, 94; women's suffrage, 166
Civil Rights Act (1875), 121
Civil Rights Act (1964), 51, 52, 94, 121, 122, 135-136, 183
Civil Rights Act (1968), 121
Civil Rights Cases (1883), 50, 116, 121
Civil War, vi, 43, 63, 67, 69, 70, 76, 77, 84, 89, 93, 102, 116, 120, 127, 128, 135, 162-163, 164, 165, 169

Claiborne, Harry E., 78
Clark, Champ, 129
Clay, Henry, 128
clear and present danger test, 129. *See also* speech, freedom of
Cleveland, Grover, 49, 97, 173
Clinton, Bill, 17, 37, 46, 67, 68, 97, 99, 118, 136, 174, 176, 181
Clinton, George, 5, 175
Clinton, Hillary, 99
Clinton v. City of New York (1998), 174
Clymer, George, 61
Coast Survey, 27
Cobb, Howell, 129
Colfax, Schuyler, 129, 175
Colorado, 49, 65, 133, 166, 172
Columbia University, 131
commander in chief, **21,** 39, 55, 60-61, 84, 98, 148, 151, 180-181
Commerce, Department of, 54, 61; secretary of commerce, 100
commerce clause, **22-23,** 27, 56, 81, 86, 87-88, 93, 147
Commerce, Science, and Transportation Committee (Senate), 82
common law, **23-24,** 60, 63, 152
Communications Decency Act (1997), 132. *See also* Internet
Communist Party, 91
compensation, 14, **24,** 25, 88, 124, 146, 150, 151, 152, 172, 177
concurrent powers, **24,** 52-53, 57, 93, 144
concurrent resolutions. *See* resolutions
concurring opinions. *See* Supreme Court
Confederate States of America, vi, 25, 116, 162-163
confederation, **24-25,** 149
Confederation Congress, 4, 8-11, 16, **25,** 30, 33, 38, 45, 54, 72, 110, 114, 136, 140, 141, 143, 177, 179, 182
confession, **25-26,** 122, 142, 157
Congress, 13, 14, 20, 24, **26-28,** 31, 55, 56, 60, 69, 80, 106, 121, 127-128, 140, 142, 144, 148, 159, 165, 166, 167, 171, 176; amendment process, 154; amendments, proposed, 3-4, 51; Bill of Rights, drafting of, 15-16; budget impasse, 118; census, 18; commerce clause, 22; composition of, 6-7, 145; and courts, 19, 57, 74, 75-76, 78-79, 137, 152; defense and war powers, 21, 39, 84, 98, 148, 179-181; District of Columbia, 41; elections, 46-47, 49, 90, 150, 161; freedom of religion, 110-111; freedom of the press, 101; House of Representatives, 64-65; impeachment, 17, 66-68; lawmaking process, 81-82; Native Americans, 85-87; powers, 7, 35, 36, 38, 45, 71, 92, 136, 139, 147-148, 164; powers denied to, 36, 40, 63, 88, 149; president, 19, 97-99, 151, 168; presidential succession and disability, 169-170; resolutions, 117; Senate, 123-124; states' rights, 134-135; territories, 141; veto, 172-174
Congress of Industrial Organizations. *See* AFL-CIO
Connecticut, 22, 28, 31, 39, 49, 61, 65,

66, 103, 109, 128, 133
Connecticut Compromise, 26, **28,** 30, 64, 81, 87, 123, 143, 145, 176
Constitution Day, 144
Constitutional Convention, vi, 4, 5, 6, 8, 15, 17, 22-23, 24, 26, 28, **29-31,** 35, 40, 47, 59, 61-62, 63, 81, 82, 84, 87, 90, 91, 94, 95, 97, 100, 106, 108-109, 113, 114, 115, 123, 125, 133, 139, 140, 141, 142, 143, 155, 159, 173, 174-175, 176, 178, 179
Constitutional Union Party, 91
constitutions, vi-ix, **28-29,** 82-83, 132
construction (interpretation of the Constitution), **32,** 70, 73, 74, 77, 90
consuls, 6, **32,** 55, 57, 60, 74, 78, 124, 137, 151, 152
Consumer Product Safety Commission, 53
Continental Congresses, 5, 8, 28, **32-33,** 40, 54, 59, 61, 87, 143
continuing resolutions. *See* resolutions
contract clause, **33-34,** 38, 44, 50, 76, 77, 103, 106, 133, 149
convention, 2, 5, 6, 8, **35,** 40, 94, 167
Coolidge, Calvin, 97, 175, 176
copyright, **35,** 81, 148
Corporation for National Service, 53
corruption of the blood and forfeiture, **36,** 153
Corwin, Edward S., 76
Cosby, William, 102
Council of Economic Advisers, 53
Council on Environmental Quality, 53
counterfeiting, **36,** 81, 147
Court of Veterans' Appeals, 74
court packing, 137
courts. *See* federal courts
Cox v. New Hampshire (1941), 11
crimes and misdemeanors, 17, **36-37,** 66-68, 78, 152
Crisp, Charles F., 129
cruel and unusual punishment, **37,** 158-159
Curtis, Charles, 175

D

Dallas, George M., 175
Dartmouth College, 34
Dartmouth College v. Woodward (1819), 34
Davie, William Richardson, 61
Davis, David, 63
Davis, John W., 129
Dawes, Charles G., 175
Dawes Severalty Act (1887), 86
Dayton, Jonathan, 61, 128
death penalty, 14, **37-38,** 43, 159
debts, 10, 11, 13, 27, 31, 34, **38-39,** 40, 41, 56, 81, 114, 115, 125, 138, 147, 149, 154, 163
Declaration of Independence (1776), vi, 28, 33, 61, 79, 88, 93, 114, 120, 144, 178
Declaration of Rights (1776), 178
Declaration of the Causes and Necessity of Taking Up Arms (1775), 33
defendants' rights. *See* accused, rights of the
defense, 7, 8-10, 17, 21, **39,** 60-61, 73, 81, 102-103, 133, 139, 142, 146, 147.

voting rights, 46-47, 95, **178-179;**
African Americans, 162, 163-164;
apportionment in House of
Representatives, 7, 46, 89-90; Black
Codes, poll taxes, and other limits on,
18, 86, 89, 94, 121, 136, 169; District
of Columbia residents, 4, 168-169;
eighteen-year-olds, 171-172; eligibility
determined by states, 145, 153;
Framers, 8, 46-47, 109, 114-115, 120;
president, indirect election, 47-50;
senators, election of, 27, 46, 165;
women, 166, 182
Voting Rights Act (1965), 86, 179
Voting Rights Act (1970), 171, 179

W

Waite, Morrison R., 19
Wallace, Henry A., 175
War, Department of, 54; secretary of
war, 25, 67. *See also* Defense,
Department of
War for Independence, vii, 5, 7, 8, 15, 33,
38, 41, 55, 59, 79, 84, 110, 113, 117,
119, 126, 138, 142, 156, 160, 178,
179, 182
War of 1812, 31, 42
war powers, 9-10, 21, 27, 39, 43, 55, 56,
81, 82, 98, 148, 149, **179-181**
War Powers Act (1973), 180
Warren, Earl, 19, 26, 51, 136
Washington, George, 17, 30, 31, 41, 60,
61, 67, 89, 90, 91, 97, 114, 142, 168,
178

Washington (state), 48, 49, 65, 129, 133
*Washington Addressing the Constitutional
Convention* (painting), 29
Washington, D.C. *See* District of
Columbia
Washington Monument, 155
Watergate, 36, 67-68, 76, 90-91, 170
Ways and Means Committee (House), 82
Webster, Daniel, 135
Webster v. Reproductive Health Services
(1989), 104
Weeks v. United States (1914), 119
weights and measures, 81, 147, **181-182**
welfare, 135, 136, 153, 159
Wesberry v. Sanders (1964), 7, 90
West Coast Hotel v. Parrish (1937), 44, 74
West Indies, 142
West Virginia, 49, 65, 133
*West Virginia State Board of Education v.
Barnette* (1943), 113
Wheeler, William A., 175
Whig Party, 91, 92
White, Byron R., 137
White, Edward D., 19
White, John, 128
White House, 42, 53, 61, 68, 91, 118,
122, 182
Willard, Emma, 183
Williamson, Hugh, 31, 61, 97, 173, 175
Wilson, Edith, 170
Wilson, Henry, 175
Wilson, James, 15, 31, 61, 62, 75, 87,
90, 94, 95, 97, 109, 114, 115, 124,
173

Wilson, Woodrow, 49, 61, 97, 99, 100,
106, 170-171
Winthrop, Robert C., 129
Wisconsin, 49, 65, 133, 135
Wisconsin v. Yoder (1972), 113
Women's Christian Temperance Union,
165
women's rights, 4, 12, 44-45, 46, 51-52,
88, 114, 163, 166, 179, **182-183**
Worcester v. Georgia (1832), 86
Works Progress Administration, 98. *See
also* New Deal
World War I, 61, 84, 102, 129, 142, 165,
166
World War II, 55, 63-64, 69, 84, 102,
148, 168, 180, 181
worship, freedom of. *See* religion, freedom of
Wright, James C. Jr., 129
writ of habeas corpus. *See* habeas corpus,
writ of
Wyoming, 7, 49, 65, 133, 166, 172, 182
Wythe, George, 61

Y

Yates v. United States (1957), 12
Yates, Robert, 5, 61, 87
Youngstown Sheet and Tube Co. v. Sawyer
(1952), 72
Yugoslavia, 181

Z

Zenger, John Peter, 102

Picture Credits

cover photographs, Library of Congress (LC) and National Archives (NA);
frontispiece, Howard C. Christy, *Signing the Constitution,* 1937, oil on
canvas, 0927.2082, from the Collection of the Gilcrease Museum, Tulsa,
Oklahoma; *page 2,* CORBIS/Bettmann; *page 3,* LC; *page 5,* LC, USZ62-
8518; *page 6,* CORBIS/Bettmann; *page 8,* LC, USZ62-26777; *page 11,*
CORBIS/Bettmann; *page 15,* Charles Willson Peale, *James Madison,* 1792,
oil on canvas, 0216.1106, from the Collection of the Gilcrease Museum,
Tulsa, Oklahoma; *page 17,* NA, RG 306 PSE, 81-2876; *page 18,* LC, U9-
22486-A #12; *page 20,* LC, F82-4509; *page 21,* NA, RG 306 SSM-4F, 63-
4118, Box 4; *page 22,* CORBIS/Bettmann; *page 27,* CORBIS/Bettmann;
page 28, LC, USZ62-1870; *page 29,* Virginia Museum of Fine Arts,
Richmond, VA, Gift of Edgar William and Bernice Chrysler Garbisch,
Photo: Ron Jennings, ©1999 Virginia Museum of Fine Arts; *page 30,*
CORBIS/Bettmann; *page 31,* LC, USZ62-1869; *page 37,* LC, USZ62-
35632; *page 42,* CORBIS/Bettmann; *page 46,* LC, USF3301-1278-M1;
page 48 (top), LC, U9-33522 #17S; *page 48 (bottom),* LC, U9-12749 #28;
page 52, CORBIS/Bettmann; *page 59,* LC, USZ62-13064; *page 67,*
CORBIS/Bettmann; *page 69,* National Archives, RG 306 PS-C, 63-1555;

page 84, CORBIS/Bettmann; *page 86,* CORBIS/Bettmann; *page 87,* LC,
USZ62-1863; *page 89,* NA, RG 306 PS-D, 61-4538; *page 94,* LC, USF33-
11961-M2; *page 96 (top),* NA, RG 306 PS-E, 83-1169; *page 96 (bottom),*
LC; *page 98,* CORBIS/Minnesota Historical Society; *page 99,* CORBIS/
Joseph Sohm, ChromoSohm Inc.; *page 102,* LC, USW3-10954-E;
page 104 (left), NA, RG 306 PS-E, 79-2974; *page 104 (right),* LC, U9-
35666-A #4; *page 106,* NA, RG 306 NT-167452c; *page 109,* LC, USZ62-
34260; *page 111,* CORBIS/Bettmann; *page 112,* CORBIS/Bettmann;
page 114, LC, USZ62-38314; *page 118,* LC, USZ62-115908; *page 122
(top),* LC, USZ62-33790; *page 122 (bottom),* NA, RG 306 PS-D, 64-3747;
page 128, NA, RG 64-M-123; *page 131,* NA, RG 306 PS-D, 70-922;
page 136, LC, USZ62-41653; *page 138,* NA, RG 306 PS-E, 77-1821c;
page 142, LC, USZ62-96268; *page 144,* NA, RG 306 PS-E, 75-282;
page 148, CORBIS; *page 155,* NA, RG 306 SSM-4B, 80-10, Box 4;
page 164, CORBIS/ Bettmann; *page 167,* LC, USA7-43100; *page 171,*
CORBIS/Bettmann; *page 173,* CORBIS; *page 178,* LC, USZ62-3460;
page 180, LC, USZ62-15187; *page 182,* NA, RG 306 PS-D, 70-2641;
page 184, NA, RG 306 PS-D, 49-12092

About the Author

Barbara Silberdick Feinberg graduated with honors from Wellesley College, where she was elected to Phi Beta Kappa. Ms.
Feinberg holds a Ph.D. in political science from Yale University. Among her recent books for children and young adults
are *Watergate: Scandal in the White House, American Political Scandals Past and Present, The National Government, State
Governments, Local Governments, Words in the News: A Student's Dictionary of American Government and Politics, Harry
S. Truman, John Marshall: The Great Chief Justice, Electing the President, The Cabinet, Hiroshima and Nagasaki, Black
Tuesday: The Stock Market Crash of 1929, Term Limits for Congress, The Constitutional Amendments, Next in Line: The
American Vice Presidency, Patricia Ryan Nixon, Edith Carow Roosevelt, Elizabeth Wallace Truman, General Douglas
MacArthur: An American Hero,* and *America's First Ladies: Changing Expectations.* She has also written *Marx and
Marxism; The Constitution: Yesterday, Today, and Tomorrow;* and *Franklin D. Roosevelt, Gallant President.* She is a con-
tributor to *The Young Reader's Companion to American History.*